# Accountability and Effectiveness Evaluation in Non-Profit Organizations

In the absence of profit, how is performance defined and evaluated?

In the absence of shareholders, who cares and how can they find out what is happening?

This volume provides new perspectives on assessing the performance of non-profit organizations whilst meeting the information needs of decision-makers, both internal, such as resource-providers, regulators and clients, and external, including boards, managers, staff and volunteers.

Whilst most discussions of accountability focus exclusively on financial accountability, this title offers a significant contribution to a relatively untouched area by combining the treatment of both evaluation and accountability from a managerial perspective.

**James Cutt** is Professor of Public Administration and Economics at the University of Victoria, Canada. He has taught at various universities around the world and held the Foundation Chair in Administrative Studies at the Australian National University. His previous publications include *Public and Non-Profit Budgeting: the Evolution and Application of Zero-Base Budgeting*, *Comprehensive Auditing: Theory and Practice* and *Public Purse, Public Purpose: Autonomy and Accountability in the Groves of Academe*.

**Vic Murray** is Adjunct Professor in the School of Public Administration at the University of Victoria, Canada. He is active in teaching, research and consulting on the problems of effectively managing non-profit organizations of all types.

# Routledge Studies in the Management of Voluntary and Non-Profit Organizations
Series Editor: Stephen P. Osborne

# Accountability and Effectiveness Evaluation in Non-Profit Organizations

James Cutt and Vic Murray

London and New York

First published 2000 by Routledge
11 New Fetter Lane, London EC4P 4EE

Simultaneously published in the USA and Canada
by Routledge
29 West 35th Street, New York, NY 10001

*Routledge is an imprint of the Taylor & Francis Group*

© 2000 James Cutt and Vic Murray

Typeset in Baskerville by Florence Production Ltd, Stoodleigh, Devon
Printed and bound in Great Britain by
MPG Books Ltd, Bodmin, Cornwall

*British Library Cataloguing in Publication Data*
A catalogue record for this book is available from the
British Library

*Library of Congress Cataloging in Publication Data*
Cutt, James, 1937–
    Accountability and effectiveness evaluation in non-profit
    organizations / James Cutt and Vic Murray.
        p. cm.
    Includes bibliographical references.
    1. Nonprofit organizations – Auditing.   2. Nonprofit
    organizations – Evaluation.   I. Murray, Victor V.   II. Title.
    HF5686.N56 C88 2000
    658′.048—dc21                                             99–087024

ISBN 0–415–21339–8

For Gwen and Shelagh

# Contents

# List of illustrations

## Tables

# Introduction

This book is a report on the results of a research project on performance measurement, evaluation and reporting in public and private non-profit organizations. The project began six years ago as a joint endeavour between the School of Public Administration at the University of Victoria in Victoria, British Columbia, and the Voluntary Sector Management Programme in the Faculty of Administrative Studies at York University in Toronto, Ontario, and was supported by a grant from the Social Sciences and Humanities Research Council in Ottawa. Graduate students at York University and the University of Victoria participated in and contributed significantly to the project. At York, Bill Tassie's doctoral thesis developed as part of the project, and some of his ideas are captured in Chapter 3. At the University of Victoria, Master of Public Administration dissertations by Geoff Dinsdale and Marti Lea Thib were written as part of the project, and their major results are contained in the case studies reported in Chapters 8 and 9. Chris Corbett's doctoral thesis developed through a partnership between this project and research in the School of Health Information Science at the University of Victoria, and his major argument is found in Chapter 12.

Although the chapters reflect a rough chronology of the project, they are primarily the story of the evolution of ideas through both conceptual development and actual practice in organizations in Toronto and Victoria. All the practical applications were in organizations in Canada, but the ideas reflect practice not only in Canada but also in the United States, the United Kingdom, Australia and New Zealand. We are confident that the problems we discovered and the ideas we developed and tested are generic to non-profit organizations wherever this form of institutional design is used to deliver services.

The foundation of performance measurement, evaluation and reporting is accountability. Chapter 1 examines this foundation as the start of the 'story line' of the project. All accountability relationships are about generating information to support decisions of some kind, and involve some sort of quasi-contractual relationship that defines shared expectations in a common currency. The major part of Chapter 1 is devoted to examining the nature of that common currency in non-profit organizations, and to describing in broad overview the evolution of our ideas about how best to define, measure and report performance in terms of that currency. Chapter 1 also situates the accountability that deals with technical or administrative performance measurement, evaluation and reporting in a broader context, relevant to both public and private non-profit organizations, of accountability in relation to political support. In short, what we define as administrative accountability to support administrative decisions is situated in the context of political accountability to support political decisions.

The information that sustains accountability relationships is generated by analytical or evaluative support systems of various kinds, and Chapter 2 reviews the variety of evaluative methods that are or might be used to provide valid and reliable information to put substance into the form of accountability relationships.

If Chapters 1 and 2 serve to set the stage, Chapters 3 and 4 describe our early attempts to 'walk the talk', to practice what we were preaching. In Toronto we set out confidently to persuade senior staff in a group of human service non-profit organizations about the significant net benefits of participating in the development of accountability information and actually using that information to support decisions; our experience is pondered at length in Chapter 3. Chapter 4 describes a concurrent adventure in Victoria where, to the accompaniment of much graduate student activity and enthusiasm, we sought to prescribe normative accountability frameworks for three non-profit organizations, one delivering social services, the second a federated funding agency that funds a number of social service non-profit organizations, and the third a cultural non-profit organization. It was, as they say, a considerable learning experience. Without foreshadowing our conclusions, suffice it to say that we discovered a great deal about the relationship between administrative and political accountability, and about the consequences of enthusiastic, normative prescription without benefit of careful consultation and testing. The good news is that we did not forfeit all goodwill with the organizations concerned, and continued to work with them throughout the project.

Unbowed, if slightly bloodied, we returned to our reflective research and classrooms to consider what had gone wrong and how we could usefully proceed. Chapter 5 reports a major effort at careful, consultative diagnosis with the various internal and external constituencies of a group of four human service non-profit organizations, including one of our early victims, about just what sort of information decision-makers had at their disposal, and what they would like to have to support their decisions. On the basis of the remarkably consistent picture that emerged from this diagnostic process, we then moved in careful consultation with the four organizations to a second attempt at prescription, indeed to a proposal for a set of general administrative accountability reporting standards designed to serve non-profit organizations across the cycle of governance and management activities from strategic planning to external reporting and evaluation. What we proposed at this stage were not standards of performance, but rather standards about the sorts and sequence of information that should be included in performance plans and reports.

Sustained by much warmer practical and academic response to our general proposals, and prompted by requests that we address in more detail some of the general information categories and indeed provide practical and specific demonstrations of how these categories could be made operational and useful in measurement terms, we continued the project by looking at providing better information about the use of resources – in short, about costs – and at the more difficult question of providing better information about what was achieved as a consequence of using these resources – in short, about results. Chapter 6 reviews the many and varied approaches to conceptualizing results, defined broadly as immediate programme consequences or outputs and longer-term consequences or outcomes. Chapter 7 describes our demonstration of the usefulness and feasibility of calculating total programme costs and unit service costs in human service organizations; by this point we had regained the confidence and support of staff and board members in the various organizations. Chapter 8 reports on the first of two case studies – the development of a set of performance logic models and associated outcome measures and methods of evaluation in one of the human service non-profit organizations that we had attempted to help, somewhat prematurely, in the activity reported in Chapter 4. Chapter 9 reports on a second case study – the development of a complete administrative accountability framework, including performance logic models, outcome measures, and approaches to evaluation, in the cultural non-profit organization we had visited earlier.

Without exception, accountability frameworks in non-profit organizations involve a multiplicity of performance measures, reflecting different concepts of success for their various internal and external constituencies. While this multiplicity is necessary, it is not sufficient to provide clear evidence for decisions at the various stages of the governance and management cycle. So the next part of the project involved trying to make sense of multiple performance measures. The most widely used multiple-component performance information framework in Canada is the 12 attributes of effectiveness framework developed by the CCAF/FCVI in Ottawa. The various agencies were all under some pressure to adopt this framework, or to show why they were not adopting it, and we set out in Chapter 10 to extend, prioritize and focus this framework in another framework that reflected explicitly the chronology of the governance/management cycle and implicitly the causal logic of non-profit programmes. Chapter 11 deals more explicitly with the matter of causal logic and the need to articulate a performance focus by examining the Balanced

Scorecard approach developed primarily for commercial organizations and then developing and adapting it for use in non-profit organizations. Two Balanced Scorecard models are illustrated, one using the CCAF/FCVI approach discussed in Chapter 10. We insisted in the Balanced Scorecard demonstrations on the development of a central performance focus to the achievement of which other performance measures were defined as instrumental. This focus served to bring some manageability, through prioritization, to the development of a core logic model and associated outcome measures.

We had then reached the stage where managers and boards considered that they had or could get much better information about choice between programmes, at the prospective or retrospective stages of the governance/ management cycle, which shared a common long-term strategic focus – in short, among programmes with a common administrative currency. What all staff and boards were faced with, however, was a next stage in which they were required to choose between programmes with different administrative currencies – in short, between apples and oranges. This we described as the problem of technical failure, and toyed for some time with the usual analytical excuse that decisions at this point were exclusively political – that is, defined in terms of a, usually implicit or concealed, currency of political support. Administrative accountability and political accountability would thus remain as two solitudes. Chapter 12 describes an attempt to build a bridge between these solitudes, and so to make some progress in resolving this problem of technical failure and concealed politics. We demonstrate a decision process in which decision-makers are provided, first, with the best available technical information about alternative programmes with incommensurable performance measures, and, second, with an ranked set of objectives to which all the programmes under consideration are addressed. Decision-makers are then required to make paired choices that reveal explicitly the common currency they are using to make choices with respect to an implicit composite utility measure of achievement of the weighted set of objectives. Decision-makers are free, of course, to use a currency that is entirely defined in terms of political support, but the relationship of such choices to the available administrative information is made explicit. Preliminary testing of this decision process suggests that this bridge between administrative accountability and political accountability can carry traffic successfully, that it can indeed offer a mechanism for informed choice that both extends the scope of decisions based on administrative information and leaves room, albeit explicit room, for decisions based on political information.

In a brief concluding section, we reflect on the lessons learned and on next steps.

# 1 Accountability

## The foundations of performance measurement, evaluation and reporting

### I General definition: accountability as shared expectations expressed in a common currency

Accountability is a fashionable word as we enter the new millennium, and is often used as an over-arching concept covering the institutions, techniques and language of performance measurement, reporting and evaluation in public organizations and private non-profit organizations. The difficulty with such generic use is that a concept that is taken to mean everything effectively means nothing. On the other hand, a general concept that is clearly defined can serve as a means of categorizing and integrating a range of related themes. This chapter attempts such a definition for the concept of accountability essentially as a framework for a set of arguments on improving the information available for decision-makers in public and private non-profit programmes and organizations.

The concept has a rich history – from Athenian democracy through biblical injunctions to the evolution of modern democratic institutions[1] but its essence has always been and remains the obligation to render an account for a responsibility that has been conferred.[2] This definition presumes the existence of at least two parties, one who allocates responsibility and one who accepts it with an undertaking to report on, and account for, the manner in which it has been discharged. Further, rendering an account, or disclosure, is a formal requirement – an obligation – through, implicitly, some specified mechanism or protocol.

This formal, hierarchical 'core' model of accountability has been extended, particularly with respect to social services provided by public organizations or private non-profit organizations, to recognize a broad range of constituencies with an interest in disclosure of information. Matek talks about disclosure of relevant information to

> all directly and indirectly responsible parties. Directly responsible parties are those to whom control of a programme or activity has been given and who can exercise sanction authority within or over the system. Indirectly responsible parties are those persons or groups

who have roles or authority within some part of the system and who can demonstrate a need for the information to order to execute their own functions effectively.[3]

The report in Canada in February 1999, of the Panel on Accountability and Governance in the Voluntary Sector also stressed multiple constituencies: 'Accountability in the voluntary sector is multi-layered – to different audiences, for a variety of activities and outcomes, through many different means. This multi-dimensional nature is the principal complexity of accountability in the voluntary sector.'[4] This extended model of accountability amounts to meeting, either by formal obligation in the core part of the model, or by choice in the wider part of the model, the information requirements of the various internal and external constituencies of a programme or organization.

Accountability defined in terms of meeting information requirements is not an end in itself, but rather a means to an end, which is always evaluation and decision-making by those who receive the information. But the decisions may vary from direct control with corresponding sanctions by those, within the core model, who receive information by formal obligation, to decisions to continue to participate in or support a programme or organization by the broader range of constituencies who receive information by choice. The mechanism or protocol through which information is communicated will correspondingly vary in the degree of formality, both with respect to the form and content of the accountability report and the extent to which verification by a third party is required to provide assurance to those who receive the reports.

Accountability as a purposeful activity is relevant only because programmes and organizations are also purposeful, and define conduct and performance required for the achievement of those purposes. Accountability in any relationship, by obligation or choice, for control or other forms of decision, formally or informally reported, verified or unverified – in short, within the core and the extended model – is defined in terms of the communication of information about conduct and performance relevant to the purposes of the programme or organization that is served by the accountability relationship. A meaningful framework of accountability must then include, within the core and the extended model, the following terms of reference: first, shared expectations about conduct and performance;[5] second, a shared language or currency in which fulfilment of those expectations will be described; third, shared criteria defined in that currency as to what constitutes fulfilment; and, finally, a means of communicating information about conduct and performance (in the shared currency and in terms of the shared criteria). Specified at the beginning of an accountability relationship, these terms of reference then define the ways in which the parties to that relation- ___ ll fulfil their obligations during and at the end of the relationship. book is about accountability in non-profit programmes and organizations in both the public and private sectors. It deals in various ways, conceptual and empirical, descriptive and normative, with how non-profit programmes and organizations meet the information requirements of relevant internal and external constituencies in accountability relationships across the chronological governance/management cycle of activities. This cycle begins with prospective activities (planning, programming and budgeting) and continues through ongoing activities (implementation, monitoring, and internal reporting and/or audit) to retrospective activities (external reporting, and external evaluation and/or audit).

The central focus of the book, descriptively and normatively, is on accountability relationships in terms of technical information, that is, on the definition of common currencies for the fulfilment of shared expectations, and corresponding criteria of conduct and performance and ways of communicating that information. There have been interesting technical developments over the last decade as to what constitutes performance and therefore can be defined as the common currencies of accountability relationships. This evolution has occurred for both commercial and non-commercial organizations in the private, cooperative and public sectors. Most of the debate has been at the level of the major product-line, or programme. The later argument is therefore defined at the programme level; satisfactory development at this level can then form the basis for aggregation to the organizational level and disaggregation to the level of the individual manager or staff member. The argument later in this chapter and in the balance of the book deals briefly with commercial programmes in the public sector – reflecting the origins in the commercial sector of some of the approaches to accountability – but primarily with defining and reporting performance in public and private non-profit programmes.

This interesting technical evolution leaves questions unanswered, and the book also explores some of the limits on specifying accountability relationships in terms of technical information, that is, the limits on specifying explicitly and implementing a common currency of performance. Some of these limits relate not so much to the technical information as to the preference of some constituencies for an alternative currency. This is the interface between what is usually described as administrative accountability (defined in technical terms about programme performance) and political accountability (defined in an alternative currency of political support). We deal briefly with this interface and acknowledge the legitimacy of an explicitly defined currency of political support at an appropriate level in the hierarchy of accountability. There are, however, other limits that are themselves technical in nature – where the current state of the art does not provide a common currency for decisions for, say, resource allocation choices between two alternative programmes. For instance, the best possible technical information on performance in, say, a youth training programme is, in our experience of the sector, still incommensurable with – that is, is defined in a different currency from – the best technical information about, say, a palliative care programme for the elderly. Where technical information cannot inform the choice, where there in no common currency – where choices are between apples and oranges – decision-makers can cheerfully fall back on implicit values, or concealed or implicit politics of various kinds. We found many examples of this problem. It is the classic prioritization problem facing those making resource allocation decisions in the executive branch of elected governments; at a more manageable level, it is what faces a regional federated funding agency in the private non-profit sector. The book explores ways of approaching this problem of technical failure and concealed politics; the approach suggested involves ways of eliciting a common currency, of revealing the values or politics of decisions. In short, we explore further technical improvement in the area of otherwise implicit politics, while acknowledging the legitimacy of explicit politics at the appropriate level in the hierarchy of accountability.

The balance of this general discussion of accountability explores in more detail the various components of the concept of accountability, proposes that the set of such concepts be defined as the necessary components of an accountability framework, considers the implementation of such a framework, and concludes by suggesting a set of criteria for its design and evaluation.

## II Elaboration: definitional details and the design of an accountability framework

The definition of accountability may be elaborated by exploring the answers to a set of questions:

1   In what form does accountability manifest itself?
2   When is accountability relevant?
3   Where is the question of accountability relevant? Is it limited to certain sectors or organizational types or applicable to all?
4   Who is accountable, and to whom is accountability due?
5   Why do those who receive accountability information need it? Alternatively, what is the purpose of accountability?
6   What kinds of information are included within the definition of accountability?
7   How is information about accountability produced, communicated, and validated?
8   How is accountability used? Are there real consequences of any kind from the discharge of the obligation to be accountable?
9   If the answers to questions 1 to 8 constitute the design of an accountability framework, the final question is How can such a framework be implemented? In short, how can an accountability framework be

taken from the stage of conceptual design to actual practical application? The definition of an accountability framework must then include both design and implementation.

These nine questions are explored briefly below, in turn.

### *In what form does accountability manifest itself?*

Accountability was defined to include shared expectations about conduct and performance, a shared language in which fulfilment of those expectations will be described, shared criteria defined in that currency as to what constitutes fulfilment, and a means of communicating that information about conduct and performance. Specified at the beginning of an accountability relationship, these terms of reference define the ways in which the parties to the relationship will fulfil their obligations during and at the end of the relationship. Accountability therefore manifests itself as information, developed, with varying degrees of formality, through the agency of a set of management information systems and associated methods of analysis and evaluation – which are discussed below under question 7. The accountability terms of reference, which set the stage for the accountability relationship, manifest themselves as information in plans and budgets; and the fulfilment of the obligations of the relationship manifests itself across the management cycle as performance reports and associated evaluations/audits over the course of and at the end of the relationship.

### *When is accountability relevant?*

Programmatic activities were defined above in a chronological management cycle, ranging from prospective activities (planning, programming and budgeting) through ongoing activities (implementation, monitoring, and internal reporting, and internal evaluation and/or audit) to retrospective activities (external reporting, and external evaluation and/or audit). A complete framework of accountability information must include the accountability terms of reference specified at the planning, programming and budgeting stage of the cycle, and the various reports/evaluations/audits provided over the course of programme delivery (the ongoing stage of the cycle) and retrospectively (at the conclusion of the cycle). The complete framework may, of course, be broken down into its constituent parts, and relevant bits of accountability information provided for these parts. So accountability information may be related exclusively to a particular activity at one stage of the management cycle, say, the strategic planning stage, and may focus on the management system that produces the strategic plan or on the operating strategic plan produced by that system, or on both. This could be seen as a formative accountability report relating to a point or period in the chronological management cycle. Such various bits of accountability information culminate in a comprehensive and summative end-of-year report that includes operating information and information about associated management systems with respect to all major management activities across the chronological management cycle. Most of the discussion in the literature about accountability focuses on the comprehensive, cross-sectional 'slice' of information which describes achievements in relation to intentions. Accountability information is, however, relevant at all stages of the management cycle, not merely cumulatively at its end.

### Where is the concept of accountability relevant?

The concept of accountability in Canada has been developed in the academic and professional literature primarily with reference to the public sector, but is relevant to all organizational and associated programmatic types, commercial and non-profit, public and private. The most recent comprehensive review in Canada[6] reflects this focus of development and scope for wider application. A major section, on accountability obligations, is devoted to exploring the accountability obligations of ministers and public servants, and thus pertains to both the public non-profit sector – public sector departments and arms-length funded institutions such as universities and hospitals – and the public commercial sector – public enterprises such as commercial crown corporations. A second, much briefer section, on accountability in certain other circumstances, broadens the discussion to the rest of the organizational universe by examining accountability in the private commercial sector and the private non-profit sector. The most thorough review at the provincial level in Canada[7] is directed exclusively at public sector departments and crown corporations, but foreshadows extension of the proposed accountability framework to arms-length funded institutions. In the private commercial sector, the topic of accountability is most commonly approached implicitly within a discussion of extending performance measurement and reporting beyond the traditional exclusive focus on financial information.[8] The discussion below of the kinds of information to be included in accountability frameworks deals with the range of organizational types and associated programmes – commercial and non-profit, public and private.

### Who is accountable, and to whom is accountability due?

Who wants this accountability information, and who has to provide it? All accountability frameworks are built around the core, hierarchical model involving two parties, one who allocates responsibility and one who accepts it with an undertaking to report on the manner in which it has been discharged; and most modern frameworks extend this core model to include a decision, by the party responsible for reporting, to meet, by choice or obligation, the information requirements of the various internal and external constituencies of a programme or organization. Although subsequent discussion is focused on the core model, the extended model and associated broader framework of reporting is always implicit, and is explicit in the discussion of the various kinds of information reported.

The hierarchical model may be addressed vertically through a variety of levels within organizations and both vertically and laterally from the highest level in organizations to external groups of various kinds. A distinction can thus be made between *internal* and *external* accountability relationships, the former reflecting the rendering of account by obligation through the hierarchical levels in an organization, from the lowest to the highest, the latter the rendering of account, by obligation or choice, from the highest level in an organization to external parties. From the bottom up within a relatively simple organizational structure, internal accountability relationships include the following: individual employees to line managers for task performance; line managers to function or programme managers for unit or cost centre performance, and function or programme managers to the senior manager – the Chief Executive Officer (CEO). Foreshadowing the next section of this discussion, the CEO requires this information for the purpose of *management control*. External accountability relationships include, in the first instance, the accountability of the CEO to the governing body (board or directors, trustees, the executive level of government, etc.) of the organization, who require the information for *governance control*. By way of qualification to the neatness of hierarchical relationships, it should be noted that in practice CEOs (presidents, executive directors, deputy ministers, etc.) have one foot in the management camp and one foot in the governance camp; the line between management and governance may therefore be unclear. In general, the governance function, exercised by governing bodies, receives the accountability of CEOs, and is, in turn, accountable to those who have assigned responsibility (and therefore accountability) to the governing body – shareholders in a commercial organization, members in a private non-profit organization, and elected representatives in public service departments. These external parties require the information for control that relates to the interest of members or constituents – which raises the question of the language or currency of reporting.

Within organizations, the currency of the accountability relationship (shared expectations, criteria of conduct and performance, and method of reporting) is defined in technical terms relating to programme performance; this may be defined as *administrative accountability*. The hierarchical accountability of governing bodies to external members or constituents may use some of the language of administrative accountability but is fundamentally defined in terms of political support, sought by those providing accountability, offered by those assigning responsibility. Where the currency of accountability is defined as political support – appointment or re-appointment of a board of directors at an Annual General Meeting, election or re-election of a government – the relationship may be defined as *political accountability*, with the objective of *political control*. The primary focus of subsequent discussion, particularly with respect to what sort of information should be reported, is on administrative rather than political accountability, and, within organizations, on the administrative account-ability of a programme manager to the CEO.

The extended model of accountability includes reporting outside the hierarchical relationship, usually by choice rather than obligation, to other constituencies within and external to an organization. For instance, a CEO may choose to provide general or specific performance accountability infor-mation internally to staff members and perhaps volunteers, and externally to customers and perhaps professional associations of various kinds. A programme manager, with the support of the CEO, could also build such voluntary accountability relationships. These extensions are in terms of administrative accountability (technical information about conduct and performance), motivated arguably by altruism or principle, but probably also by interest in successful programmatic and organization performance over the longer term; Chapter 11 deals specifically with the contribution of reporting broadly to various internal and external constituencies to long-term organizational performance. The governing body might also choose to provide information to a range of constituents broader than those with a direct political relationship; in this case the motivation could again be seen as simply principled – the 'right thing to do' – but is also likely to be related to longer-term considerations of building political support.

Two final matters remain to be discussed in this section: the matter of whether individuals or organizations should be held accountable; and the distinction between objective and subjective accountability.

Should individuals or organizations be held accountable? Although the issue can become complex, the most appropriate answer is implicit in the previous discussion. In the final analysis, organizations are made up of individuals, and only individuals can be entrusted with specific respon-sibilities and therefore held accountable. It should also be stressed that accountability is limited by the extent of responsibility and corresponding delegated authority. Managers cannot be held accountable for matters over which they have no authority or control. The issue has important implications for the definition of managerial performance and associated accountability; to illustrate, managers should not be held accountable *directly* for the outcomes of programmes in the community where these outcomes are affected by variables beyond the authority and control of managers. This point is worth pursuing on the distinction to be drawn between responsibility and accountability. Formally, managers should not be held directly *accountable* for matters for which they are not *responsible*, that is, matters over which they do not have authority and control. It can, however, be argued that management accountability can be extended to include the establishment of management systems and the performance information produced by those systems in areas beyond management's responsibility. For instance, senior management in post-secondary institutions should be accountable for the establishment of management systems to collect longitudinal outcome information on matters such as graduate employment success, and career and income growth, even though neither credit nor blame can be attached to managers for the operational information on those performance measures.

Much of the discussion about accountability, and indeed its generally rather negative context, reflects the concept of *objective accountability* – a formal requirement to account imposed by one party on another as the counterpart to assigned responsibility. The implication is that individuals must be coerced to be accountable and will only go as far as required. But there may be more to accountability than the measured mile. *Subjective accountability* reflects the moral character, and associated personal standards, of administrators, and operates voluntarily and thus in a more positive context with respect to their own sense of responsibility. Such subjective accountability may also, of course, reflect adherence to broader, and in some cases very formal and objective, professional ethics and standards. The appropriate conclusion is probably that the line between objective and subjective accountability is a fine one, that they are generally complementary, and that the ultimate safeguard in any accountability relationship is the subjective accountability of the administrator. This reassuring conclusion does not weaken the case for establishing formal, objective accountability frameworks. The point is captured delicately but unequivocally by LeClerc:

> Accountability, as a personal trait and as a logical response to expecta-
> tions and pressures, will not naturally lead to the institutionalization of
> formal accountability regimes. This is in spite of the growing number of
> officials, managers, and members of governing bodies who do adhere to
> the appropriate values and are imbued by a sense of responsibility and
> accountability. Good faith and a noble disposition are not sufficient.[9]

### Why do those who receive accountability information need it? What is the purpose of accountability information?

Accountability information is needed as an aid to decision-making about actual and intended performance. At the various levels of management, accountability information (formative and summative) is used internally, i.e. within the organization, as an instrument of internal accountability for the purpose of *management control* across the management cycle of activities. Planning and budgeting information is necessary to establish 'accountability terms of reference' (ends and means for the management cycle), and formative and summative information across the management cycle is necessary to monitor, evaluate, and report performance in relation to established ends and means, and, if necessary, to make adjustments to both ends and means. At the governance level, senior management and boards need the range of formative and summative accountability information to make decisions about past and potential performance (i.e. as an instrument of internal accountability at the highest level for the purpose of *governance control*) and are likely to require assurance – through internal validation of some kind, such as an internal audit – that the information they have been given by management is complete and accurate. Senior management and boards also require accountability information, particularly summative information, to meet external accountability requirements to shareholders and other external constituencies; in turn, these external constituencies are likely to need assurance (and at this level the provision of assurance is generally not optional) through external validation of some kind such as an external audit, that the information they have been given for the exercise of *shareholder control* (and control by other external constituencies) is complete and accurate. The concept of shareholder control may be generalized to *political control* where the currency of the relationship is defined in terms of political support.

In the extended model of accountability, the purpose of control of various kinds does not obtain for those constituencies to which management and/or boards choose to provide information. Voluntary choices by management to provide accountability information to staff members may be related to the purpose of creating a happier and better-informed staff and therefore ultimately to the purpose of improved programmatic or organizational performance. Providing information to customers would more obviously be related to building customer loyalty and increasing demand for the product or service, and therefore also to organizational performance. Provision of information by boards to external constituencies other than those whose direct political support is sought may be seen in terms of widening the base of political support.

### What kinds of information are included in the definition of accountability?

Implicit in the discussion to this point is that responsibility is assigned by one party to another for 'performance' of some sort, and that accountability requires the communication of information about that performance. But how is performance defined? In short, what is the required scope of accountability information?

The general parameters around that scope were proposed in section I. A meaningful framework of accountability must be defined in terms of shared expectations about conduct and performance expressed in a shared language or currency, shared performance criteria defined in that currency, and a means of communicating information, in the shared language and associated criteria. This section is addressed primarily to the matter of a shared language or currency of performance – with illustrative criteria of performance – with respect to administrative accountability. It does not elaborate on the currency of political accountability, which will be expressed through various expressions of political support such as voting in elections or Annual General Meetings. In short, the focus of this section is on the categories of information, general and specific, that constitute the language or currency of administrative performance and accountability. Chapter 5 in this book addresses specifically the question of general standards of administrative performance reporting – in effect, general standards of accountability – for non-profit organizations, with respect to both content and form.

The scope of administrative accountability information can be defined cumulatively at two levels: a basic level dealing with conformity to or compliance with processes and procedures, without explicit reference to programmatic or organizational objectives and operations – defined as *procedural accountability*, and common to all programmes and organizations; and a second level related explicitly to the achievement of programmatic or organizational objectives and methods of operation – defined as *consequential accountability*, and defined differently for commercial and non-profit programmes and organizations.

The focus of this book is on public and private non-profit programmes and organizations, but much of the evolution of accountability in such areas is either common to, or is derived from, concepts and practices relating to accountability in commercial organizations, public and private. The following discussion therefore begins with general coverage of both commercial and non-profit programmes and organizations, and then moves quickly through matters specific to commercial programmes and organizations as a basis for dealing in more depth with non-profit programmes and organizations.

*Procedural accountability*

For all programmes and organizations, public and private, commercial and non-profit, the structure of accountability information is built on a foundation of basic financial information. Managers are accountable for completeness and accuracy in the representation of financial information in the form of financial statements during and at the end of the management cycle in relation to budgeted financial information at the beginning of the cycle. In the light of budgeted financial information, this level of accountability represents shared expectations about accurate and complete representation of financial information across the cycle. The shared currency is obviously financial, and the criteria of accuracy and completeness are the set of criteria that make up Generally Accepted Accounting

Principles (GAAP). This set of criteria is well developed and refined for commercial programmes and organizations, private and public; variations on the theme for public and private non-profit programmes and organizations have also evolved recently.[10] As the foundation of accountability information – part of the required core of information for all organizations – the financial statements prepared at the end of the management cycle are generally subject to verification, with respect to completeness and accuracy using GAAP, through financial audit. The concepts and methods of analysis that sustain the production of this accountability information are found in financial accounting; and those that sustain its verification in financial auditing.

A second element of procedural accountability requires managers to monitor and report across the management cycle the compliance of their programme or organization with the wide variety of authorities (statutes, regulations, by-laws, administrative regulations, etc.) to which they are subject. This component of procedural accountability is frequently part of the required hierarchical framework of accountability – though legislative requirement – for public commercial and non-profit programmes and organizations, and is increasingly commonly used voluntarily as part of the extended framework of accountability by private commercial and non-profit programmes and organizations. In this case, the shared expectations relate to compliance with the set of authorities determined at the beginning of the cycle, the currency is demonstrated legal compliance – again, especially in public sector programmes and organizations, subject to verification through external compliance audit – and the concepts and methods of analysis that sustain this accountability information are found in law, particularly administrative law, and in the various sub-sets of law relating to compliance with authorities in such areas as employee safety, human resource policies, etc.

*Consequential accountability*

In all commercial programmes and organizations, public and private, financial information across the governance/management cycle provides evidence not only of procedural accountability with respect to its completeness and accuracy, but also of consequential accountability. The budgeted and actual statement of income and expenses provides information about intended and realized net income (accounting profit). This single measure, accounting profit, or revenue minus expenses incurred in the earning of that revenue, reflects on the revenue side the monetary value ascribed by purchasers to the products/services sold, and on the expenses side the monetary value of the resources used by the programme/organization to make the product or service available for sale. In the language that will be used later for non-profit programmes and organizations, profit thus reflects explicitly effectiveness or the achievement of objectives, and implicitly efficiency or the use of resources in the pursuit of these objectives. Performance analysts use financial ratio analysis of the statement of revenue and expenses to provide comparative analysis of the profitability of the programme and organization, and financial ratio analysis of the statement of financial position to provide comparative analysis of liquidity and solvency. It is common in comparative assessments of the performance of commercial programmes or organizations – such as those provided regularly in business magazines like *Business Week* and *Fortune* – to provide a comprehensive picture of commercial performance, including, for instance: market value; dividend yield; earnings per share; sales (and sales growth); profit (and profit growth); net margins; return on invested capital; and return on equity. With respect to commercial performance, the shared expectations relate to profit and its related measures, the currency is financial, the criteria are defined in terms of targets and relative performance, and the means of communication is defined in terms of interim financial statements over the course of the cycle and audited annual statements at the end of each annual cycle. What all this amounts to is that the financial results of commercial organizations provide rich evidence of consequential accountability.

However, there has been some interesting development over the 1990s in the scope of information reported under the head of commercial performance. This development reflects to some extent an acknowledgment of the extended definition of accountability and the interests of wider constituencies in information of various kinds, but deals primarily with a more sophisticated definition of performance over time within the traditional, focused hierarchical definition. What this line of development entails is an acknowledgment of a variety of kinds of non-financial information that are related to financial performance. One version of this approach, 'Measures that Matter',[11] includes the following indicators: Execution of Corporate Strategy; Quality of Strategy; Ability to Innovate; Ability to Attract Talented People; Market Share; Quality of Executive Compensation; Quality of Major Processes; and Research Leadership. Implicitly these factors are all seen as contributing to long-term profitability. A more formal and sophisticated variant – the Balanced Scorecard approach[12] – acknowledges the richness of financial information, but also stresses that comprehensive information on performance for the organization as a whole or for specific products (programmes) should include not only financial results but also information in three other categories: customer results; internal business process results; and innovation and learning results. The information on non-financial results in a commercial organization is envisaged explicitly not as an end in itself but rather a means to an end. Information about customers, business processes, and innovation and learning are drivers of future financial performance, and are thus instrumental in long-term financial performance. In its developed form, the Balanced Scorecard approach is much more than just a checklist of relevant information at any given performance measurement stage; rather it is a logic model, a dynamic, chronologically and causally integrated, model of organization performance, focused on the strategic long-term objective of profit maximization.

Chapter 11 demonstrates an adaptation of the Balanced Scorecard for use by public and cooperative commercial organizations using explicit inclusion of the non-financial objectives or constraints – strategically specified – which limit long-term profit maximization. Essentially, the Balanced Scorecard is reformulated in constrained optimization terms, where the strategic objective is specified as profit maximization subject to required targets or limits in a series of non-financial areas which do not contribute to but formally constrain the long-term financial objective. An obvious example would be a requirement placed on a public commercial organization to operate a specified service without charging any user price. In this case the shared expectations include targets with respect to the various constraints, the currency of performance includes not only financial results but also specific technical information with respect to the various non-financial constraints, the criteria are defined as financial targets and technical targets for the various constraints, and the means of communication is defined in terms of interim and final reports on the achievement of financial and technical targets.

To summarize, for all commercial organizations, private and public, the Balanced Scorecard approach is *longitudinal* in that it is focused on a long-term strategic objective, and *lateral* in that its includes a set of categories of information (and associated performance measures) which, through a specified set of chronological and causal relationships, are assumed to drive long-term financial performance. For public and cooperative commercial organizations, additional information on non-financial constraints forms part of the system.

For decision-makers in private commercial organizations, choice among alternative decisions can therefore be clearly informed by technical information that is commensurable. It is defined in a common numeraire or currency – the long-term financial consequences. There is, of course, room for judgement – models are imperfect, assumptions can be varied, uncertainty is pervasive – but at least choices are among apples and apples. In short, there is a common, technical currency, and a common criterion of success (long-term profit maximization) expressed in that currency, for decisions among alternatives. Financial budgets and financial reports across the management cycle provide a common means of communication. Things are a little more complicated in public and cooperative commercial organizations because of the absence of a common currency for the various constraints, but at least core constrained optimization decisions are informed by a common currency.

For public, cooperative and private non-profit programmes and organizations that provide services without charge or at a charge that covers

only a small proportion of costs, the definition of consequential accountability is more complex. Financial results, which provide the core
performance information in commercial programmes and organizations,
provide much more limited information in non-profit organizations. If
services are not sold, the revenue side of the financial statements simply
describes the various sources of funding used by the organization, and
does not represent the valuation of organizational services by consumers.
So financial statements in non-profit programmes and organizations say
nothing, by definition, about consequential accountability, and provide
information only at the basic procedural level – the completeness and
accuracy of information on financial sources and uses. This is, of course,
an important category of information and constitutes the first level of
accountability information, as described above.

In the absence of a (relatively) simple profit measure, consequential
accountability for non-profit programmes in both the private and the public
sectors deals broadly with two components which jointly provide a non-
profit surrogate for commercial profit: first, and comparable to financial
costing information in the commercial sector, information on the use of
financial (and other) resources to provide services; and, second and quite
distinct from revenue information used in the commercial sector, information on the service results (in non-financial terms) achieved by that use.
This whole area can be broadly summed as value for money – the surrogate for profit in organizations that do not sell their products. Value for
money in its most basic formulation was developed by legislative auditors
in the public sector, and focused on measures of resource utilization
(efficiency) and measures of the attainment of intended results (effectiveness). Formally, the authorized definitions are as follows: *efficiency* refers to
the use of financial, human and physical resources such that output is
maximized for any given set of resource inputs, or input is minimized for
any given quantity and quality of output provided; *effectiveness* refers to the
achievement of the objectives or other intended effects of programmes,
operations or activities.[13] Shared expectations in this approach to consequential accountability would thus be defined in terms of efficiency
and effectiveness targets, the currency and associated criteria of success
would be in definitions of efficiency and effectiveness appropriate to the
programme or organization in question, and methods of reporting would
include on an ongoing and annual basis the achievement of efficiency and
effectiveness targets.

As for commercial organizations, accountability information for non-
profit organizations thus included multiple components, arranged in a
*lateral* way: two components, financial results and compliance with authorities, dealing with procedural accountability, and two components,
efficiency and effectiveness, dealing with consequential accountability or
value for money. In these first formulations, there was no attempt to link
chronologically or causally the lateral components of the information

framework into a logic model of organizational performance, nor any attempt, at least explicitly, to formulate a unifying strategic, long-term objective. Financial accountability and accountability for compliance with authorities (both procedural) and accountability for value for money in its two components, efficiency and effectiveness (both consequential) constituted the structure of broad-scope or *comprehensive accountability* and its verification counterpart, broad-scope or *comprehensive auditing*, developed first in Canada by the Office of the Auditor General in Ottawa, and emulated in a variety of ways by other legislative auditors and private professional service firms. In practice, the two major components of broad-scope accountability and auditing were treated separately, and continuing debate focused on development of the consequential component of accountability.

The next stage in the development of accountability information in non-profit organizations saw the development of a broad definition of accountability which included the financial component of procedural accountability, excluded the compliance component, and elaborated extensively on the set of categories or relevant information within the value-for-money component of accountability. The CCAF/FCVI – formerly the Canadian Comprehensive Auditing Foundation (Fédération Canadienne de Vérification Intégrée) – in Ottawa published in the late 1980s its proposed set of 12 attributes of what was generically described as 'Effectiveness'.[14] The set of attributes used to elaborate the old concept of value for money was designed to reflect the perspectives of the various constituencies of programmes and organizations; in short, it was designed to address an extended definition of accountability. The proposed attributes included the following set of categories of information, including both management systems and operating results: Management Direction; Relevance; Appropriateness; Achievement of Intended Results; Acceptance; Secondary Impacts; Costs and Productivity; Responsiveness; Financial Results; Working Environment; Protection of Assets; and Monitoring and Reporting. All but one of these (Financial Results) refers to an elaboration of value for money with respect to non-profit organizations; it should be noted that the approach was also used for public commercial organizations, in which case the financial results would also be consequential in nature. The CCAF/FCVI attributes were designed as a basis for auditable representations by management across the set of information categories. Shared expectations were therefore defined in terms of targets in these categories, the currency and associated criteria of success were defined in measures appropriate to the programme or organization in question, and methods of reporting defined in terms of representations by management – similar to financial statements produced by management – on an ongoing and annual basis dealing with the achievement of targets in the various attributes.

The CCAF/FCVI attributes were not prioritized or arranged as a model of performance, either causally or longitudinally. In Chapter 10 we have attempted both a prioritization and a longitudinal or chronological reclassification of the twelve attributes, as well as an extension of the set of attributes, to reflect the governance/management cycle from strategic direction to external reporting and evaluation/audit.

As the CCAF/FCVI attribute approach evolved over the 1990s, a related and parallel development – dealing with actual performance measures or indicators within relevant categories of performance information – introduced explicitly the longitudinal dimension. Both government and private funders of cultural and social non-profit organizations required measures of performance that began with inputs, continued through processes, and then dealt with consequences in various stages, ranging from traditional tangible measures of output to impact or outcomes in the community over various periods of time (a common distinction is into initial, intermediate and final or ultimate outcomes). By definition, this approach introduces an explicit longitudinal dimension to information, and an implicit causal logic model of programmes. This evolution was reflected in the specification of shared expectations that included outcomes, and a corresponding extension of the currency, criteria, and methods of reporting with respect to consequential accountability in non-profit programmes and organizations. The development of approaches to outcome measures, and two illustrations of their application – one in a human service non-profit organization, the other in a cultural non-profit organization, are presented in Chapters 6, 8, and 9.

The performance picture presented by an elaborated version of the CCAF/FCVI attributes that includes rearrangement and prioritization of the information categories over the management cycle, the articulation of performance measures within each information category, and the extension of each performance measure longitudinally and causally, is rich and varied, meeting in an extended accountability framework the accountability information needs of the variety of constituencies of non-profit organizations including funders, clients, and other interested parties outside the organization, and governance and management within the organization. But it is also a very complex and unfocused picture, unlike the inexorable focus on long-term profitability, unconstrained or constrained, that provides a common currency of performance for decision-makers in private and public commercial organizations.

In the next stage of our work to date we proposed to introduce explicitly the question of focus. We did this by building on our work with both the Balanced Scorecard and the CCAF/FCVI attributes. The four major information categories used in the Balance Scorecard – financial results, customer results, internal business process results, and innovation and learning results – are all clearly relevant, suitably defined, for public and private non-profit organizations and their service delivery programmes. But long-term profitability will obviously not do as the long-term strategic objective to which information in all these other categories contributes. But some alternative strategic objective must be defined as the necessary focus of an optimization strategy; only one thing can be optimized at a time, albeit subject to specified constraints. Our conclusion was that the long-term strategic focus of non-profit organizations and programmes had to be defined in constrained optimization terms. That focus was long-term cost-effectiveness (or cost-utility) – literally, bang for the buck, where a defined over-arching non-monetary service objective was maximized for a defined financial budget constraint. Other constraints could also be defined, but the core constraint, the one necessary for the definition of the objective to be optimized, is the available budget. So we redefined the Balanced Scorecard approach for non-profit organizations and programmes to begin with the specification of a long-term strategic service objective in relation to a predicated long-term budget constraint. This constraint might be exogenously specified by a funder, or might be wholly or partly subject to fund-raising activities by the organization; in either case, the long-term strategic focus is on doing as well as possible in a service objective for a given budget. Information collected over the management cycle would include the four traditional categories of the Balanced Scorecard, supplemented by ongoing performance in the major service objective and performance in achieving the expected budget.

Reflecting on the richness of the CCAF/FCVI attribute approach, particularly developed as suggested above, we decided to recast the remodelled CCAF/FCVI approach as an alternative Balanced Scorecard. The approach paralleled that defined for the traditional Balanced Scorecard, except that the range of information collected across the management cycle was now defined as the set of CCAF/FCVI attributes, extended longitudinally, and brought together causally and longitudinally in the optimization of long-term service effectiveness for a given budget. An increase in the richness of the information available for management, which, in Canada, has become somewhat familiar and comfortable with the CCAF/FCVI approach, is bought by some increase in complexity. Nevertheless the whole model is still reduced ultimately to a constrained optimization, and all relevant performance information must be related causally and longitudinally to that long-term cost-effectiveness. These developments for non-profit programmes and organizations of the original Balanced Scorecard and of the CCAF/FCVI attributes as an alternative Balanced Scorecard are described in Chapter 11.

How practical are these developments of richer consequential accountability information for non-profit programmes and organizations? For non-profit organizations that share the same long-term cost-effectiveness objective, say, a group of youth agencies working on a shared youth training objective, decision-makers facing choices among alternative programmes could make these decisions using technical information that is commensurable. For a given budget, which programme offers the best long-term effectiveness score? It is clearly a matter of being approximately right, but at least technical information provides the common basis for decisions – apples versus apples, not apples versus oranges. The problem becomes more complex where long-term objectives are different.

We found ourselves at a stage where, at least in principle, decision-makers in non-profit organizations with a shared long-term cost-effectiveness objective could allocate scarce resources – that is, use the available budget – using technical information on long-term cost-effectiveness. However, the difficulty came either within one organization with different programmes, or for a central funding agency (public or private) dealing with organizations and programmes with different long-term objectives. This was the point at which technical information failed us. Decisions still had to be made, of course, but they could not be based on clear technical information. This led to some interesting situations.

In many cases, decision-makers actually resisted and resented the development of technical information even up to the level defined above where clear choices could be made using that information. Our research demonstrated clearly that they actually preferred to make the decisions using implicit values, often justified as some sort of political process. In any event, it was concealed politics; these research results are reported in Chapter 3. Our position here was that this sort of decision-making process was fine as long as the technical information available for choice was fully available to interested constituencies. Decision-makers could then be held *politically* accountable for their selected deviations from the set of choices derived from technical information. The snag is obviously that decision-makers are usually very reluctant to make that information available.

A second and larger difficulty is that the current state-of-the-art in technical performance measurement cannot fully inform some choices. Where technical information cannot inform the choice, where there is no common currency, where choices are between apples and oranges, decision-makers can cheerfully fall back on implicit values, or concealed politics of various kinds. We found many examples of this problem. It is the classic prioritization problem facing Cabinet decision-makers in elected governments. At a more manageable level, it is what faces a federated funding agency in the private non-profit sector, or a regional health board in the public non-profit sector. What happens at this level is that the technical people concede, and decisions are made (for decisions must always be made) in a political process – again implicit values, concealed politics. Our first, well-intentioned but, as events unfolded, rather naive attempts to cast some light on such politics are discussed in Chapter 4.

We proposed to address this problem of technical failure and concealed politics in the following way. Given the best technical information available – and we have been at pains to suggest that this can become quite good – and revealed, technically based, choices and associated rankings among comparable programmes (with a common long-term objective), decision-makers would now be invited to allocate in an open process a given budget using explicit ranking (ordinal) choices among paired alternative programmes with different long-term objectives; an alternative approach would be to invite decision-makers to assign a cardinal score on a prescribed utility scale. In effect, we were asking decision-makers to reveal a common currency, comparative utility with respect to an over-arching objective to which the different programmes all contributed. For instance, a federated funding agency board – carefully defined to incorporate the perspectives of all interested parties, and informed by, first, a carefully generated set of prioritized community objectives for, say, a three to five year period, and, second, the best technical information available on different programmes – could make an explicit ranking based on its assessment of the contribution of various programmes to the set of prioritized community objectives. Such a process, with careful attention to voting procedures and openness, makes very clear what values, what common currency, what performance utility measures, obtain in decisions. There is still room, of course, for pure politics – passion and prejudice of various kinds – but decision-makers are fully accountable for the exercise of such a prerogative in the proposed process. The first trials of our approach, in social service agencies and regional authorities, are very encouraging. It is no longer a matter of labouring at technical information up to the point when choices are between apples and oranges, and then consigning decisions to an undefined, but certainly closed, political process. Rather, it is a matter of producing the best possible technical information, acknowledging the apples versus oranges limits of technical information, and then designing a decision process that elicits a common currency, that reveals the values or politics of decisions. Decision-makers are well informed in this process, but the currency of their decisions is explicit, and they are fully accountable for their decisions in the light of that currency. The design of these approaches – to eliciting a common currency and an illustrative application are presented in Chapter 12.

### How is information about accountability produced, communicated, and validated?

Given the desired scope of performance for which managers are to be held accountable, the necessary information about performance is produced by a set of management systems using a variety of analytical/evaluative methods. These management systems and associated methods of analysis amount to the management information systems which give substance to the structure of accountability across the cycle. Chapter 2 deals with methods of analysis. This section deals briefly with the management systems served by these methods. This topic is well served in the literature.[15] The Auditor General of British Columbia proposes an accountability framework that includes the financial and compliance elements of procedural accountability, and a general approach to consequential accountability defined as 'operational results', which actually builds into the traditional concepts of efficiency and effectiveness some of the additional richness of the CCAF/FCVI attributes. To serve that framework, the Auditor General describes the necessary management information systems across the chronological management cycle. These systems range in order from: first, strategic planning and policy development; second, business planning and programming; third, budgeting, including performance measurement and targeting, human resource planning systems, and administrative and financial control systems; fourth, information systems for monitoring performance; fifth, programme evaluation and performance reporting systems, including internal and external validation (audit) systems; and, finally, incentive systems including resource allocation at the programme level and compensation at the individual level. In short, the concept of comprehensive accountability, procedural and consequential, is put into practice by an aligned set of management information systems, integrated across the cycle of management activities.

Communication occurs across the cycle of management activities and culminates in formal external reporting. For such management systems as strategic planning and budgeting, communication can be taken to refer to both the *internal* information processes by which plans and budgets are developed, and whatever *external* communication is required. Monitoring and reporting systems are designed for the purpose of internal and external communication to defined constituencies about actual compared to planned performance. So also evaluation and audit systems, internal and external, produce information designed for particular constituencies.

The last part of the question is concerned with validation. Diagrams on accountability relationships are generally triangular in nature. One corner of the triangle is occupied by the person assigning responsibility and to whom accountability is due, the second corner by the person who is assigned responsibility and who therefore owes accountability to the first person, and the third by the person who serves the accountability relationship by performing the evaluation/audit function. The role of the third party, whether as part of an internal management system or as an external evaluator/auditor, is to provide assurance to the client, the one to whom accountability is due, about the discharge of responsibilities by the person who owes accountability. This is done either by attestation to the completeness and accuracy of accountability reports produced by the manager who owes accountability, or, in the absence of any such report, by direct evaluation by the evaluator/auditor of the manager's performance and subsequent evaluation/audit report to the client. Attestation has a long tradition for financial statements provided by managers, and is becoming commoner for broad-scope performance information as managers move towards making formal representations on these matters. The CCAF/FCVI approach was specifically designed to provide for an auditable set of representations by management across the range of attributes. Managers would provide the report about shared expectations in the agreed currency (or currencies reflecting the various attributes) and in terms of the agreed criteria, and auditors would attest to the completeness and accuracy of that information.

### How is accountability information used? Are there real consequences of any kind from the discharge of the obligation to be accountable?

While there is little debate that accountability is by people to people, it is common to discuss accountability frameworks in conceptual or technical terms and to forget that accountability frameworks have behavioural implications. An accountability framework that had no real consequences for programmes or individuals would be little more than a costly administrative nuisance and would not be taken seriously. The behavioural effects here would be undesirable in two senses: first, managers would be diverted from presumably meaningful to meaningless activity; and, second, managers would certainly become cynical about accountability and possibly therefore about their use of resources and the results achieved by that use. An accountability framework that did have consequences at the programme and individual level would be meaningful and desirable provided two conditions were met. First, the incentives built into the real consequences should be rationally and fairly linked to desired performance. Second, the measurement system used to assess performance should be carefully designed to reflect and promote desired performance; managers will manage to the measurement system provided, and inappropriate measures will lead managers in the wrong direction. The management systems that deal with real consequences (such systems as the compensation and related work circumstances of managers, and those related to resource allocation to programmes or organizations) are therefore integral in the design of accountability frameworks; they are also integral to the implementation of accountability frameworks – which is the last question to be addressed in the definition of an accountability framework.

### The implementation of an accountability framework

This topic is discussed thoroughly in the literature.[16] These sources discuss the various issues to be addressed in implementing or 'marketing' an accountability framework, and point to the importance of an actual implementation strategy and action plan for any proposed accountability framework.

The discussion is closely tied to the matter of real consequences discussed above. The argument broadly is that implementation of an accountability framework in non-profit programmes and organizations does not merely mean a change in existing processes; rather it requires a major shift in corporate culture. Those at all levels of the hierarchy within the core accountability framework, say, in a private non-profit organization, members of the organization, board members, volunteers, the CEO, programme managers, and staff, must be convinced of three conditions if the accountability initiative is to be successful. First, performance information is important to both those preparing it and those receiving it and will be the basis on which decisions are made. Second, performance information will have a direct impact on the way business is conducted. And, third, performance information will be used fairly, that is, in a balanced rather than selective manner. With specific reference to public programmes and organizations, the Auditor General of British Columbia proposes seven preconditions for success. The seven preconditions are as follows: the objectives of the reform must be clear and consistent; expectations and communication of the reform must be well managed; actions must demonstrate the commitment to making reform successful; delegation of authority must be accompanied by a proportionate enhancement of accountability; accountability must serve to influence governance – accountability is not an end in itself; a culture shift, where results are valued over process, must occur at all levels; and the public (and the legislators who represent them) must exercise tolerance for error as the public sector learns to adapt to a new way of managing.[17]

## III Criteria for the assessment of accountability frameworks

By what criteria can accountability frameworks be assessed? The first and most obvious criterion is that the constituencies *to whom* accountability is due and *from whom* it is owed, i.e. accountability relationships, must be clearly defined. The remaining criteria deal with *what* sort of information is provided, *how* that information is *produced, communicated* and *validated*, and how the information is *used*, i.e. the *real consequences* resulting from the discharge of accountability obligations. These three matters are dealt with in turn, with most emphasis – reflecting the complexity of the issue and the extensive discussion offered in section II and in the literature – on what information is provided.

Are there standards or principles for what information should be provided, i.e. for accountability reports? The literature deals with the subject in a variety of ways. Standards occur at three levels:

First, standards for the *kinds of information* which should be included in accountability reports. Classic examples of this are the Value-for-Money Auditing Standards proposed by the CICA,[18] the set of 12 attributes produced by the CCAF/FCVI,[19] the Balanced Scorecard for commercial organizations[20] and the accountability framework proposed by the Office of the Auditor General and the Committee of Deputy Ministers in British

Columbia.[21] In general, the consensus is that accountability information is multi-dimensional, for commercial as well as non-commercial organizations, reflecting the variety of constituencies for information, that the traditional 'accountability core' of audited financial statements needs to be supplemented by additional information about financial performance, and a variety of non-financial information, and that information is needed about financial and non-financial operating targets and results and also about management systems and practices (such as financial control systems and marketing systems). Chapter 11 offers a set of standards for accountability information in non-profit organizations. Standards for types of information provide the currency of accountability relationships.

Second, standards or *criteria of performance* for each type of information. This is the 'performance indicators' part of the picture. There *are* clearly defined and generally accepted criteria for the financial statements part of accountability reports, but no such agreement on performance criteria for either financial or non-financial performance. What is clear, however, is that meaningful accountability reports must provide performance information as measures *or* representations of some kind against established criteria or benchmarks – which might be, for instance, budgetary targets or competitive standards. Criteria of performance expressed in the agreed currency are required to make operational the shared expectations that are the basis of accountability relationships by specifying what constitutes fulfilment of these expectations.

Third, standards in the form of the *qualitative attributes* of the information presented. Again, there is broad agreement on the set of attributes for financial information[22] and, agreeably, these standards are relatively generalizable to non-financial information. They include: *relevance* (for decision-making), *comparability* (cross-sectionally and longitudinally), *reliability* (including verifiability), and *understandability* (to the various users).

One approach to a *generic template* on the 'What information is provided' question would be to retain the useful distinctness of the three perspectives outlined above within an integrated set of criteria dealing with *content* and *form*. The following proposed approach begins with a general criterion and elaborates its components in a set of specific criteria and sub-criteria.

At the most general level, accountability reports should provide to decision-makers on a timely basis information that is sufficient and appropriate in content and understandable and accessible in form to discharge accountability obligations and provide for governance and management control.

The question of *timeliness* is self-evident; the questions of content and form bear elaboration.

The question of content may be dealt with under the heads of *sufficiency* and *appropriateness*. The criterion of sufficiency refers to the quantity of information provided, and may be further broken down into two sub-criteria: *completeness* and *succinctness*.

Completeness requires that the information be both comprehensive and operationally useful, that is, that the various kinds of information that are significant to the various users for decision-making be provided, and that the information be provided in relation to defined performance criteria. For public and private non-profit organizations, completeness from the perspective of, say, the CEO and the board (the primary internal users) requires information that provides for accountability and control with respect to procedural matters (complete and accurate financial information – in relation to accepted accounting principles – and compliance with authorities – again in relation to established regulatory criteria) and also with respect to consequential matters (the use of resources and the achievement of organizational objectives in relation to criteria). Various approaches to defining this comprehensiveness were outlined above, and a specific attempt at a set of standards is offered in Chapter 5.

Given completeness, the second sub-criterion of succinctness requires that significant information be presented in the appropriate degree of detail, where appropriateness would reflect such matters as the degree of significance (to key users), any particular sensitivities that may obtain – for instance, relating to the privacy of client information – the resources necessary to obtain that information, and any definitional or other structural changes from information previously presented. If the general content criterion of completeness defines what should be in the information provided, the related criterion of succinctness requires that only significant information in the appropriate level of detail be provided, and therefore defines what should not be in the information provided. It can also be argued that succinctness should require that, to the extent possible, the various information components should be presented in such a way that, first, priorities are made clear, and, second, that they provide a graphic or dynamic representation or 'story' of the organization over the management cycle rather than just a static cross-section. Chapter 10, on an adaptation of the CCAF/FCVI attributes, attempts such a representation.

Appropriateness refers to the quality of the information provided. It reflects the extensive material in the literature on the qualitative characteristics of information, and can be broken down into a set of sub-criteria. First, *validity* requires that the information represent accurately what it purports to represent – for instance, how were the statistics on client satisfaction obtained? Are they representative? Or even illustrative? Second, *reliability* requires that information be verifiable to the extent possible, that is, that the same information would be obtained by repeated investigations or by different investigators. Validity and reliability can be taken to include such matters as the reasonableness of assumptions used in deriving information. The notion of verifiability can also be extended to include actual verification, referred to above as validation or audit, by a third party in order to provide assurance about information. Ideally, internal information should be internally verified by, say, an internal audit management system, and external information, should be verified by external audit – including not only the universal external audit of financial statements but also external verification of value-for-money information. In short, verifiability can be seen as auditability, and auditability can be formally extended to include the conduct of audit and the expression of an audit opinion. *Comparability* requires that information of a comparative nature be presented – all performance is relative – and that such information be consistent over time and among similar organizations. For any public or private non-profit organization, information within one year should be comparable – e.g. output achievements should reflect directly output targets – information should be comparable across years, and information should be presented for similar organizations (to establish some external comparability). Finally, *objectivity* requires that information be balanced and free from bias of any kind. The clear identification of sources and methods for obtaining information is obviously essential; without demonstrated objectivity, accountability information may be, or may be perceived to be, little more than a smokescreen.

With respect to structure or form, the two criteria adduced in the general definition were *understandabilty* and *accessibility*. Understandability refers to the cogency, clarity, and readability of the information presented – and would be enhanced by the attempt at a 'moving picture' representation suggested above – and accessibility refers to the provision of assistance to users in such forms as summaries, graphics, indexing, and cross-referencing.

These generic criteria are intended to provide the basis on which an external assessor or auditor could attest to the fairness with which accountability information is presented. The analogy is obviously with the reference to 'fair presentation' used in the traditional short-form auditor's opinion on financial statements.

There is very limited explicit discussion in the literature about criteria for the remaining issues, but reasonable criteria can be inferred from the role played by these other components of an accountability framework.

With respect to the *production* of accountability information, the following criterion can be inferred. Given the required scope of accountability information, the aligned set of management information systems designed to produce that information must be in place, integrated across the management cycle, and operating effectively.

With respect to the *communication* of accountability information, a similar criterion can be inferred. For the defined scope of accountability information across the management cycle, and the defined requirements of the various internal and external constituencies for (users of) accountability information, a set of management systems with respect to both internal and external reporting must be in place, integrated across the management cycle, and operating effectively.

With respect to *validation* of accountability information, the criterion follows that: first, for internal accountability, given scope and defined internal constituency requirements, management systems be in place and operating effectively to plan, conduct and report on evaluations/audits of internal accountability information, and thus to provide assurance to internal users about completeness and accuracy; and, second, for external accountability, given scope and defined external constituency requirements, management systems be in place to provide for external evaluation/audit of external accountability information, and thus to provide assurance to external users about completeness and accuracy.

With respect to the *use* of accountability information, the general criterion follows that management decision-making systems incorporate accountability information in the decision-making process. Two more specific criteria can be inferred. First, internal accountability information must be used by management for internal management control decision-making in a manner consistent with organizational objectives and the corresponding responsibilities and objectives prescribed to management, and must be correspondingly used by senior management and boards for internal governance control decision-making. Second, external accountability information must be correspondingly used by external constituencies, particularly shareholders.

With respect to *real consequences* from the discharge of accountability obligations, the obvious general criterion follows that management systems be in place to translate accountability information into real consequences at the programme level, with respect to, say, continuance and resource allocation, and correspondingly at the individual level with respect to, say, promotion and compensation. More specifically, a wide range of behavioural criteria could be adduced. Two illustrative criteria follow. First, the incentives built into the real consequences should be rationally and fairly linked to desired performance. And, second, the measurement system used to assess performance should be carefully designed to reflect and promote desired performance; managers, being human, will manage to the measurement system provided, and inappropriate measures will lead managers in the wrong direction, i.e. away from behaviour consistent with organizational objectives.

## Notes

1 P. Day and R. Klein, *Accountabilities: Five Public Services* (London, Tavistock Publications, 1987). G. LeClerc, et al., *Accountability, Performance Reporting, Comprehensive Audit: An Integrated Perspective* (Ottawa, CCAF/FCVI, 1996). Dwight Waldo, CEPAQ-ENAP, 'Debats sur L'Imputabilite', Actes du Colloque sur L'Imputabilite, Chateau Mont St. Anne, Quebec, 9 et 10 juin, 1983.
2 Report of the Independent Review Committee on the Office of the Auditor General (Ottawa, Information Canada, 1975), 9.
3 S.J. Matek, *Accountability: Its Meaning and its Relevance to the Healthcare Field* (Hyattsville, Maryland, US Department of Health, Education and Welfare, 1977), 10.
4 Panel on Accountability and Governance in the Voluntary Sector, *Building on*

*Strength: Improving Governance and Accountability in Canada's Voluntary Sector* (Ottawa, Panel on Accountability and Governance, 1999), 14.
5  Day and Klein, *Accountabilities*, 5. Matek, *Accountability*, 14.
6  G. LeClerc, et al., *Accountability*, Chapters 5 and 6.
7  Auditor General of British Columbia and Deputy Ministers' Committee, *Enhancing Accountability for Performance: A Framework and an Implementation Plan* (Victoria, BC, Office of the Auditor General, April 1966). Canadian Institute of Chartered Accountants, CICA Handbook Section 1000, Financial Statement Concepts, Auditor General of British Columbia and Deputy Ministers' Committee, 1996.
8  R. Kaplan and D. Norton, *The Balanced Scorecard* (Cambridge, Mass., Harvard Business School Press, 1996).
9  LeClerc, et al., *Accountability*, 59.
10  Canadian Institute of Chartered Accountants, Public Sector Accounting and Auditing Committee, *General Standards of Financial Statement Presentation* (Toronto, CICA, 1995). Canadian Institute of Chartered Accountants, *Not-For-Profit Financial Reporting Guide* (Toronto, CICA, 1998)
11  Ernst and Young LLP, *Measures that Matter* (Boston, Mass., Ernst and Young Center for Business Innovation, 1998).
12  Kaplan and Norton, *Balanced Scorecard*.
13  Canadian Institute of Chartered Accountants, Public Sector Accounting and Auditing Committee, *Value-for-Money Auditing Standards* (Toronto, CICA, 1988), 2.
14  CCAF/FCVI, *Effectiveness Reporting and Auditing in the Public Sector* (Ottawa, CCAF, 1987).
15  R.N. Anthony and D.W. Young 1999, *Management Control in NonProfit Organizations*, 6th edn (Boston, Mass., Irwin/McGraw-Hill). Canadian Institute of Chartered Accountants, Financial Statement Concepts. Auditor General of British Columbia and Deputy Ministers' Committee, *Enhancing Accountability*.
16  Anthony and Young, *Management Control*. Canadian Institute of Chartered Accountants, Financial Statement Concepts, 43–54. Auditor General of British Columbia and Deputy Ministers' Committee, *Enhancing Accountability*.
17  Canadian Institute of Chartered Accountants, Financial Statement Concepts. Auditor General of British Columbia and Deputy Ministers' Committee, *Enhancing Accountability*, 45.
18  Canadian Institute of Chartered Accountants, *Value-for-Money Auditing Standards*.
19  CCAF/FCVI, *Effectiveness Reporting*.
20  Kaplan and Norton, *Balanced Scorecard*.
21  Canadian Institute of Chartered Accountants, Financial Statement Concepts. Auditor General of British Columbia and Deputy Ministers' Committee, *Enhancing Accountability*.
22  Canadian Institute of Chartered Accountants, *General Standards*. Financial Accounting Standards Board (US), Statement of Accounting Concepts, No. 1, *Objectives of Financial Reporting by Business Enterprises* (Washington, FASB, 1978).

# 2 Generating information to serve accountability relationships

## Evaluation methods and processes

## I Introduction

As we have seen in Chapter 1, accountability is the process for meeting the information needs of those to whom one is responsible (either legally or morally). These needs involve information about possible futures, current actions and the results of past actions. This chapter deals with evaluative approaches for generating the accountability information needed by decision-makers across the management cycle.

Those who have been crying out for 'more and better accountability' in the non-profit sector often complain that key stakeholders such as donors, policy-makers or client groups do not know enough about how effectively and efficiently an organization or programme has been performing. Fears are expressed that money is being wasted or that a particular service is ultimately of no value in improving the conditions it was intended to improve. Therefore, the process of improving the non-profit sector through better accountability must start with evaluation before looking ahead at future challenges and opportunities.

While the need for more and better evaluation may be clear, actually carrying it out in accordance with the ideals laid down in Chapter 1 is not so easy. Many problems and pitfalls arise, which can discourage the process from getting started, distort the results it produces and lead to its rapid abandonment soon after it begins.

The chapters to follow present several pieces of research which show what actually takes place when those seeking accountability attempt to evaluate the performance of the programmes, organizations or larger systems in which they are interested. The picture that emerges from this research is not an especially positive one. Many problems are revealed and yet decisions on funding, programme changes, staffing, and other matters must be made and they will be based, in part, on some kind of assessment of the impact of past practices. For this reason, the remainder of this book examines a variety of specific efforts to move the accountability dialogue into a more open and rational discussion of how decisions will be reached.

This chapter sets the stage for the research reports that follow by intro-ducing basic concepts in evaluation, describing the ideal model of the evaluation process and pointing out the technical and human problems that commonly result in a less than ideal process.

## What is evaluated?

A great deal of confusion can arise between evaluators and evaluatees because the latter does not understand what the former is trying to eval-uate. It is therefore crucial to know the *level* of evaluation being undertaken. These levels are:

- Individual
- Programme, organizational unit or function
- Organization
- Larger social system

Individual evaluation focuses on the performance of individuals in their jobs. The evaluation is usually against standards set down in a job descrip-tion or goals contained in a personal performance plan.

The next level of evaluation focuses on elements *within* an organization such as a programme, an organizational unit (department, section or subsidiary) or a function such as human resources or marketing. Examples of evaluation at this level are assessing the success of a programme for reducing substance abuse by teenagers, or the effectiveness of a marketing department created to boost attendance at symphony concerts, or the impact of a management function, such as planning, on the operation of the organization.

Non-profit organizations are made up of many programmes and functions all designed to achieve the overall mission of the organization. Certain evaluators are interested in assessing the performance of the total organization in achieving its mission and less in the state of each of its programmes. For example, many United Ways (federated funding organi-zations which operate throughout North America) want evaluations of the whole organization because that is what they fund. Conversely, certain government departments who contract with non-profits for the delivery of specific programmes will be focused on the programme level of evalua-tion and care little about the rest of the organization in which the programme resides.

Finally, any given social need or issue is usually addressed by a number of organizations and programmes. The system level of evaluation looks at how the efforts of various interested parties (sometimes called 'actors') collectively impact an issue. This broader perspective has two levels of analysis, referred to here as 'jurisdictional' and 'sectoral' evaluation. Juris-dictional evaluation measures processes or results at the geographical or political level. For example, the assessment of the quality of life of residents in a country, province, or community is an example of jurisdictional evaluation. Sectors are areas of common activity directed towards a particular social or economic end. Evaluation at the sectoral level focuses on the status of the issue or end-goal that the activities are attempting to address. The United Nations' assessment of global child poverty is an example of sectoral evaluation. The Canadian Council on Social Development's annual monitoring of the nature and extent of child health and well-being in Canada is another example. In system-level evaluations, evaluators are not interested in how any one organization deals with an issue but rather in the status of the issue itself.

## Types of evaluation

The ideal evaluation process is one that provides incontrovertible evidence that something has done what it was intended to do. The questions an evaluation process seeks to answer sound simple on the surface. For example, an organization is created to help recent immigrants adjust to their new land. Does it succeed? A programme is developed to help children appreciate art. Does it do that? Often the questions raised are more complex, such as: which organization or programme can make the greatest contribution for a given cost; or, which can achieve a given level of effectiveness at the least cost? These value for money questions are key in the minds of investors (e.g. funders) who want to see the greatest return on their investment. For example, if a funder has only a limited amount of money to devote to the cause of helping the blind, it wants to put that money to work in a way that will have the greatest impact on that cause. Hence, the funder will want comparative evaluative data in order to make its decision. The different types of evaluation given below can help to answer these questions.

### Outcome evaluation

The ultimate objective of evaluation is to make a statement about outcomes – the end result of the activities that are being evaluated. To achieve this, the evaluation effort is focused directly on getting information on specified outcomes. As will be seen, all forms of evaluation have their problems and one of the most serious of these for outcome measurement is that outcomes may differ over time and be more difficult to measure the further they are from the programme or intervention, both in time and causally. One, therefore, has to be aware of long-term, intermediate and short-term outcomes. For example, an organization created to help street youth may have as the outcome it ultimately desires an increase in the chances that 'children at risk' today will be self-supporting, emotionally healthy and contributing members of society when they become adults. This long-term outcome may not be feasible to measure in terms of available time and resources. But a more modest intermediate outcome could be the percentage of the organization's clients who complete a high school education by age 20, compared to a matched sample of other street youth who do not participate in the organization's programmes. Finally, it may be possible only to get at relatively short-term outcomes; for example, the number of the organization's clients who re-establish contact with their families and are not charged with any violations of the law in a 12-month period following programme completion.

*Process evaluation*

It is intended that outcomes, at least in part, should result from a specific set of processes followed or activities undertaken by the evaluatee. As a result, some evaluations attempt to measure the occurrence of activities, or clusters of activities. For example, programmes to help fishermen who have lost their employment due to the decline of fish stocks may measure the number who take special retraining courses, the number and kind of courses available, and the quantity and quality of information provided about alternative sources of employment. The inference is that if these activities are performed well more fishermen will manage to make a successful transition to a new kind of employment. Similarly, an art gallery may seek to assess the success of a special exhibition by counting the number who attended, evaluating the quality of the exhibition catalogue as judged by art experts, and counting the number of press releases produced and column inches of space devoted to the exhibition in local newspapers. If the evaluator's focus is on a leadership function, such as the way the board of directors governs the organization, a process evaluation would seek to measure various aspects of the way it runs its meetings, how it goes about setting goals for the organization, or the roles and responsibilities of its committees.

*Input evaluation*

Processes cannot occur without the initial investment of financial, human and technological resources to make them happen. Therefore, it is possible to perform an evaluation of these inputs. For example, how much money was put into a given project; how many person-hours were devoted to it; how much computer technology was put in place; how much management time was invested in developing the project, etc. Here the inference is that, without the inputs of money, people and technology, the activities cannot occur which, in turn, means that the outcomes cannot be achieved.

## How is evaluation carried out?

In order to answer the question, 'What was the result of past actions?' an evaluator must work through four distinct stages in the evaluation process:

- Designing the evaluation system;
- Choosing data collection methods;
- Developing standards for assessing the data; and
- Interpreting and using the results of the evaluation.

In designing the system, the questions must be asked:

- Why is this being done? (e.g. is it for formative or summative purposes?)
- What is to be evaluated? (e.g. programmes/functions, organizations or systems?)
- What type of evaluation will be used ? (e.g. outcome, process or input?)
- Who will do it and when? (e.g. will outside evaluation experts be used? Will the evaluatees be involved?)

For data collection, the choices are between:

- quantitative (e.g. numerical counts, questionnaire surveys)
- qualitative (interviews, focus groups, observations, case studies)

The evaluation standards must be developed in consideration of:

- How will the evaluator know what the results mean?
- What is success and what is failure?
- What will indicate that a problem exists?

There are two basic kinds of standards: *absolute standards* are previously identified targets against which the programme, organization or system is measured that allow clear indications of how close the evaluatee has come to the specified standards; and *relative standards* which, rather than using a priori targets, allow an evaluatee's results to be compared with the results of others or to the evaluatee's results from some previous period. *Benchmarks* are comparisons to results achieved by others. The evaluation result may be better, the same as or worse than the others, but there is no known absolute standard. *Time-based* comparisons look at the results achieved by the evaluatee across a range of time periods (months, years). The evaluation result is a trend in performance over time that is rising or falling.

*Analysis and Action*, interpreting and using the results, requires answers to the following:

- Why did this result occur? (Was it because the evaluatees were poorly selected or trained? Was it because of a change in conditions beyond their control? Was it due to inadequate funding? Was it due to poor management?)
- What do these results tell us about what can be done better? (Should something be changed? Should the programme be dropped? Should more money be invested?)

## The role of logic models in evaluation

An evaluation system, either implicitly or explicitly, confronts certain problems that inevitably appear when the process is undertaken. They are the 'logical fallacies' in evaluation. Evaluators who commit these fallacies run a high risk of reaching erroneous conclusions. What are they?

### The measurement inference fallacy

This occurs when an outcome is inappropriately inferred from the measurement of a process or an input. For example, an agency claims that the problem of youth unemployment is being solved because there has been an increase of 25 per cent in the number of youths taking employment counselling. In this case, one method of evaluation (counting the output of counselling) is used to infer conclusions more directly reached by another method (outcome measurement). Another version of this fallacy occurs when a measurement is assumed to be a valid representation of the thing measured when this may not be the case. For example, a survey of the attitudes of older people about the importance of fitness shows a great increase in the belief that fitness is important. This is taken as an indicator that the goal of increased fitness levels for seniors is being achieved. The measurement of attitudes is taken as an indication of behaviour.

### The level of focus fallacy

In this case the performance of a whole organization is inferred from the performance of a programme; or the performance of both of these is inferred from the performance of a single individual. For example, an evaluator may conclude that organization X is not successful because it is being led by an executive director who has a reputation of being ineffective in another organization. Or an art gallery is assumed to be achieving its mission of enlivening and enriching the human spirit through art because a special exhibition (one of its programmes) broke new records for attendance.

### The side-effects fallacy

Evaluation is ultimately about measuring results. The results measured are usually those specified as the goals of a programme, organization or larger system. The problem is that the actions taken to reach the goals may create important unanticipated secondary effects (usually called side effects), which are not measured. For example, an agency may have the output goal of raising more money. An evaluation measures this but fails to note that the money was raised by entering into a number of programmes that are unrelated to the organization's mission.

Evaluation systems may attempt to overcome these common problems through system design. The designers seek to make clear what they think are valid links between processes and outcomes and between programmes and organizational mission. They also try to predict possible side effects and create measures to capture them. The results of all this are called the 'logic models' for the evaluation system. As we will see, some systems never make these connections explicit, some simply recommend that they be created for each application of the system, and some create a logic model that addresses one of the fallacies but not the others (e.g. for measurements but not levels or side effects).

## II The ideal evaluation process

The ideal evaluation process is the same process as that used in the natural sciences to discover new truths about the physical world. It is known as the scientific method. It can be illustrated by describing in a simplified way how the effectiveness of a new drug is evaluated.

The process begins with a claim, or hypothesis, about what the new drug is intended to do (and not do). This is a statement of its goals or objectives. For example, it may be to control pain due to headache with no side effects for at least twelve hours. Usually after many tests on animals, the drug is tested on people. The drug is administered to a group of people with headaches (the condition it is meant to treat) and a placebo is administered to a matched sample in a 'double blind' design in which the participants and those performing the test do not know who is getting which treatment. All other conditions that might influence the onset, duration or severity of headache pain are controlled for in the evaluation design, as well as all possible undesirable side effects the drug might cause. If all goes well, the drug takers show better results than those who were given the placebo. After repeating the same test a number of times, and getting the same positive result, the evaluators conclude that the drug is effective and safe.

From this example, it can be seen that the ideal evaluation requires:

(1) A clear statement of its objectives. They should be S.M.A.R.T.: Specific, Measurable, Achievable, Relevant and Timebound.

(2) A clear statement of the desired outcomes – both positive effects and the absence of negative 'side effects' – which means creating indicators or measures that fully reflect the desired outcomes and possible side-effects; and a process for interpreting the results of these measurements, i.e. what 'good', 'average' or 'poor' results are. (This means there must be one or more pre-established, absolute standards against which performance can be measured in a given time period, or relative standards that allow comparisons with others or with the evaluatee over time.)

(3) A choice of methods for producing the data on the indicators which are timely and feasible to use in terms of cost and effort. They must also be valid (measure what they intend to measure) and reliable (produce consistently accurate results every time they are used).

(4) Logic models of the types discussed above. There are two basic logic models required:

1   'measurement' logic models make clear the assumed links between input indicators and process indicators, process indicators and outcome indicators, and outcome indicators and goals. They should also identify the other factors that affect the indicators at each stage but are not directly controllable by those responsible. These are the 'constraints' discussed in Chapter 1 within which the evaluatee must work. Finally, they should attempt to predict possible side-effects and show how these will be measured. The generic structure of a measurement-based logic model is shown in Figure 2.1.

2   'level of focus' logic models link evaluations between levels. That is, they make explicit the links between evaluations of individuals, programmes or organizational units, organizations and systems or sub-systems. The generic structure of level-based logic models is shown in Figure 2.2.

## III  Problems with the ideal evaluation process

Even in the world of scientifically designed studies of drug effectiveness, things can go wrong. Unfortunately, cases like the Thalidomide scandal in the 1960s in North America (a drug approved for reducing nausea during pregnancy which subsequently caused thousands of birth deformities) are not rare. In the case of the evaluation of people, programmes, functions, organizations or systems in the non-profit world, there are significantly more pitfalls and difficulties. They arise from two basic sources:

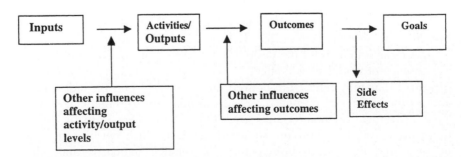

*Figure 2.1* Generic measurement logic model.

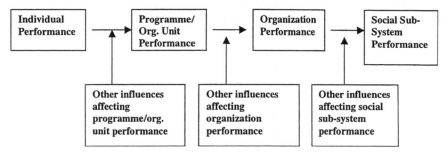

*Figure 2.2* Generic level-based logic model.

• Those that are due to inherent technical difficulties in the design that can cast serious doubts on the conclusions of the evaluation; and
• Those that are the result of the psycho-social reactions that occur when people are subjected to evaluation by others.

### Technical problems with the evaluation process

While the ideal evaluation process ought to start with a clear statement of goals, in reality arriving at such statements is often very difficult. Developing even clearer statements of outcome indicators that fully and unambiguously reflect these goals is even more difficult. For example, at the system level, the aim of a government department may be to improve the 'quality of citizenship' of the population by 'ensuring a high level of appreciation of our heritage'. Many museums, ethnic associations, historical site preservation groups and other organizations exist to help achieve this general goal. But the difficulty of creating a clear and widely shared definition of 'appreciation of our heritage' is formidable. At the very least there will likely be considerable disagreement among evaluators and the various evaluatees about the definition.

Once goals are stated clearly, the connection between goals and outcomes may seem a simple enough technical challenge yet the history of evaluation is rife with examples of failure at this stage. For example, an external funder may want to evaluate an immigrant aid organization's programme for teaching English to non-native speakers. The goal of these classes is to get as many non-English speaking immigrants as possible to some predetermined standard of proficiency in English, for a given sum of money. It is easy to conclude that a logical outcome indicator for this goal might be 'the number of non-English speaking immigrants who complete the course with a mark of 60 per cent or better on a standardized English test'. One of the easiest ways to achieve this goal is to select only those who already have some English language skills and who have the time and resources to attend the classes. As a result, many immigrants who most need the help, but who can't attend class regularly or are deemed slow learners, may be systematically excluded.

The methodological problem is that the choice of only a few specific outcome measures often cannot begin to capture the full range and complexity of the effects caused by the programme, organization or system interventions. How does one create measures that fully reflect the mission of an art gallery to 'enliven and enrich the human spirit through exposure to art' or even of a simple programme in a community service agency 'to improve the quality of life of frail elderly seniors' in its district?

Once outcomes are established, methods must be put in place to obtain the desired data, such as statistical reporting systems and attitude measurement systems. These methods are often exceedingly difficult and costly to create and maintain over time. A large percentage of non-profit organizations have little or no money to invest in developing sophisticated evaluation tools, nor do they have the skills to implement them. For example, measurement of the success of the Boy Scout movement in creating better citizens should probably require follow-up investigations of former scouts at intervals throughout their adolescence and adulthood and compare them with a similar group of non-scouts. Just keeping track of the addresses of the former scouts after a few years can be difficult enough in a primarily volunteer organization, let alone the other difficulties of following a control group and getting valid measurements of citizenship.

While creating evaluation systems is fraught with technical problems, interpreting the results of what they produce is even more difficult because of the logical fallacies identified earlier. This is due to the inherent weakness of the logic models (either implicit or explicit) on which the evaluations systems are based.

*Problems with measurement logic models*

Sometimes, for practical reasons, all that can be gathered are input and/or process data. As Figure 1 shows, however, the connection between engaging in certain activities and producing certain outcomes is influenced by other conditions not controllable by those carrying out the activities. It may seem obvious, for example, that, if the United Way in a community launches a 'new and improved' publicity campaign to increase donations and donations actually increase 7 per cent over the previous year, then that result was due to the new campaign. But what if, over the same period, the economy had improved such that people felt more secure and able to donate? Conversely, if donations do not increase, does this mean the new campaign was a failure? Not necessarily. Perhaps if there had been no new campaign, there would have been a more serious decline in donations due to an economic downturn or increased competition from other fund-raisers.

*Problems with level-of-focus logic models*

Because of the methodological difficulties of measuring things at the organization-wide and system-wide levels, some evaluators suggest that only programmes should be evaluated because only programmes have sufficiently specific and measurable objectives. The problem is that programmes themselves are ultimately only means to larger ends. They are meant to contribute to the overall mission of an organization, or of a larger social system, usually along with many other programmes. Indeed, some evaluators want to be able to compare relative costs and benefits among related programmes, so there is at least an implicit logic model that links levels. However, these links are often not explicitly stated and therefore frequently not tested. This means that a programme may be shown to be a great success on its own terms, but it may actually not be all that good when compared to other programmes in the organization, or when compared to other programmes contributing to the larger system mission. Finally, even if the level-of-focus logic model is tested in some way, the problem of the contaminating influence of unknown or uncontrollable variables can arise to confuse the interpretation of the results. So 'proving' that programme X provides more 'bang for the buck' than programmes Y or Z becomes exceedingly difficult.

*A special word on 'best practices'*

There is a long-standing belief among management consultants and academics that certain practices work better than others, thereby producing more successful outcomes. The problem has been that years of research have failed to prove conclusively that these 'best practices' actually produce the results claimed for them over long periods of time and across different organizations. This leads to the phenomenon of 'fads' where various practices are presented as 'the answer', but then are found wanting and are replaced by another set of sure-fire techniques. The general failure of fads is not to say that best practices do not exist, only that they do so within a certain context – personal, historical, cultural, economic, political or technological. This means they are idiosyncratic; what works for one programme or organization may not work for another. The one universal 'best practice' is a commitment to developing an information system that reveals when improvements are necessary and leads to the search for those improvements that are effective for that particular situation.

## Psychosocial problems with the evaluation process

*The 'Look good avoid blame' and 'goal displacement' phenomena*

Most people prefer to succeed and, if there is a failure, prefer not to be seen as responsible for it. This is the 'Look good avoid blame' (LGAB) mindset. Formal evaluation processes often proclaim that they are not being carried out for the purpose of judging those responsible (i.e. that they are formative rather than summative). The intent is to simply reveal any problems that might exist and provide information to help resolve them. The difficulty is that, in spite of all the assurances to the contrary, many evaluatees believe in their hearts that, if an evaluation reveals problems, they will be blamed; or, conversely, if the evaluation results are positive, they can take the credit. The behaviour of elected officials when economic conditions improve or worsen is only one of the more vivid examples of this tendency.

Therefore, when an LGAB attitude prevails, the evaluation process is likely to be a 'political' one. The evaluatees will focus on whatever the evaluation indicators are and will do what they can to show the desired results. Or, if the results look bad in spite of their efforts, they will go to whatever lengths are necessary to explain the results as being beyond their control. This self-serving tendency is well recognized in the system of public auditing of finances. It is predicated on the belief that a certain percentage of people who are responsible for other people's money might be tempted to be less than accurate in accounting for its use. Hence the evaluators have created the separate, specialized and highly controlled profession of public accounting and a system of auditing to provide assurance that money has been spent as the providers intended it to be spent. The problem is that more complex evaluations of goal attainment are not amenable to the application of the kind of rigorous standards that are used in tracking financial expenditures.

As we have seen, outcome indicators often fail to capture the full intent of goals. When the LGAB phenomenon is operating, these inadequate indicators become substitutes for goals as the evaluatees seek to 'look good'. This is known as the 'goal displacement' phenomenon. The case of the immigrant aid organization offering English language training discussed above illustrates this point. The indicator chosen to represent the goal – number of successful course completions – became the goal while the real goal of helping as many people as possible learn English was forgotten. In this case, goal achievement was actually harmed by the temptation to admit only those applicants with a high potential for success.

*Subjective interpretation of reality (SIR) phenomenon*

The other key psycho-social tendency which creates major problems for evaluation systems arises when evaluation data must be interpreted and explained. We have already seen how frail the logic models are which underlie evaluations. When it comes to analysing almost any aspect of human behaviour, there are too many variables and there is too little control over those variables to permit solid conclusions about causal connections. For every human behaviour, there are many theories offered as explanation, few of which can be conclusively proven. This is one of the reasons for the constant flow of new ideas in fields such as child rearing, managing people, education, how to handle chronic welfare dependency and the treatment of mental illness.

In spite of the lack of fully proven theories, however, decisions about complex social problems must be made. For example, every day governments, funders, and agency executives must choose to create or change policies with respect to foster parenting for children at risk, or whether to start or terminate a programme aimed at reducing violence among school children. Those who make such decisions would usually say they make them on the basis of empirical evidence, but since such evidence is inevitably inconclusive, they also base them on their pre-existing beliefs and attitudes about 'what works'. In other words, most evaluation results are interpreted subjectively and different people can interpret the same data many ways.

The combination of the LGAB and SIR phenomena makes it likely that the evaluation process will be a 'political' one. Some evaluatees may resist evaluation in the first place because of the fear that it will reveal poor results for which they will be blamed. Others may attempt to distort the evaluation data once the process is implemented so the data will make them look good. And, both evaluatees and evaluators may interpret the final results to support predetermined positions.

## *Recent research on evaluation processes: what really goes on*

The next two chapters present reports on a 5-year research project which observed and recorded evaluation efforts in nine non-profit organizations in two Canadian cities. (Research by others into evaluation is reviewed in Chapter 3, where the research project is introduced.) These studies focus on the relationship between external evaluators and evaluatees. The evaluators are stakeholders who provide funds for the organizations that were studied.

# 3 Recent research on accountability relationships and evaluation

## What really goes on?

## I Introduction

The concept of organizational effectiveness is elusive, contested and particularly difficult to grasp in non-profit organizations.[1] Yet with funding constraints and calls for enhancing accountability mechanisms, there are increasing pressures to 'tighten' and 'rationalize' criteria and processes for evaluating such organizations. But what really goes on when evaluators set out to make judgements about the effectiveness of non-profit organizations?

Reviews of the literature on organizational effectiveness have tended to show it as falling within distinct camps, with little overlap between them. One of the most common distinctions has been between those theorists and researchers who view evaluation as an intendedly rational process, and those that view it as an essentially political process.[2] 'Rational' in this sense refers to formal processes for establishing that means lead to preferred ends. 'Political' refers to informal processes by which parties seek to gain support for, and avoid conflict over, their personal aims and ambitions.

The former school is represented primarily by those coming out of positivistic management science and professional evaluator backgrounds. Its representatives work with the assumption that facts about performance can be ascertained, and, while subsequent judgements may be fallible, they can be brought as close to the 'truth' as possible.

The majority of those working with a 'political' perception of the evaluation process tend to represent the post-modern schools of organizational theory.[3] They believe that evaluators and evaluatees often have different objectives, and that there is much that cannot be measured objectively. Therefore evaluation is simply a process in which parties attempt to negotiate an interpretation of reality in which the subjective views of the side with the most power tends to dominate.

What is missing in the literature is a point of view that considers the possibility that both perspectives on evaluation have some validity. Both 'rational' and 'political' elements can be at work at the same time during the evaluation process, but as yet there is little empirical research to show how this interweaving might occur. Accordingly, this chapter examines how members of three distinct funding organizations evaluated the same two agencies in Toronto. In doing this it identifies critical underlying dimensions of the 'organizational effectiveness' construct, and shows the ways in which evaluators unconsciously use them in reaching conclusions on agency effectiveness.

The research used a qualitative design to examine the funding–evaluation relationships between non-profit social service agencies and their main funders. Data collection and analysis entailed a grounded theory approach,[4] in which researchers attempted to minimize a priori theorizing about the situation. Researchers interviewed individuals in the funding and funded organizations that were involved in processes related to agency evaluation and funding. In addition, they observed various meetings within agencies and between agencies and funders, and reviewed contemporary and historical documents. A framework for describing evaluation processes emerged from the data, and this framework was then used to interpret the funders' evaluations of agencies. One of the funders studied is a Canadian provincial government ministry, one is a municipality in that province, and the third is a federated funding organization (FFO). The ministry had annual expenditures in the order of $8 billion (all figures are in Canadian dollars) and funded several thousand social service agencies, including about 500 in Toronto. The municipality provided about $14 million in funds for some 300 agency-operated programmes in this city. The FFO distributed about $40 million to some 205 agencies in the city.

The two agencies studied are called the 'professional institution' (PI) and the 'community development agency' (CDA). Based on terms people used in referring to them, PI, an organization with roots in the nineteenth century, is a multi-service, multi-branch agency that provides services to families and children throughout the city. Its annual budget at the time of the study in 1993 was in the order of $9 million. Of this, it received 49 per cent from the ministry, 11 per cent from the municipality, 15 per cent from the FFO and the rest from other sources. It provided child welfare services on behalf of the ministry and municipality, children's health services on behalf of the ministry, and counselling services on behalf of the municipality and the ministry. The FFO provided core funding for the agency, a member agency of the federation. CDA established in the mid-1980s, provides services for families with children in high-need neighbourhoods from one location in a specific area of the city. At the time of the study its annual expenditures were under a half million dollars, of which it received 46 per cent from the ministry, 6 per cent from the municipality, 5 per cent from the FFO and the rest from other sources.

The choice of the particular funders and fundees as subjects of the study was dictated by necessity. In practice, it is quite difficult to persuade organizations to allow in-depth observation of how decisions are made about such important matters as funding. In this instance the funders gave permission only on the condition that organizations which they deemed to be 'not troublesome' would be studied. We were able to persuade one large, well-established organization and one small 'emerging' organization to allow themselves to be made subjects of the study. It must be empha-sized, therefore, that, because of the constraints in the selection of the research subjects, no generalizations regarding all funder–fundee evalua-tion processes are possible.

Rather than starting with an overview of the data, this chapter first briefly describes the organizational effectiveness evaluation framework that emerged from the research. It then uses the framework as the basis for describing the general approaches to evaluation used by each of the three funders. How they evaluated the two agencies is then presented. The chapter concludes with a discussion of the implications of the research for practice and theory.

## A multidimensional framework for understanding evaluation processes

The primary insight derived from this close examination of evaluation processes was that the parties involved may often differ in terms of the scope, focus and method of evaluation. For example, the scope of the eval-uation; what they evaluate, that is, the focus of the evaluation; and how they evaluate, that is, their evaluation methods. The parties are not always explicit about their positions on these dimensions of evaluation processes. Each evaluator (and often there are several) and evaluatee tends to make implicit assumptions about answers to these questions of the 'who, what, and how' in the evaluation process. We suggest that this is one reason that the process so often is viewed as 'political' rather than rational.

Figure 3.1 depicts the conceptual framework illustrating the scope, focus, and method dimensions of the evaluation process.

### Scope dimension

The scope of evaluation refers to the identity of the entity being evalu-ated. Three common identities found during our study of the two agencies and three funders were programme, system, and agency.

In general, a programme is an organized set of activities and resources directed towards common goals related to providing services. Although the concept can be vague and programme boundaries are not always clear,[5] the participants in the research found it easy to distinguish between the concepts of programme and those of agency and system. For example, they would talk about how it is necessary to evaluate the 'English as a second language programme' in an agency offering many services for recent immigrants who did not speak English.

The second aspect of the scope dimension is the agency. An agency is an incorporated non-profit organization that receives funding to serve the

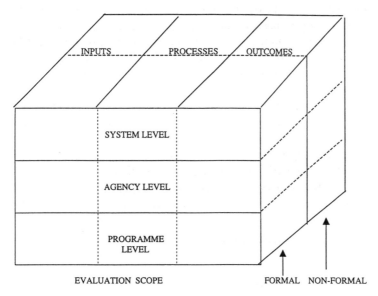

*Figure 3.1* Effectiveness evaluation framework.

needs of one or more constituencies. The evaluation of agencies addressed the overall performance of the agency and all the activities carried out to administer it. Evaluators focusing on the agency level would make comments such as 'I like that agency; it is a no-nonsense, business-like organization'.

The programme/agency dichotomy appeared straightforward in the research data. A third element of the scope dimension was not as evident initially, but in the eyes of certain funders, was obvious once identified. This was the 'system'. The system is an abstraction, but it generally means the agencies or programmes in aggregate together with their funding mechanisms and regulations. The system addresses a designated geographic area such as 'long-term care for the elderly ill in Scotland', 'the drug problem in San Francisco', or 'Canadians with handicaps'. It is a combination of elements with its own distinct identity.[6] At the system level, evaluation efforts are directed at assessing how well the system as a whole is working.

### *Focus dimension*

Focus, what is being evaluated, is the second dimension of the evaluation framework. Three aspects of evaluation focus that emerged from the data were inputs, processes and outcomes. These have been defined in detail in Chapter 3.

## Method dimension

The method dimension, how an evaluation is carried out, is the third dimension of the evaluation framework. The research revealed two types of evaluation methods used by evaluators, which we have labelled formal and non-formal.

One view that emerged from the data was that respondents believed evaluations should be done as 'scientifically' as possible, that is, by applying formal methods, again as described in this chapter.

For example, the use of budgets to control expenditures is a type of formal evaluation. It has a process focus and is aimed at the programme or agency level. The budget is made up of predicted expense levels for certain activities that represent the criteria for judgement. Evaluation is based on how well budget targets are met. A more typical example of outcome-focused formal evaluation at the programme level would be 'before' and 'after' measures of a family therapy programme on spouse abuse. The formal approach is 'technically rational' and attempts to use scientific methods as the basis for the evaluation decision.

Evaluation is about judgement. It became clear in our research that evaluators were constantly making judgements about others using non-formal methods. Sometimes evaluatees were fully aware of the process and the methods being used: these were the formal evaluations. But often the basis on which judgements were reached was not explicit. We called this the non-formal method of evaluation. When interviewed in-depth, most evaluators said they felt that the judgements they made in non-formal ways were arrived at as 'rationally as those based on formal methods' and were as valid. But this was not perceived in the same way by those being evaluated.

There appeared to be two common non-formal methods being used: reputation, and congruence with values. Reputation is what is generally believed about a specific agency, programme, or group of similar agencies or programmes. Reputation appears primarily at the agency level of analysis and is based on the opinions of groups the evaluator considers important. An agency's reputation can come from the opinions of others and/or from judgements the evaluator has made in the past. The implicit assumptions are that what representatives of organizations in associational networks (e.g. other agencies, other funders, umbrella groups) believe about the agency or programme is important for judging outcomes or processes, and that one can accept these beliefs as valid judgements.

Values-based evaluation arises from deeply held beliefs about what a system, agency, or programme ought to be like. Such beliefs often are taken for granted in such a way that they are not explicitly articulated as criteria for judgement. Judgements are made without formal measures being taken, and the evaluatees are not always officially notified that they are being judged against these criteria. If they are notified, they might not be told how much weight is being placed on the criteria or what an acceptable performance standard would be.

Examples of a reputation-based, non-formal evaluation would be comments such as the following: 'I hear Agency X has been made a United Way-supported agency; that shows you how good their work must be.' 'We can't support Art Gallery Y any more; everyone says it has completely lost touch with where art is going.'

An example of a system-level, non-formal, values-based evaluation is the belief that it is inefficient for two or more agencies to provide similar services to the same clientele, that is, that service duplication is to be avoided unless parallel services are warranted. Unquestioning belief in this proposition then leads certain agencies to be judged negatively because they are part of an 'inefficient' system. An agency-level example is a belief that 'ethno-specific' agencies are better at serving the particular ethnic groups they represent than are 'mainstream' agencies. The mainstream agency, with multiple programmes, only some of which may be ethno-specific, may thus be judged ineffective simply because it is not ethno-specific. An example at the programme level is the belief that clients ought to participate in developing and providing the services they need. This would lead programmes seen as not encouraging client participation to be evaluated negatively.

To summarize, the effectiveness evaluation framework shows various ways in which misunderstandings and contradictions can arise between an evaluator and evaluatee, between two or more evaluators, or even within a single evaluator organization. One can be evaluating at a programme level while another is assuming that the agency is the level to use. Often the espoused rhetoric of evaluators is that they are interested only in outcomes although, in fact, the actual focus in on processes. A major problem arises when a formal evaluation method is used while at the same time – only without formal recognition – a non-formal evaluation process based on reputation or value congruence is at work.

The evaluation framework comprises three dimensions, each of which has components. We recognize that any given evaluation may use a mix of components. For example, it may be based on information from programme, agency, or systems levels; may focus on both processes and outcomes, and may have used formal and non-formal methods. One of the reasons evaluation is so often seen as 'political' is that the parties involved misperceive, or are unaware of, the particular mix of approaches being taken.

## Evaluation processes of three funding organizations

The three funding organizations studied in this research funded many of the same non-profit social service organizations in the city in which the research took place, including the two agencies covered in this chapter. The following are brief descriptions of the three funding organizations as described by their representatives.

First, according to ministry respondents and official documents, the *ministry*'s formal role was that of province-wide policy and standard setting and broad system management in the area of social services. District offices managed the 'local system', 'corporate' units in the province's capital city supported and guided district offices, and non-profit social service agencies delivered mandated services, services defined in terms of ministry programmes. The government determined the services needed in the process of developing legislation and defining related services. Government representatives viewed agencies as agents of the state, providing services under contract (that is, a service plan and legal agreement) to the ministry to meet public objectives.

Second, municipal staff said that the *municipality* had a role as an architect and planner of community services for the geographic area of the city. It had established funding mechanisms in three areas: children's aid society funding for agencies providing child welfare services; purchase of counselling service contracts for agencies to provide counselling to people on low income; and grants to agencies to deliver certain specified social service programmes (e.g. for seniors, immigrant women, etc). There were evaluation processes associated with each funding mechanism.

Third, representatives of the *federated funding organization* indicated that their role in evaluating and funding agencies, was to ensure that funds meet vital needs in the community (defined as the city in which they operated) with maximum efficiency, and to promote future donations by the public by offering the assurance that agencies receiving funding were effective. FFO staff provided the overall guidelines for evaluating and funding agencies, with panels of volunteers applied to individual agencies. The FFO's allocations committee considered evaluations of individual agencies, as well as other factors, in deciding on the distribution of funds to agencies across the system.

### How the three funders approached the scope dimension of evaluation

The locus of the *ministry* was on social problems and issues province-wide. Both its political masters and its administrative chiefs tended to see the world in terms of issues such as services for 'children at risk', welfare for the indigent and unemployed, services for the disabled, etc. They therefore viewed individual agencies primarily as vehicles for the delivery of programmes designed to deal with 'their' issues. While they expressed concern if any given agency did a poor job of programme delivery, they tended to look at things from a 'system-wide' level. For them, system-wide meant, for example, the views of the electorate and the media concerning the condition of children at risk in the province as a whole. While ministry leaders expressed a desire to be able to assess the outcomes of programmes at the individual agency level, in practice (as will be seen below) they were doing little to bring this about during the period of study and remained primarily responsive to system-wide conditions.

An example of the ministry's concern for the system rather than individual organizations or their particular programmes, was the often repeated belief that there was 'too much infrastructure' and that there could be a more efficient administration of service delivery through 'integration and rationalization of the delivery system' and the 'amalgamation' of agencies. Given no political opposition, they would have proceeded to do this irrespective of the performance of any given agency. In practice they could move only slowly in this direction because of opposition in the communities that would be affected by such moves.

The *municipality*'s approach to the scope of evaluation differed somewhat between its three areas of activity. It had made a broad policy decision to work with the provincial ministry to support children's aid societies operating in its jurisdiction and to pay local agencies for providing family counselling to low-income earners. This meant their concern was 'top down' (in that decisions on funding were not significantly influenced by the delivery agencies) and system-wide at the level of the city. In practice, they did little or no evaluation of these two areas of activity but depended on the ministry both for funds and evaluation.

In the area of grants, the perspective changed. The scope was much more 'bottom up' and focused on the agency. Agencies would apply to the city for grants in support of specific programmes which it (the agency) believed were needed by the community in which it operated. If the agency could make a sufficiently persuasive case, the city would provide a grant. At the time of the study, the city was undertaking an intensive review of its grant-making process aimed at giving it a more top-down system-wide emphasis (i.e. depending less on individual agencies to define community needs) but this had not yet been completed.

The *federated funding organization* differed significantly from the government ministry in that it focused primarily on the agency. System considerations entered the picture when it came to deciding which agencies would receive funding. It had its own assessment of community needs, and attempted to avoid duplications, etc. However, once an agency was accepted for funding, evaluation emphasized the agency's overall performance in meeting the needs it had claimed it would be meeting when it was accepted. Evaluations by volunteer citizens' panels occurred every two years with ongoing agency contacts with FFO staff taking place in the intervening period.

Like the municipality, the FFO at the time of the study was becoming more concerned about system-wide matters in that agency evaluations were not the only consideration in deciding on funding. Efforts were being made to develop a plan for allocation based more on an assessment of overall community needs. For example, there were several discussions about whether to reallocate some funds from large 'established' agencies to newer, 'emerging' ones which might be 'closer' to the communities they were created to serve.

## Approaches to the focus dimension

From a focus perspective, the *ministry*'s evaluations primarily addressed processes. The ministry and agencies signed formal agreements that set out what services agencies would provide. These agreements constituted a contract and district office staff then monitored these contracts to 'maintain regulations', and to identify the need for action if an agency deviated from the terms of the contract. There was a specific focus on compliance with legislation for licensed programmes. Whether or not licensing was involved, programme supervisors looked at how agencies ran programmes. 'Following the rules' and 'compliance with regulations' was the main message.

At the time of the study, corporate staff had task forces at work developing 'accountability projects' which were aimed at adding an outcome focus to evaluations of agencies and programmes. These projects were looking for outcome indicators for specific service areas. Various stakeholder representatives were participating in these projects, such as ministry staff, service consumers, agency officials, and advocacy groups. The intent was that the indicators developed would be used to compare the performance of programmes across agencies. By the time of writing, however, they had still not managed to make the conversion from process to outcome focused evaluation. The focus of evaluation in the *municipality* was also primarily on processes, with relatively little attention paid to outcomes. Criteria for agency eligibility to provide programmes funded by the municipality addressed the organization of the agency and how it conducted its business. For evaluating programmes already funded, municipal staff focused on agency management, how programmes met community needs, and the extent that the agency represented its community. Examples of statements of what was considered important were 'to work in the language of the community', and hiring 'staff who are connected to communities'.

Even when the municipality set out to review its whole system of grant making it concentrated on process. The mandate of the expected new grants system would be to provide community-based services that address critical social needs in a way that promoted equitable access. The key objectives of the new grants system, as presented in the review committee's report, were to be: 'flexibility, stability, accountability, effectiveness and collaboration'. However, the question of how these processes would connect to outcomes such as reduced homelessness, better-integrated immigrants, etc. was not discussed.

The *federated funding organization* had an interest in increasing the focus of its evaluations on outcome measurement but the current emphasis, like the other two, was on processes. For the agency-level reviews that panel volunteers conducted, the FFO had established evaluation criteria though they did not specify how they were to be measured, nor what standard an agency had to achieve in order to be judged as excellent, average, or poor. Of the 40 criteria established, all were process oriented. For example, there were 15 criteria addressing management processes; 9 looked at the agencies' support for the FFO; and 9 addressed the accessibility of the agency for community members. Ten criteria were grouped under the headings 'agency effectiveness' but even here the focus was on whether the agency possessed processes that might yield outcome achievement rather than the outcomes themselves.

At the system level there was also a focus on processes. Although there was work underway to examine relations between the structure of the system and system-level outcomes, the focus of system-level evaluation was on how the system was structured and how it operated, rather than on the effects of the system on those receiving services. For example, evaluation of the system addressed whether funds were allocated where the need is greatest. This was manifested in discussions on whether 'established' agencies were receiving too great a proportion of funds, limiting the ability of the system to meet emerging needs through 'new' agencies. Questions arose from some as to whether established agencies were too 'professionalized' and insufficiently 'community-based', and whether they were 'culturally appropriate' in terms of the board and staff composition. On the other hand, other FFO staff argued that larger, established agencies had the expertise and stability required for the effective provision of services. While the issue of the relative effectiveness of large versus small agencies was debated, it was seen as unresolvable at present due to the lack of impact assessment and outcome measures.

### Approaches to the methods dimension

The *ministry*'s evaluation methods varied. Formal evaluations were a part of district staff responsibilities. Staff described these formal processes as including reviews of service plans and licensing, as well as reviews of funding application documents and other materials submitted by the agencies along with legal agreements. These reviews were based on requirements established in legislation, and involved the application of standardized procedures for reviewing documentation. In the few cases where an agency would come to the notice of the ministry because it had got into trouble with some of its stakeholders, other formal processes were followed, such as programme reviews.

Many of the ministry staff interviewed said that it was desirable to avoid subjectivity in evaluations. However, there were also non-formal evaluation processes in use. Those interviewed admitted that an agency's reputation could be a factor in evaluation, albeit an informal one. Lacking programme outcome measures, district staff would rely on their impressions of agencies. Many staff said they had heard comments and complaints about agencies, and described how 'you know from the community how an agency is doing'. Others said they sometimes heard about 'incidents' from clients who received programme services that agencies delivered. They also had contacts with other funders and umbrella organizations, through which they picked up information on agencies and programmes. Thus staff got to know their agencies and programmes based on their day to day contacts with them and what others told them.

The ministry's institutionalized values also constituted a part of its non-formal evaluation method. This was evident primarily at the system level. As noted above, many of those interviewed said that the ministry preferred a stable social service system with a relatively smaller number of large multi-programme agencies that provide mandated services in compliance with regulations. 'Amalgamation' and 'integration' were buzzwords at the ministry, although there was no empirical evidence on the relationship between the extent of system amalgamation and integration, and system effectiveness.

In so far as the *municipality* evaluated its purchase of counselling service contracts, it followed the practice of the ministry by simply ensuring that the terms of the contracts were being adhered to – a formal administrative exercise. The evaluation of grants, however, was much more informal. Essentially the staff member designated as responsible for a given grant talked to agency representatives about the programme in question to get a sense of whether there were any problems with it. They also mentioned that they occasionally discussed grant-receiving agencies with other agencies and community groups as well as the FFO and ministry colleagues.

Several staff members expressed a desire for a more formal set of criteria and measurement tools to aid them in this process and hoped that the recently completed review of grant making might lead to this increased formalization.

Formal reviews of agency performance were a distinct aspect of *federated funding organization* evaluations. The FFO had established criteria for evaluating member agencies, and a similar approach to evaluating temporarily funded agencies. Staff members mentioned that there were ongoing efforts to improve these. Another one stated 'we are committed to performance-based allocations'. The FFO trained its volunteer panel members in the application of these methods, and a staff expert supported each panel.

Panel members used 40 official written criteria as the basis for their discussions that led to an overall grade for the agency's performance. They described how technical expertise was available for each panel (e.g. finance, labour relations), and how panel evaluations paid particular attention to financial management issues. The panel's evaluation of agencies had to support its funding recommendations. A higher level FFO committee reviewed and challenged panel recommendations in order to help achieve consistency across panels, with final approval of evaluating and funding coming from the FFO's board.

Non-formal methods were also in use, however. Although agency reputation was not formally a part of FFO evaluations, FFO staff did consider it. As one interviewee said, 'a good evaluation takes reputation into account', and FFO staff would hear about specific agencies from the community of consumers and other agencies. In addition, volunteers and staff talked about the allocation of funds by type of agency (e.g. established or new) and by geography (e.g. suburbs or downtown). This reflected a perception of reputation associated with the type of agency, as opposed to specific agencies.

Often there was continuity in the composition of the volunteer panels from one year to the next. This allowed for the retention of impressions of agency effectiveness from year to year. Further, panel members received the evaluation reports of previous panels which indicated how the FFO had viewed an agency in the past. Staff also communicated their perceptions of agency reputations; for example, the researchers were informed by several staff members that that the agencies included in this research were well-performing agencies.

Unofficial estimates of an agency's congruence with values provided a second aspect of the FFO's non-formal evaluation method. While panels had formal criteria to guide their evaluation and funding decisions, FFO staff could affect the interpretation and importance of these criteria in their communication with a panel. For example, the presence of 'anti-racism' policies in an agency and an estimation of its ability to survive if funding were reduced were heavily weighted informal criteria. The 'fit' of agency activities with the FFO's mission also entered into evaluation and funding decisions, as did the equitable allocation of resources across geographic communities and types of agency. There was also considerable weight given to how well individual agencies represented their communities in their activities. For example, those interviewed felt that an agency should focus on empowering those it serves (rather than concentrating on providing professional treatment), to contribute to community development.

FFO staff members interviewed reported a general interest in promoting a system that reflected the city's diversity. They believed that the social services system should be diverse and representative of local communities. This took the form of a discussion about 'hastening the shift in resources' from large, mainstream agencies to smaller agencies, where funds were 'desperately needed'. Some interviewees indicated that the proportion of funding that large agencies received might not reflect the overall needs of the community, and disempowered groups might not be represented by the large agencies. Some referred to large agencies as being relatively slow to change and inefficient in comparison to small ones.

Another system-level value expressed by some FFO interviewees was that the FFO should try to minimize the duplication of services. For example, it was felt that a small agency wishing to provide a new service should first approach an existing agency for support. The smaller agency should only provide the service if the larger one did not provide similar services in a culturally appropriate way or if there was sufficient 'critical mass' to justify a small agency providing services already provided elsewhere. The result of this complex evaluation process was that the evaluation of a given agency based on its own merits might not match the evaluation of it in terms of its contribution to the desired social service system in the city.

### Summary

The similarities and differences in the general approach to evaluation taken by the three funding organizations can be summarized as follows. All tended to focus on processes rather than outcomes though each differed in terms of *which* processes they would emphasize. They also all used both formal and informal methods of evaluation but, again, they varied in terms of the formal criteria they applied and the non-formal values for which they sought congruence in agencies. Finally, they differed along the scope dimension in terms of the extent to which they approached evaluation from a 'top-down', system-wide perspective. Given these general approaches to evaluation, we now look at how they manifested themselves in the case of the two funded agencies, and consider how evaluation and funding decisions were connected in each case.

### The professional institution

The *ministry* saw PI (the family services agency (see p. 43)) as an institution for delivering certain of its province-wide programmes on a contract basis. Hence, at the corporate level, it instructed its district staff to ensure that PI was complying with the terms of these contracts. This meant it wanted to see evidence that the money given was being spent for the purpose for which it was designated. Clear, on-time reporting of the information was valued. In the course of doing this, the district staff got to know PI's leaders well and formed unofficial perceptions of them as efficient and professional. At the corporate level, officials had a preference for large, multi-programme agencies that could help rationalize the delivery system for their programmes. Though they didn't see PI as all that large, they did respect it for being multi-programme and efficient. No effort was made to formally assess the outcomes of PI's efforts.

In spite of rhetoric within the ministry espousing the desirability of tying funding decisions for agencies to demonstrated track records as effective and efficient programme-deliverers, no connection existed in practice. The funding decision for the year in which the study was conducted was based on an across-the-board, system-wide policy decision to hold increases to 1 per cent. Evaluations of specific agencies were not considered.

As far as the *municipality* was concerned, since it was not approached by PI for money from its grants programme, there was little in the way of any kind of evaluation carried out. The contracts under the Children's Aid and Family Counselling programmes were based on a generic model developed by the ministry and they depended on the ministry to monitor compliance. The Family Counselling contract in particular had been in place for years and received only cursory monitoring. Nevertheless, the municipality staff responsible for the programmes delivered by PI had strong informal relations with them and they, too, perceived the agency as very efficiently and professionally run. Unlike the ministry, however, they had a predilection for agencies which were 'community based' and performed a community development function, especially in under-privileged areas of the city. Given this non-official criterion for evaluation, PI was perceived as established, mainstream and 'in touch with community needs though not community based'.

Like the ministry, the municipality's decision on funding for PI in the year of the study was not related to the evaluation of performance. It was again based on a policy decision to provide the same across-the-board increase for all mandated programmes.

The *federated funding organization*, unlike the other two funders, did attempt to evaluate PI as an agency rather than just some its programmes. The volunteer allocations panel, applying the FFO's 40 process-oriented criteria, judged the organization to be 'well run', 'impressive' and 'professional'. These conclusions were based on PI's written and oral presentations, also its reputation revealed by past evaluations and staff input. At the higher levels, where evaluations were used as part of the basis for funding decisions, non-official criteria were brought into play by senior staff. These were derived from a system-wide perspective of community needs and emphasized the desirability of smaller, newer, more ethno-specific agencies focusing on more needy groups. On these grounds, PI was seen as too large and 'mainstream'.

As far as funding was concerned, in the year of our study the funding decision for PI was a 0 per cent increase, and this can be linked to the FFO's perception of PI's effectiveness. The decision was a compromise between those who wanted to cut its funding in order to redistribute it to newer, smaller agencies closer to those more in need and those who wanted to increase it because PI was so effective and efficient in what it did.

### The community development agency

The *ministry* partially funded three of CDA's main programmes but, in terms of evaluation, its concern was primarily with ensuring compliance with the terms of the contracts through standardized reports. There was a designated contact with a regional office staff member and this person got to know the Executive Director and her staff. Through these informal contacts and discussions with others who knew the agency, the ministry liaison official felt CDI was very effective in meeting the needs of the women and children in the numerous ethnic groups who made up the community in the agency's catchment area. As she said: 'I believe in what they are doing because I've seen it work'. No formal examination of outcomes was ever undertaken however. As with PI, there was no connection between CDA's favourable evaluation and funding; the latter being governed by system-wide policies.

The *municipality* was a partial funder of only one programme through its grants process. As such, it took very little interest in CDA in a formal sense. Evaluation was very informal, conducted by the staff member designated as the liaison person with CDA. She depended entirely on non-formal means – reputation, informal conversations with the CEO, etc. One of the unofficial criteria held by municipality granting staff was a predilection for agencies that worked closely with community members and attempted to develop a 'sense of community' among those involved in their programmes. They assessed CDA as especially effective in this area, citing as evidence its record of 'spinning off' a number of autonomous grass-roots community groups from its activities.

Again, the decision on funding was based on system-wide criteria. The CDA had its grant renewed with no increase or decrease because that was the policy directive for the kinds of programmes the municipality was supporting.

The *federated funding organization*, although giving the CDA a grant of about $23,000 for the year of our study, was not a regular supporter of it. This funding came under a special 'short-term developmental' funding scheme. In theory, CDA could have been dropped or incorporated into the regular 'FFO member' group. But, in practice, it had remained in the special category for five years because the FFO had not been able to increase its donations sufficiently and it had been unable to decide on dropping existing regular members to be replaced by newcomers.

Nevertheless, CDA did go through an evaluation by a volunteer allocation panel. Though the panel had difficulty understanding its somewhat vague 'community development' mission, it was impressed by the evidence of support provided by several community members who came to the evaluation meeting. FFO staff were also ideologically predisposed to value CDA's closeness to the community, its client empowerment orientation and multi-ethnic programme base.

Most FFO managers would like to have been able to bring CDA into the member group, but could not find a way to do so. As a result it maintained its status as a temporary recipient and the size of its contribution with no change.

## *Summary*

A composite picture of the image of an effective agency emerges from the combined perspective of the three funders as they looked at the two agencies in our study. An effective agency would be one that: is large, established and multi-service, yet ethno-specific and small; innovative but stable; has a board comprising people willing to sign contracts and be responsible and liable for the agency's activities, yet representative of diverse communities, including recent immigrants and disempowered groups; and is able to provide specific services that meet government mandates, yet determine the services to provide based on the needs of local communities.

This agency would contribute to a system that has fewer agencies and less infrastructure, yet would encourage new agencies and reallocate resources to do so if necessary. It would not duplicate existing services, but would recognize where parallel services are warranted and develop them. It would be funded based on its performance, subject to funder policies on funding, and provided it did not divert funds from other agencies, regardless of their performance.

In other words, agencies receive contradictory messages from funders, that are difficult to resolve. Funders are constrained in their ability to coordinate their evaluation activities due to differences between them in the nature of their evaluations, and agencies may find it difficult to satisfy more than one funder's definition of what constitutes a good agency due to these differences.

An interesting aspect of this situation is that, despite these seemingly irreconcilable differences, representatives of the funders all agreed that the two agencies, PI and CDA, were 'good agencies'. This conclusion emerged despite the contradictions in the funder approaches to evaluation and despite the differences in the nature of the two agencies in question. In other words, the funders' evaluation frameworks-in-use can accommodate contradictions and funding organizations can 'speak out of both sides of their mouths'.[7]

## II  Conclusions

### *Implications for practice*

There are implications for practitioners from this situation. From both the agency and funder perspective, the implications relate to how to address the paradox that contradictory evaluation frameworks present.

For an agency, rather than trying to resolve or negotiate the paradox, the approach may well be to accept it and deal with it as it is. The agency, particularly the executive director, can be seen as a juggler,[8] and possibly a manipulator of funder perceptions. The two agencies involved in this research illustrate this juggler–manipulator role. For example, PI could depict itself to the ministry as a large, multi-programme agency that integrates various programmes and sources of funding, and in doing so, achieves economies of scope and scale in the delivery of services, services it provides in compliance with state regulations. To the FFO, it could depict itself as a set of local offices that respond to local conditions, under a shared administrative arrangement provided by the overall organization, allowing for collaboration between local offices in client referrals and the administration of activities.

The CDA could depict itself to the ministry as an established, stable member of the local social services system, providing a range of services in accordance with ministry requirements. To the FFO and the municipality, it could depict itself as a community-based agency that represents disadvantaged groups, representatives of which are involved in the agency's administration. At the same time, each agency would do the minimum required to meet the requirements of formal funder evaluation processes, as evaluations themselves appear to have little relation to funding decisions.

From the perspective of the funding organizations, an awareness of the results of this research could lead to a consideration of whether to change the contradictions within and between them in terms of what they emphasize in evaluations. As a minimum, each can become more aware of how agencies may react to their non-formal approaches to evaluation. In addition, they can consider ways to increase inter-funder collaboration in agency evaluation processes. Such collaboration could range from agreeing to a standard form and content for agencies to describe their structure operations and results where each funder could then interpret in its own way, to seeking agreement on common formal and non-formal bases for evaluation and a joint application of the resultant evaluation processes.

### *Implications for theory*

Researchers agree that organizational effectiveness is a central theme and an implicit or explicit variable in a wide range of theories on organizational behaviour.[9] There are many ways to operationalize the organizational effectiveness construct, with different ways leading to different theoretical predictions and empirical results. The construct has evoked considerable debate in recent years, with researchers noting the conceptual disarray and contradictions related to it.[10] It is particularly elusive in the non-profit sector.[11] We would suggest that Figure 3.1 provides one way of understanding in more detail how and why evaluation can come up with such different conclusions when they seek to assess the effectiveness of non-profit organizations. Starting with different assumptions about who they are evaluating (scope), they proceed with differing perspectives as to what should be evaluated (focus), and then carry out the task using different methods. Particularly important are the non-formal methods involving the influence of reputation and the extent to which the evaluatee's activities are seen as congruent with deeply held values and beliefs.

The findings of this research also have implications for that branch of organizational studies known as institutional theory. Underlying much of the institutional theory literature is the assumption of a homogeneous institutional environment.[12] This research covered agencies that provided similar social services in the same city, each receiving funding from the same three funders, including co-funding for some programmes. While there was some isomorphism in the funders' approaches to effectiveness evaluation, there was considerable fragmentation in the evaluation–funding environment.

More recently, institutional theorists have addressed the existence of multiple and diverse institutional belief systems, noting that there can be multiple institutional environments that impose conflicting demands on an organization which makes conforming to their implicit demands more complex. This leads to partial or selective conformity. The extent to which the institutional environment is fragmented, with each fragment having its own connections to an organization, may contribute to crises of the organization's legitimacy in the community as it attempts to respond to conflicting institutional demands for 'appropriate behaviour'. One of the ways organizations can seek to maintain their legitimacy in this confusing situation is through symbolic management practices, such as 'ceremonial conformity' with demands from more powerful institutions on which they are dependent. This is an especially common practice when the inspection and evaluation by external actors is itself primarily ceremonial. The organization is granted legitimacy if it *appears* to conform with social norms, values and expectations, regardless of considerations of technical efficiency or outcome effectiveness.[13]

The above appears to be what occurred in the situation reported in this chapter. Because evaluations had little or no real impact on funding in the three funder organizations, both the evaluators and evaluatees tended to treat the formal evaluation process in a 'ceremonial' fashion. Each side went through the motions knowing the outcome didn't matter much. On the other hand, larger questions of the worthiness or legitimacy of the two fundees were determined by non-formal means occurring through the contacts of funder representatives designated as liaison figures for each agency. Though not reported here in detail, it might be mentioned that agency leaders also had an intuitive appreciation of the formal 'ceremonial' evaluation process and the non-formal reputation check and value congruence tests to which they were subjected. For this reason they worked hard at meeting all the requirements of the formal process while also seeking to influence the non-formal process in a variety of ways.[14] To date, the literature on institutional theory has not adequately explored this subtle distinction between the formal and ceremonial processes, and non-formal processes by which powerful figures in an organizational field bring influence to bear.

The research reported here took place at a time of change in the relationships between the funders and fundees, a change chiefly characterised by declining funds to distribute. This had prompted all of the funders to proclaim rhetorically their desire for more 'rational' evaluation processes that focused much more heavily on outcomes. By the time the study ended, little connection had been made between the rhetoric and the actual practice. It remains to be seen, if changes actually *were* made to the formal evaluation systems, if there would continue to be a gap between the formal system and non-formal value congruence-based evaluation. The determinants of the nature and extent of the divergence between formal and non-formal evaluations over the long term remain to be studied.

## Notes

1  P.S. Goodman and J.M. Pennings 'Critical issues in assessing organizational effectiveness', in E.E. Lawler, D.A. Nadler and C. Camman (eds) *Organizational Assessment: Perspectives on the Measurement of Organizational Behaviour and the Quality of Work Life* (New York, John Wiley and Sons, 1980). V. Murray and W. Tassie, 'Evaluating the effectiveness of non-profit organizations', in R.D. Herman (ed.) *The Jossey Bass Handbook of Non-profit Management and Leadership* (San Francisco, CA Jossey Bass, 1994). R.E. Quinn and J. Rohrbaugh 'A spatial model of effectiveness criteria: towards a competing values approach to organizational analysis', *Management Science*, 29: 3 (1983), 363–77. J.G. Simon, 'Modern welfare state policy toward the non-profit sector: some efficiency-equity dilemmas', in H.K. Anheier and W. Seibel (eds) *The Third Sector: Comparative Studies of Non-Profit Organizations*, (New York, Waiter de Cruyter, 1990). M.E. Taylor and R.D. Sumariwalla, 'Evaluating non-profit effectiveness: overcoming the barriers', in D.R. Young, R.M. Hollister, V.A. Hodgkinson and associates (eds) *Governing, Leading, and Managing Non-profit Organizations* (San Francisco, CA, Jossey Bass, 1993). A.R. Williams and C. Kindle, 'Effectiveness of non-governmental and non-profit organizations: some methodological caveats', *Nonprofit and Voluntary Sector Quarterly*, 21: 4 (1992), 381–90.
2  F. Heffron *Organizational Theory and Public Organizations* (Englewood Cliffs, NJ, Prentice-Hall, 1989). R.D. Herman, 'Nonprofit organization effectiveness: at what, for whom, according to whom?', *Nonprofit and Voluntary Sector Quarterly*, 21: 4 (1992), 411–15. Murray and Tassie, 'Evaluating the effectiveness of non-

profit organizations'. Quinn and Rohrbaugh, 'A spatial model of effectiveness criteria', 363–77. W.R. Scott, *Organizations: Rational, Natural and Open Systems* (Englewood Cliffs, NJ, Prentice-Hall, 1987).

3 M. Alvesson and S. Deetz, 'Critical theory and postmodernism: approaches to organizational studies', in S.R. Clegg, C. Hardy and W. Nord (eds) *The Handbook of Organization Studies* (Thousand Oaks, CA, Sage, 1996).

4 B.C. Glaser and A.L. Strauss, *The Discovery of Grounded Theory: Strategies for Qualitative Research* (Chicago, Ill., Aldine Publishing, 1967).

5 R. F. Adie and P. G. Thomas, *Canadian Public Administration* (Toronto, Prentice Hall, 1987), 167.

6 R. Znaniecki *Cultural Sciences: Their Origin and Development* (New Brunswick, NJ, Transaction Books, 1980), 219.

7 G. Morgan, *Imaginization* (Newberry Park, CA, Sage Publications, 1994), 127.

8 J. Cutt, D. Bragg, K. Balfour, V. Murray and W. Tassie, 'Nonprofits accommodate the information demands of public and private funders', *Nonprofit Management and Leadership*, 7: 1 (Fall 1996), 45–67.

9 K.S. Cameron, 'The effectiveness of ineffectiveness', *Research in Organizational Behaviour*, 6 (1984), 235–85.

10 Cameron, 'The effectiveness of ineffectiveness' 235–85.

11 Williams and Kindle, 'Effectiveness of non-governmental and non-profit organizations', 381–90.

12 T. D'Aunno, R.I. Sutton and R.M. Price, 'Isomorphism and external support in conflicting institutional environments: a study of drug abuse treatment units', *Academy of Management Journal*, 34: 3 (1991), 636–61.

P. DiMaggio and W. Powell, 'The iron cage revisited: institutional isomorphism and collective rationality in organizational fields', *American Sociological Review*, 48 (1983), 147–60.

13 B.E. Ashforth and B.W. Gibbs, 'The double-edge of organizational legitimization', *Organization Science*, 1: 1 (1990), 177–94 K.D. Elsbach and R.I. Sutton 'Acquiring organizational legitimacy through illegitimate actions: a marriage of institutional and impression management theories', *Academy of Management Journal*, 35: 4 (1992), 699–738. W.R. Scott and J.W. Meyer, 'The organization of societal sectors', in J.W. Meyer and W.R. Scott (eds) *Organizational Environments: Ritual and Rationality* (Newbury Park, CA, Sage, 1992).

14 A.W. Tassie, V.V. Murray, J. Cutt and D. Bragg, 'Rationality and politics?: what really goes on when funders evaluate the performance of fundees?', *Nonprofit and Voluntary Sector Quarterly*, 7: 3 (September 1996), 347–65.

# 4 The use of information in the accountability relationship
Further evidence of human problems in the evaluation process

The research reported in the Chapter 3 presented a detailed examination of what can go on in an accountability relationship between funders and fundees in the non-profit sector. The focus was on how the former actually evaluated the performance of the latter over the course of a year. However, the larger project of which that chapter was a part had another objective, in addition to simply documenting existing processes.

In the spirit of 'action research', the plan called for sharing the results of phase 1 of the study with the actors in the process – the key figures in the funding organizations and the CEOs in the organization being funded. The intent was then to work with them in overcoming some of the problems revealed by the data.

It was assumed that both funders and fundees would appreciate an opportunity to use the information we provided to jointly produce a more rational and more effective evaluation system. This chapter tells the story of two such feedback efforts carried out by the researchers. The first involved feedback given to the funders and fundees in the organizations referred to in Chapter 3. The second focused solely on the *internal* use of feedback information by two Victoria-based organizations which formed a second phase of the study.

## I Responses of funders and fundees to information about their accountability relationship

Chapter 3 reported on our study looking at how three major funders (a provincial government department, a municipal government department and a federated funder) arrived at its judgements about the performance of two social service organizations in a large Canadian city. Four received a significant amount of their funding from the three funders. This study was subsequently expanded to include two additional social service organizations: one, a large family services organization comparable to 'PI'; and the other, a small 'grassroots' organization similar to CDA.

The findings for the other two organizations were similar to those reported in Chapter 3 for 'PI' and 'CDA'.

## The funders' evaluation processes

In terms of the scope of evaluation, two of the funders did not consider the agencies as a whole but looked only at specific programmes for which they had provided designated funds. The third funder did emphasize overall agency performance. One funder was more interested than the others in the state of the overall system in which agencies operated rather than the performance of any specific agency.

In terms of what was evaluated (focus), all three funders said they *wanted* to emphasize outcomes or results but, in fact, they looked almost exclusively at processes – whether the fundee followed certain procedures and carried out certain actions in the course of spending the money. Measures of activity (processes) were also examined, e.g. number of clients served, number of counselling sessions held, etc. Each funder varied somewhat in terms of what procedures were to be followed and how they were to be reported.

In terms of how evaluations were carried out (method), the formal evaluation procedures used consisted mostly of ensuring that the fundees reported on required matters, (e.g. financial reporting) although each funder had somewhat different reporting requirements. One of the most significant findings was that a major influence on a funder's judgement about a fundee was the application of two non-formal methods of evaluation. One involved making use of the unofficial reputation of the agency based on past experiences with it and the reports of various respected individuals in the funder's network. The other involved an informal check of the extent to which the evaluate behaved in ways congruent with certain unofficially held beliefs and values. For example evaluators in one funding organization had a belief that too much money was being given to large 'mainstream' organizations and not enough to small, new, ethno-specific organizations for visible minorities. This belief was never communicated as part of the official evaluation process nor was it clear what weight would be placed on this criterion. Conversely, the leaders in another funding organization held an implicit belief that a proliferation of small single-issue agencies was inefficient and that, from a larger system perspective, there should be greater rationalisation through mergers, joint ventures, etc.

### The fundees' responses to being evaluated

All were aware of the differences in approach of the three funders. They both complained about the extent to which the same information had to be repeated in making their formal reports and applications, though they assiduously complied with all aspects of this process.

The large mainstream organizations were also aware of the non-formal aspects of evaluation, particularly the way they were being judged with respect to non-official criteria based on congruence with certain values and beliefs. Their response to this was to attempt to make changes in order to meet these criteria on the one hand, and to form an informal coalition of other large agencies to influence one funder not to punish them for not being small and ethno-specific.

### Phase 2 the action research effort

When phase 1 of the research project was completed, the results were summarized in a relatively brief (25-page) report. This was sent first to the three funding agencies for their comment. The intention was to first ensure that all parties accepted the basic factual accuracy of the account of the year's activities. The next step was to arrange meetings between the funders and fundees in order to explore their willingness to undertake a one-year pilot project. The purpose of the pilot project would be to 'negotiate' an agreement on what was to be evaluated and how, using the phase 1 data as the starting point for discussion.

The process of getting the funders to accept the phase 1 report as 'accurate' was a lengthy one lasting eight months. It involved meetings with each funder between which were long periods while they 'considered' the document. In truth, it appeared not to be a high priority matter and was put on the 'back burner' until one of the researchers pushed for a meeting.

The major reaction to the document was in relation to its discussion of the influence of reputation and non-formal estimates of value congruence on the judgements of the evaluators. The existence of these influences clearly implied that the process was not entirely carried out through the formal and official evaluation methods. The federated funding organization was particularly upset because the word 'political' was used to describe the process. As one of those interviewed said: 'The use of our (formal evaluation) criteria helps keep politics at bay'. Their fear was that if information reached the public suggesting that judgements of the worthiness of fundees was based in part on non-rational and non-formal methods it could affect donor contributions.

Once this funder agreed to a revised wording of the report with all references to 'political process' removed, it was passed to the two fund-seeking organizations for comment. Meetings with them were held over the next four months. While they disagreed with very little in the report, they were also generally pessimistic about the extent to which the funders would be interested in changing the process. One agency CEO went so far as to state that he, at least, did not particularly want a more open and up-front evaluation process. He felt his agency did better managing the non-formal aspects of evaluation in their own way through existing contacts.

Finally, some 15 months after the action research phase was begun, a meeting of representatives from the three funders and four agencies was held to explore the possibility of a pilot project to jointly develop improvements to the evaluation system. While much information was exchanged on the current funding environment and discussions arose on various possible options for joint activities related to evaluation, in the end, nothing was agreed upon. As one executive director commented: 'Nothing here grabs me'. The meeting broke up with the understanding that, if any of the parties, either alone or with others, wanted to explore further how practical use might be made of the phase 1 results, they would get in touch with the researchers (i.e. 'Don't call us, we'll call you'). Subsequently, no such calls were received.

## *Analysis*

The interesting question is: if funders are so interested in more and better evaluation of outcomes (as they publicly claim to be), why did this particular group of them not take advantage of an opportunity to actually do something about it? Similarly, since the fundees claimed to be equally interested in pushing the funders to 'get their act together' and take a more homogeneous approach to evaluation, which they would have a voice in shaping, why did they respond apathetically to the proffered project?

In the broadest sense, the most likely explanation is that the parties did not feel it was in their interests to pursue the opportunity offered. Other claims on their time and energy were clearly believed to be more important. There are various reasons for this. One obvious possibility is that the parties in this study did not believe the researchers were competent or trustworthy enough to do the job of facilitating the project (though no direct evidence of such a belief was detected).

Another explanation is that the representatives of the funders present at the meetings were not the top echelon decision-makers in their respective organizations. All reported to higher level managers. Perhaps for their superiors the goal of improving evaluations in the manner proposed had little priority. Also, for the two government funders, the main concern was for system-wide performance, rather than the actions of individual agencies.

More broadly, it is possible that the rhetoric calling for more and better evaluation is only that. Few funders really want it in practice because, at an almost sub-conscious level, there is the suspicion that deeply held values and beliefs about how fundees ought to operate which diverge from official criteria might surface and be challenged.

Perhaps if the fundees studied had had a long record of poor performance (i.e. very bad reputations) there might have been more interest. Alternatively, if the funder's top managers had been under significant pressure from powerful stakeholders such as politicians to do more about evaluation than give speeches about it, the pilot project might have gone ahead. In other words, only when there are significant externally imposed rewards for change, or penalties for retaining the status quo, might there appear a more serious willingness to change.

From the point of view of the fundees, the explanations for their not trying to push for the pilot project are slightly different. One is that they quickly perceived the indifference among the funders at the joint meeting and, as a result, decided it was not worth their while to try to push for change. A long period of socialization in which the message is 'they have the power and there's no point in fighting it' is a difficult mindset to overcome.

It was also possible that, at least for the large mainstream agencies who had not at that time suffered serious funding cuts relative to others, they preferred the process they knew with all its political subtlety rather than what might emerge from the proposed project. It was clear from the researcher's presentation that an objective of the next phase would be to seek agreement on actual performance measures, what weight they would have, and how they would be interpreted. The hope was the parties would then use them for several years. No matter how equitable the negotiating process, this could seem a threatening prospect.

Clearly more research is necessary into when, or if, an openly negotiated evaluation process can be developed and implemented between organizations in power dependency relationships to one another. On the basis of the present exploratory study, the barriers are formidable.

## II Responses to information about accountability relationships within non-profit organizations

The attempt to persuade three funding institutions to enter into open negotiations with four of the organizations they jointly fund for the purpose of improving evaluation systems did not succeed. In part this was because the parties perceived that the process was primarily a 'political' one that involved the funders' ideological positions and personal networks which the fundees felt more comfortable working with than a more technically rational approach.

We now present a similar case but from a somewhat different perspective. The same large research project that examined how funders evaluate fundees in Toronto had a second component based in Victoria, British Columbia. This segment focused primarily on the role of the non-profit manager in the evaluation process.

The action research project there aimed at implementing a more comprehensive and open approach to the evaluation of non-profit organization performance. The effort was focused this time solely on the *internal* processes used within organizations. The accountability relationship was between various organizational members. By means of interviews and document analysis, the existing evaluation process was examined within three organizations: a federated funding organization (FFO), a mental health service and an arts organization. These existing processes were then compared to an 'ideal' process based to some extent on that developed by the Canadian Comprehensive Auditing Foundation (see Chapters 1 and 10). These comparisons were intended to form the basis of discussions among the researchers, the CEOs, their management teams and board chairs in an effort to develop a general framework which all could use as the basis for developing a better evaluation of organizational performance as well as communicating results to key internal and external stakeholders.

## *A logic model of performance accountability*

Figure 4.1 summarizes the first version[1] of a logic model which was proposed as a tool by which CEOs could evaluate the performance of their organization as (a) a way of holding their subordinates accountable, and (b) a form of accountability reporting to those to whom they are in turn accountable (e.g. board of directors and external stakeholders). It is based on the concept of the *management cycle* through which the organization's leaders ought to move as they carry out their responsibilities. Virtually all normative teaching on management maintains that, to be successful, the leaders of organizations ought to: (1) develop a set of strategic priorities for the organization; (2) convert these into a set of operational plans for each organizational unit and level; (3) oversee the implementation of these plans; (4) evaluate the results by analysing a series of performance reports; and (5) communicate results to those to whom one is accountable.

It should be noted that it is *not* being argued that all managers actually go through these stages; only that doing so will, other things equal, improve organizational performance. The logic, broadly speaking, is that organizations perform better when there is a clear vision and set of prioritized goals; when each of its units knows what part it must play in reaching the organization-wide goals (i.e. has an operational plan); when the actions taken to implement plans are 'tracked' through various information systems and these systems produce information which results in an indication of the extent to which operational objectives and strategic goals have been reached; and when the analysis of these results becomes a critical part of the input for the next round of the management cycle.

It is realized that there is no research evidence definitively proving that perfect execution of each of these stages of the management cycle will result in a more successful organization; indeed, unanticipated or irremediable conditions can occur which can damage an organization in spite of the excellence of its management. Conversely, some organizations can

| MANAGEMENT CYCLE | MANAGEMENT SYSTEMS & ATTRIBUTES | MANAGEMENT INFORMATION |
|---|---|---|
| Strategic Context | Strategic Planning<br>- responsiveness<br>- relevance | Values<br>Mission Statement<br>Strategic Plan<br>- service delivery objectives & targets<br>- resource acquisition objectives & targets |
| Operational Plans & Budgets | Management Direction<br>- operational planning<br>- budgeting<br>- appropriateness<br><br>Quality Assurance | Operational Plan<br>- tied to strategic plan<br>- best practices<br>Programmes<br>- objectives<br>- targets<br>- indicators<br>Budgets<br>- revenue targets<br>- expenditure targets |
| Internal Management | Compliance<br>People Management<br>Protection of Assets<br>General Administration<br>Financial Management | Compliance targets<br>Staff & volunteer management targets<br>Asset protection targets<br>Administration targets<br>Financial management targets |
| Performance Reporting | Monitoring & Reporting | Compliance Statements<br>Financial Statements<br>Performance Report:<br>(a) Service delivery & resource acquisition:<br>- intended results: outputs, impacts & outcomes<br>- secondary impacts<br>- client & community acceptance<br>- costs & productivity<br>- quality<br>(b) Internal management:<br>- intended results<br>- costs & productivity |
| Evaluation | Internal Evaluation/Audit<br>External Evaluation/Audit | Evaluation/Audit Reports |

*Figure 4.1* Performance reporting model for evaluation.

succeed thanks to a very propitious environment, and yet be run by managers who adhere to very few of the elements of the cycle. The best that can be argued is that excellence in carrying out each stage of the cycle will increase the probability of organizational success.

In the case of non-profit organizations in particular, with no single 'bottom line' equivalent of return on investment for shareholders as the chief indicator of success, reporting on how well the various stages of the management cycle are carried out can serve as an accountability report to critical stakeholders.

The second column of the accountability framework indicates the kind of *management systems* that need to be in place in order to carry out each stage in the cycle. Column 3 notes the 'products' of these systems, such as plans, budgets, reports or measures that are used eventually to produce the evaluation of the organization's performance (stage 4). The details of these two columns will not be explicated here but will become clear in the discussion of results.

## Methodology

The methodology for this phase of the action research project was a follows: As noted above, the three organizations that agreed to participate in the study were a service organization for persons with mental illness, an arts organization and a federated funding organization (FFO). For the mental health and arts organizations, the study focused on the internal processes and systems used by management to evaluate the performance of the organization. In the case of the FFO, the focus was on the system used in making decisions on the allocation of the money collected in its fund-raising programme to its member agencies. The plan agreed upon in each case was that researchers would proceed in the following steps:

1   Gather information on formal evaluation systems currently in place using the accountability framework guideline. The framework was to be reviewed and discussed with the CEO before data gathering began.
2   Prepare a report summarizing the results of the data gathering in terms of the framework thereby showing what management systems and processes were in use and what kinds of information was being gathered.
3   Discuss this report with the CEO in terms of how adequate the formal evaluation system was. An exploration of non-formal evaluation processes would also occur at this time. It was realized that, at this point, the CEO would probably bring others in to the discussion.
4   Given a general agreement among all those participating as to areas of the formal evaluation system that could be improved, a mutual exploration of ways to do this would be carried out between the 'evaluators' and the 'evaluatees' with the researchers acting as facilitators.

## How the three non-profit organizations fared in terms of the accountability framework

Some of the common patterns emerging from the three organizations with respect to the framework shown in Figure 4.1 were the following:

- Strategic plans existed and were formulated in terms of goals to be achieved but these were not prioritized, nor was there any attempt to specify measurable targets to be worked towards; for example the art gallery did not attempt to set an attendance figure to aim for.
- There was little attempt to explicitly derive operational plans from strategic plans, e.g. by expressing operational objectives in terms of the language of strategic goals and priorities. Nor did they identify specific measurable targets.
- Budgets were not integrally linked to operational plans or strategic plans. The budgeting process appeared to be carried out in traditional ways that had little connection to the strategic planning process.
- None of the organizations had developed comprehensive systems for routinely gathering and disseminating information on the organization's compliance with legal and regulatory requirements, value-for-money auditing, outcomes or asset protection (risk analysis). As a result accountability reports in these areas were minimal.
- Benchmark data from other comparable organizations were not available on a regular basis over time.
- External accountability reports for outside stakeholders were not prepared other than an annual report to grant makers (which mostly documented how the money they provided was spent.)

### The action research process – feedback and follow-up

In each of the three organizations studied, the process initially followed by the research team was much the same though the reactions to it were not. Initial meetings were held with the Executive Directors (or, in the case of the FFO, the chair of the Allocations Committee) to explain the nature of the project, discuss its potential advantages and what would be required. In all cases, our reception was welcoming and enthusiastic. Subsequently, one of the researchers visited the sites as often as necessary to gather the data on the management systems in use and obtain copies of the kind of information they generated (plans, reports, etc.). These were then compiled in the form of a written report in the mental health organization and the FFO. (A different approach was taken with the arts organization as will be noted below).

### The federated funding organization

As noted above, the project at the FFO focused solely on the organization's allocation process – the means by which it was decided how much each of their member organizations would receive of the donations collected by the organization. This focus was chosen because the Allocations Committee was initiating a new system that they called the 'zero base' method of making allocations. With this process, all applicants would be considered as starting with nothing (no allocation) and would have to justify their grant by means of the evaluation data required by the new system.

For a number of reasons too complex to describe here, the system had many problems with it, not the least of which were that most of the member-agencies did not possess enough of the required information in the form desired, nor did they receive extensive training in how to work with the new system. As well, there were no prioritized objectives for use as a basis for the allocation decisions. As a result, the new system proved almost useless and the decisions were eventually made on the basis of the knowledgeable, but more subjective, impressions of the Allocations Committee members.

When the allocation process was over, our observations were summarized in a short written report using the framework outlined in Figure 4.1 as a guide. This report was provided to the committee so that they could read it before we met with them to discuss ways we might work together in the future to help improve the system. As it turned out, several of the committee members reacted extremely negatively to the written document perceiving it, not as a simple description of what information was, and was not, collected and how it was used, but as a strong criticism of the Committee and its support staff. At the meeting with the Committee, the research team attempted to explain the purpose of the report as simply a basis for discussion; however it became apparent that several key members had reached the unchangeable conclusion that we were only interested in destructive criticism. As a result, we were not able to proceed with the next phase of the project.

### *The mental health organization*

The same general process was followed as with the FFO: an initial meeting, in this case with the Executive Director and the Board Chair, to explain the framework and how it would be used as the basis for gathering information. Again, the information was gathered and summarized in a short (8-page) report pointing out what was being done and not done in this organization in terms of the framework. By comparison with the FFO, the MHO came somewhat closer to possessing the requisite systems and producing the information needed though there were still significant gaps such as no linkage between the strategic plan and either budgets or operational plans, no prioritization of objectives or specification of targets, etc.

The next step in this case was a meeting with the ED to discuss the report which, again, had been given to her beforehand. In this instance, the response was one of calm acceptance and some attempt to explain why the gaps existed. For example, the gap between strategic plans and operational plans occurred because funding came to programmes making it impossible to link them systematically to strategic priorities. The researchers' understanding was that a subsequent meeting would be held to discuss the next steps in how to improve the evaluation process, possibly with board and other management members present.

There followed a period of no contact for some two months at which point we phoned. We were informed that our report had been presented by the ED to a meeting of the Board who had difficulty understanding what it said. The ED admitted that she was herself not clear about its significance and seriously doubted it was worth her spending more time on as she had so little to spare already. It was decided that the report would be studied by one board member (an academic economist) who would attempt to assess its potential value. This information was passed to one of the research team in a distinctly distant and 'chilly' tone, quite unlike her usual warm style of interaction. The researchers then requested a meeting with both the ED and the Board member in an effort to clarify the problem. At this meeting it emerged that the report was again viewed as critical, not neutral, in tone; that the framework was perceived as too academic and that the ED was convinced that there would be little point in exploring further information needs. Following the meeting a clearer understanding appeared to exist and an agreement was made to meet once more to discuss the organization's information needs. The results of subsequent research with this organization are reported in Chapter 8.

### The arts organization

The approach taken by the CEO of the arts organization was some-what different. After our initial meeting to explain the project, the framework and the possible outcomes, she asked that we then meet her full managerial team plus the board chair, about ten people in all. At this meeting we again described the project and its methodology. A number of requests for clarification were asked. The data were gathered but, because of the reaction to the written reports in the other two organizations, nothing was written for internal distribution. Instead, the research team met again with the Director to present its findings orally in the form of a discussion, using the accountability framework as a guide. Even in this case, however, the attempt to proceed with the development of a 'better' accountability system met passive resistance. Eventually progress was made in gaining agreement to proceed with a limited form of *programme* evaluation and internal and external accountability reporting. This is reported in Chapter 9.

### Discussion: what is going on here?

A few conclusions about the evaluation dimension of the accountability relationship emerge from these three action research initiatives.

First, however much the parties in an unequal power relationship might subscribe to the desirability of more and better formal accountability processes in the abstract, they are much less interested in it in practice, both as evaluators and evaluatees. When it comes down to actually spending time working on improvements in this area, they tend to see such efforts as too time consuming and 'not worth it'.

Second, the first effort at bringing funders together to explore more rational evaluations processes revealed that there a was a great deal of perceived power in informal knowledge. It is recognized by all that those who make decisions about the fate of those dependent on them will make evaluative judgements with or without the aid of formal information systems. If non-formal methods have been used in the past and either of the parties believe they led to adequate decisions, the temptation is to retain such methods. EDs can convince themselves they have power in informal knowledge and funders can convince themselves they 'know' how their fundees are performing on the basis of similar non-formal knowledge. These convictions are likely to be sustained so long as the organization in question avoids disastrous events.

Third, in spite of continuous assurances to the contrary, there is a strong tendency for formally developed information to be taken as a form of personal criticism. It is often assumed that such reports will be used as a club to beat people with, not as a thermometer to impartially reveal problems for discussion. Hence the tendency will be to avoid formalized information systems if possible.

Fourth, evaluation texts insist that there should be a distinction between 'formative evaluation' and 'summative evaluation'. The former is meant to help solve problems (the approach of the action researchers in this project), while the latter is more judgemental. The possibility of making and sustaining this conceptual distinction in practice, however, seems fraught with difficulties. In the final analysis, there is a high probability that most evaluation will come to be perceived as adversarial to some degree. Most people suspect that if formative evaluations reveal unsatisfactory performance it will be stored up and used against the evaluatee at some point either in a formal summative evaluation or informally. Hence it is better to minimize all types of formal evaluative activity.

There are, of course, other explanations for the lack of success in achieving 'negotiated' improvements in evaluation systems. They mainly have to do with the processes followed by the action researchers in these studies. It seems clear that written reports are not effective for example. A number of other inadequacies in the intervention process followed by the researchers may have existed. It is also possible that the accountability framework is not the best vehicle to use as the basis for discussing areas needing improvement. Subsequent efforts to move ahead with these organizations focused first on what new kinds of information the CEOs would like to help them 'tell the story' of their organization to various stakeholders. The results of this approach are discussed in Chapter 5, and, specifically for the mental health organization and the arts organization in Chapters 8 and 9.

## Note

1   A more elaborate version of this model was developed over the course of the research and is presented in Chapter 5.

# 5 Taking the next step

Developing general standards of performance reporting for non-profit organizations

## I Introduction

In the light of our experience with the two non-profit organizations (NPOs) – one in the cultural sector, one in the human service sector – discussed in Chapter 4, we licked our wounds and pondered the, mainly negative, implications of going into discussions with agencies with a predetermined normative model of what information agencies should have if they were to live up to our high standards of internal and external accountability. Suitably humbled, we decided that a more modest, and more thorough, approach would be to start from the bottom up, ask agencies what information they currently had, and what they would like to have, and use this as a basis for some normative suggestions – for prescription that would be rooted in agency experience and needs. The opportunity arose to do detailed case studies of four human service NPOs – those described below, and the mental health organization discussed in the previous chapter – in Victoria, British Columbia (BC).

The objective of this part of the research is therefore to develop a proposal for a set of standards for performance reporting in human service NPOs; the argument is addressed primarily to client service programmes, but is also adapted to include fund-raising programmes. Interest in the subject reflects the increasing role that NPOs in BC are being required to play as the provincial government retreats from the delivery of social services, and arose specifically from the wide variety of forms of performance reporting in the absence of reporting standards, and the associated difficulties faced by NPOs in accommodating the varied and changing information requirements of public and private funders, and other users of performance information such as clients, volunteers, management and staff.

Conceptually, the paper draws on three of the perspectives on accountability discussed in Chapter 1: What accountability information is needed? When is it needed? And by whom is it needed? With respect to the first question, in broad terms we excluded procedural matters related to compliance with authorities and divided accountability information into two categories: financial information of a procedural nature; and consequential information about value for money. The second question we treated by dealing with information across the various stages of the management cycle.[1] We dealt with the third question by building around a traditional core model of accountability a wider framework of internal and external constituencies with an interest in the performance of the organizations in question.[2]

The intended contribution of the paper is the development for major stakeholders in human service NPOs in BC, Canada – with, of course, an aspiration to generalizability to like organizations elsewhere in Canada and in other countries in which human services are delivered by NPOs – of a set of performance information reporting standards that reflect how organizations work across the management cycle. The standards for reporting are not standards of performance. But they are intended to contribute to both better accountability and better organizational performance, and to provide a framework for the next logical stage which would be the development of criteria of success – standards of performance – for each kind of performance information included in the reporting framework.

## II  Methodology

### Research questions

Project fieldwork was conducted in four human services NPOs, through an analysis of available documentary evidence and interviews with internal and external stakeholders. The following research questions were addressed:

1   What sorts of performance information are considered necessary across the management cycle by the various internal and external stakeholders?
2   Given the information that is considered necessary, do internal and external stakeholders feel that they get sufficient information to make decisions about organizational performance?
3   In the light of answers to the first two questions, which describe current practice, is it feasible to prescribe general standards for reporting consistent and comparable performance information?

### The four organizations

*Capital Mental Health Association (CMHA)* provides programmes and rehabilitation services for persons with mental illness and their families. Its mandate is threefold: to alleviate the distress of persons with mental illness by offering social, vocational, educational and residential rehabilitation programmes; to promote the mental health of the greater community; and to encourage and facilitate integration of persons with illness into the general community. It offers six programmes with an annual operating budget of approximately $1,800,000.

*Esquimalt Neighbourhood House (ENH)* provides programmes to foster the growth, development and well being of individuals and groups in the community. Clients of ENH are primarily single-parent, low-income families, mostly headed by women. Seven major programmes are offered for an annual operating budget of approximately $530,000.

*Vancouver Island Multiple Sclerosis Society (MSS)* helps people with multiple sclerosis and their families to maintain and enhance the quality of their lives. Its key objectives are to assist multiple sclerosis sufferers and their families on Vancouver Island; to cooperate with interested groups to provide a home for multiple sclerosis patients and allied neurological diseases in the Province of British Columbia; and to raise funds for research into the cause of, and cure for, multiple sclerosis. The five major programmes are offered for an annual operating budget of approximately $750,000.

*Silver Threads Service/Meals On Wheels (STS/MOW)* comprises two organizations with distinctive mandates and client groups. STS provides opportunities through services and centres to enhance the quality of life for seniors. Clients include people aged 55 or over, many of whom live alone. The eight programme areas are offered for an annual operating budget of approximately $660,000.

MOW is a community service that provides and delivers nutritionally balanced meals to people who are convalescing, as well as to sick and/or elderly people who can no longer cook for themselves and would otherwise have to move to an institutional setting. The annual operating budget is approximately $390,000.

(Budget data relate to interview time in early 1996.)

### Framework for analysis

The general framework for analysis is illustrated in Figure 5.1. The two axes define the constituencies for information and the timing question: when information is available in the management cycle. The relevant constituencies include the key internal and external stakeholders who are users of information, and the management cycle identifies the sequence of events where information users require specific types of information. The column headings in Figure 5.1 refer to the major internal and external users of performance information. Internal users include the Executive Director (ED), the governing board, staff, and volunteers other than those serving on the governing board. External users include funders of various kinds, the various categories of service users (customers, clients), and other

| INFORMATION ACROSS THE MANAGEMENT CYCLE | | | INFORMATION USERS | | | | | | |
| --- | --- | --- | --- | --- | --- | --- | --- | --- | --- |
| | | | INTERNAL | | | | EXTERNAL | | |
| 1. General Stage of Cycle | 2. Specific Stage of Cycle | | ED | Board | Staff | Volunteers | Funders | Clients | Other |
| Prospective Information on Operational Programmes (a) | PLANS | Primary and Support Spending Programmes | | | | | | | |
| | | Fundraising Programmes | | | | | | | |
| | BUDGETS | Financial (b,c) | | | | | | | |
| | | Performance Levels (b) | | | | | | | |
| Ongoing Information During the Delivery of Operational Programmes | PRIMARY SPENDING PROGRAMME DELIVERY | Financial | | | | | | | |
| | | Performance Levels | | | | | | | |
| | FUND RAISING PROGRAMME DELIVERY | Financial | | | | | | | |
| | | Performance Levels | | | | | | | |
| | SUPPORT SPENDING PROGRAMME DELIVERY | Financial | | | | | | | |
| | | Performance Levels | | | | | | | |
| Retrospective Information on Operational Programmes | YEAR END REPORTING | Financial | | | | | | | |
| | | Performance Levels | | | | | | | |
| | EVALUATION AND AUDIT | Financial | | | | | | | |
| | | Performance Levels | | | | | | | |

(a) Operational programmes (activities) include the following: first, two categories of primary programmes that are externally focused, the first providing services to clients, the second financing programmes for clients by raising operating funds from different contributors; and, second, support programmes, such as staffing, marketing, and general administration which provides services internally to primary programmes. Capital funding and spending programmes are not included.
(b) Accountability for performance is divided into two categories: first, narrow or procedural, which is exclusively financial in scope, and includes such information as line-item budgets and financial statements; and second, broad-scope or consequential, which includes both financial, and non-financial information about efficiency – how resources are utilized – and effectiveness – the nature and achievement of programme objectives.
(c) Financial budgets include both revenue (sources of funds) budgets and expenditures (disposition of funds) budgets.

*Figure 5.1 (a)* Performance information by information user in NPOs: framework.

relevant users such as government regulators, professional associations, and external auditors and evaluators.

The row headings are used to classify performance information across the management cycle. The first level of classification defines performance information in three broad categories – prospective, ongoing, and

retrospective. The information refers exclusively to operational programmes. Operational programmes (or activities) include primary and
support programmes. Primary programmes are externally focused and
include client service programmes and fund-raising programmes. Support
spending programmes, such as human resource management and general
administration, provide services internally to the primary spending and
fund-raising programmes. Prospective information is divided into two
sequential categories: information on strategic and operational planning
of both primary and fund-raising programmes, and the translation of planning information into budgets. Budgets are defined at two levels, which
reflect the two levels of accountability (procedural and consequential); the
first is limited to financial information, and the second is performance-
oriented. This distinction between financial and performance information
is pursued across the management cycle in Figure 5.1(a) for each of the
three sub-categories of ongoing information (primary spending programmes, fund-raising programmes, and support programmes) and the
two subcategories of retrospective information (year-end reporting, and
evaluation and audit).

## *Applying the framework*

A total of 62 semi-structured interviews were conducted across the four
organizations, including the four EDs, three board members (including
the President and the Treasurer) from each organization, 26 staff members,
11 non-board volunteers, 6 funders (including the United Way – the
Victoria version of the generic federated funding organization (FFO)
discussed in Chapter 3 – and 5 government funding departments), 9 clients
(three of whom participated indirectly through a group interview conducted
by a clinical staff member and observed by a researcher); and 2 in the
'other' category (a representative from each of the Office of the Comptroller
General of the Ministry of Finance and the Office of the Auditor General).

In the interviews, respondents were asked to identify the following: (a)
the kinds of performance information they considered necessary for decisions; (b) which categories of necessary information they considered most
important (core) and which of a supplementary nature; (c) within the necessary categories, whether information currently available was sufficient for
their decisions; and, (d) whether there were any areas where their interpretation of performance information might be in conflict with that of
other users. Responses were classified according to the following scale: 0
indicates that information in this category was not perceived as necessary;
1 indicates that information was perceived as necessary but insufficient;
and 2 indicates that information was perceived to be both necessary and
sufficient.

Further analyses revealed supplementary and core information gaps identified by users across the cycle, and some areas of performance information

where interpretation by different users might be in conflict. A second and more normative level of analysis combined the additional insights obtained by the researchers on information deficiencies and possible areas of conflict not identified by the respondents, with a cross-check using the set of 12 attributes of organizational effectiveness proposed by the CCAF/FCVI[3] to arrive at a set of general standards for reporting performance information in human service NPOs.

## III  Results and analysis

Within each respondent group across the four organizations there was virtual unanimity on what information was available and on information gaps; the responses are therefore presented and analyzed in aggregate.

### *What information do respondents consider necessary, and do they have enough of it?*

Figure 5.1(b) illustrates the initial findings about performance information and information gaps across the management cycle. Gaps were identified when users indicated that they considered information necessary but had insufficient to make decisions. The seven groups of respondents were asked to use the three-point scale (0, 1, and 2) to indicate what information was necessary and whether it was sufficient. Respondents were also asked to prioritize information by indicating what information they considered core, or more important, and what they considered supplementary. Each of the 98 cells in Figure 5.1(b) contains 0, 1, or 2, as described above. Respondents described 38 cells (39 per cent) as unnecessary, 22 cells (22 per cent) as necessary and sufficient, and 38 cells (39 per cent) as necessary but insufficient. Of the total, 45 cells (46 per cent) were considered core information; but only 14 core cells (33 per cent) contained sufficient information, leaving 31 of the 38 information gaps in core areas. The following discussion briefly describes the findings for each group of respondents.

The EDs and boards were the two groups that felt themselves to be most in need of information. EDs defined 13 of 14 information categories as necessary, and 11 as core information. However, in only 3 of these 11 did they have sufficient information, and they were all in financial areas. EDs thus defined 8 core information gaps, and 1 supplementary information gap.

Boards also defined 13 of 14 cells as necessary, and 11 as core information. Of these, only 4 provided sufficient information, and again only in financial areas. Boards defined 7 core information gaps, and 1 supplementary information gap.

Staff defined a total of 9 necessary cells, and 7 as core information. However, only 2 of the 7 provided sufficient information, and they were financial in nature. There were thus 5 core information gaps, and 2 supplementary information gaps.

| INFORMATION ACROSS THE MANAGEMENT CYCLE | | | INFORMATION USERS | | | | | | |
| --- | --- | --- | --- | --- | --- | --- | --- | --- | --- |
| | | | INTERNAL | | | | EXTERNAL | | |
| 1. General Stage of Cycle | 2. Specific Stage of Cycle | | ED | Board | Staff | Volunteers | Funders | Clients | Other |
| Prospective Information on Operational Programmes (a) | PLANS | Primary and Support Spending Programmes | 1 | 1 | 0 | 0 | 1 | 0 | 0 |
| | | Fundraising Programmes | 1 | 2 | 0 | 0 | 1 | 0 | 0 |
| | BUDGETS | Finanical (b,c) | 2 | 2 | 2 | 0 | 2 | 0 | 2 |
| | | Performance Levels (b) | 1 | 1 | 1 | 0 | 1 | 0 | 1 |
| Ongoing Information During the Delivery of Operational Programmes | PRIMARY SPENDING PROGRAMME DELIVERY | Financial | 1 | 1 | 1 | 0 | 1 | 0 | 0 |
| | | Performance Levels | 1 | 1 | 1 | 1 | 1 | 1 | 0 |
| | FUND RAISING PROGRAMME DELIVERY | Financial | 2 | 2 | 0 | 1 | 2 | 0 | 0 |
| | | Performance Levels | 1 | 1 | 0 | 1 | 1 | 0 | 0 |
| | SUPPORT SPENDING PROGRAMME DELIVERY | Financial | 1 | 1 | 1 | 0 | 0 | 0 | 0 |
| | | Performance Levels | 1 | 1 | 1 | 0 | 0 | 0 | 0 |
| Retrospective Information on Operational Programmes | YEAR END REPORTING | Financial | 2 | 2 | 2 | 2 | 2 | 2 | 2 |
| | | Performance Levels | 1 | 1 | 1 | 1 | 1 | 1 | 1 |
| | EVALUATION AND AUDIT | Financial | 2 | 2 | 2 | 0 | 2 | 2 | 2 |
| | | Performance Levels | 0 | 0 | 0 | 0 | 0 | 0 | 0 |

(a) Operational programmes (activities) include the following: first, two categories of primary programmes that are externally focused, the first providing services to clients, the second financing programmes for clients by raising operating funds from different contributors; and, second, support programmes, such as staffing, marketing, and general administration which provides services internally to primary programmes. Capital funding and spending programmes are not included.

(b) Accountability for performance is divided into two categories: first, narrow or procedural, which is exclusively financial in scope, and includes such information as line-item budgets and financial statements; and second, broad-scope or consequential, which includes both financial, and non-financial information about efficiency – how resources are utilized – and effectiveness – the nature and achievement of programme objectives.

(c) Financial budgets include both revenue (sources of funds) budgets and expenditures (disposition of funds) budgets.

LEGEND
0 = not necessary, 1 = necessary but insufficient, 2 = necessary and sufficient

▓ = CORE INFORMATION ☐ = SUPPLEMENTARY INFORMATION

*Figure 5.1 (b)* Performance information by information user in NPOs: initial findings.

Volunteers in both client service and fund-raising had limited information needs, primarily related to performance results. Of the 14 cells, they
chose 5 as necessary, with 4 as core information. Gaps occurred in all 4
core areas; volunteers received sufficient information only about financial
year-end reports.

Funders defined 11 cells as necessary and 8 as core information. Of the
8, 3 cells show sufficient information, all financial. Of the 7 gaps identified, 5 were core and 2 supplementary.

Clients, like volunteers, had very focused concerns, in this case primarily
with information relating to client service results. They considered 4 of
14 cells necessary and 2 as core information; for both core areas they
received insufficient information.

Finally, other users considered only 5 of 14 cells as necessary, and 2 as
core, in both of which they received sufficient information. Two information
gaps were identified in the supplementary information category.

### What additional information is needed to complete the picture?

A second and more normative level of analysis incorporates, first, the insights
obtained by the researchers over the research process and, second, those
obtained by considering the 12-attribute approach designed by the CCAF.

The first set of changes is shown by a '3' in the cells of Figure 5.1(c),
which should be seen as supplementary to Figure 5.1(b). The first proposed
extension relates to planning information. While both EDs and boards
acknowledged their need for more and better information for planning,
they considered such information for primary and support programmes
to be general rather than core in nature; further, boards considered that
they had sufficient information on fund-raising. Both the interviews and
the analysis of documentation suggest that a strategic planning process is
the foundation of a successful formal management control system for both
spending and fund-raising programmes. This process would establish organizational values, mission, strategic objectives and priorities, and strategic
programming as vital to the establishment of clear and consistent performance accountability terms of reference across the management cycle. For
EDs and boards this broader information – a strategic plan which is regularly monitored and updated – is shown on Figure 5.1(c) for both spending
and fund-raising programmes, and the core status of fund-raising information assigned by EDs, boards and funders in Figure 5.1(b) is extended
to spending programmes. Staff did not feel they needed this information,
but the interviews made it very clear that a strategic plan that did not
involve staff would be of very limited value. For spending programmes
this information is thus designated as necessary core information for staff
(in the four organizations, staff are not directly involved in fund-raising).
This recommendation on the importance of strategic information is made

INFORMATION USERS

| INFORMATION ACROSS THE MANAGEMENT CYCLE | | | INTERNAL | | | | EXTERNAL | | |
|---|---|---|---|---|---|---|---|---|---|
| 1. General Stage of Cycle | 2. Specific Stage of Cycle | | ED | Board | Staff | Volunteers | Funders | Clients | Other |
| Prospective Information on Operational Programmes (a) | PLANS | Primary and Support Spending Programmes | 3 | 3 | 3 | | 3 | | |
| | | Fundraising Programmes | 3 | 3 | | | | | |
| | BUDGETS | Finanical (b,c) | | | | | | | |
| | | Performance Levels (b) | 3 | 3 | 3 | | 3 | | |
| Ongoing Information During the Delivery of Operational Programmes | PRIMARY SPENDING PROGRAMME DELIVERY | Financial | | | | | | | |
| | | Performance Levels | 3 | 3 | 3 | 3 | 3 | 3 | |
| | FUND RAISING PROGRAMME DELIVERY | Financial | | | | | | | |
| | | Performance Levels | 3 | 3 | | 3 | 3 | | |
| | SUPPORT SPENDING PROGRAMME DELIVERY | Financial | | | | | | | |
| | | Performance Levels | 3 | 3 | 3 | | | | |
| Retrospective Information on Operational Programmes | YEAR END REPORTING | Financial | | | | | | | |
| | | Performance Levels | 3 | 3 | 3 | 3 | 3 | 3 | |
| | EVALUATION AND AUDIT | Financial | | | | | | | |
| | | Performance Levels | 3 | 3 | 3 | | 3 | | |

(a) Operational programmes (activities) include the following: first, two categories of primary programmes that are externally focused, the first providing services to clients, the second financing programmes for clients by raising operating funds from different contributors; and, second, support programmes, such as staffing, marketing, and general administration which provides services internally to primary programmes. Capital funding and spending programmes are not included.

(b) Accountability for performance is divided into two categories: first, narrow or procedural, which is exclusively financial in scope, and includes such information as line-item budgets and financial statements; and second, broad-scope or consequential, which includes both financial, and non-financial information about efficiency – how resources are utilized – and effectiveness – the nature and achievement of programme objectives.

(c) Financial budgets include both revenue (sources of funds) budgets and expenditures (disposition of funds) budgets.

LEGEND
3 = nnormative recommendations

[shaded box] = CORE INFORMATION    [open box] = SUPPLEMENTARY INFORMATION

*Figure 5.1 (c)* Performance information by information user in NPOs: completing the picture.

despite some recent reservations on strategic planning.[4] Mintzberg's concerns are primarily directed to formalism, inflexibility, and excessive faith in quantification.

Turning to the area of budget information, EDs, boards, staff and funders all acknowledged that they had insufficient information in the core area of budgeted performance levels in spending programmes, but no consistent pattern of improvement emerged. This whole question of consequential accountability information at the budgeting stage is designated in Figure 5.1(c) (row 4) as requiring improvement. The following two lines of improvement are suggested. First, responsibility centre budgeting should match direct and controllable costs for each responsibility centre manager with the corresponding output measures, in terms, wherever possible, of efficiency or productivity standards. Currently, formal output information is limited to client numbers, and there is ample scope (anecdotal evidence abounds) for incorporating quality by using, for instance, success rates and client (or client family) satisfaction. Second, programme budgeting should match full programme costs, including allocated costs, with programme output and outcome measures that reflect programme effectiveness. Longitudinal information on outcomes in the community, such as family stability and client employment success, is more elusive and more difficult to match with programme costs, but is nevertheless a fundamental part of information on effectiveness; it was very clear from the discussions with funders that they believed their grants were buying community outcomes. Such responsibility budgeting and programme budget information would establish the consequential accountability terms of reference for both responsibility centre managers and the organization as a whole.

Monitoring this broader performance information for primary spending responsibility centres and programmes is shown (Figure 5.1(c), row 6) as important for EDs and as the basis of ongoing internal reporting to boards and staff, external reporting to funders, and internal and external reporting to volunteers and clients. Monitoring broader performance information for support spending centres and programmes is primarily of internal interest. EDs, boards and staff all designated this area as necessary but insufficient, but again with no consistent view on improvements. The interview process in all four organizations underlined the importance of more formal management systems and associated cost and output information in internal support systems such as administration, marketing, and, particularly, human resource management. This proposed improvement is shown in row 10 of Figure 5.1(c). Ongoing information on fund-raising is primarily financial, and EDs, boards and funders all designated this area as necessary and sufficient (row 7, Figure 5.1(b); only volunteers required more information. But all four groups acknowledged insufficient information on performance levels other than purely financial, such as coverage of, or success rates in, different target markets. A more formal set of cost and non-financial output measures for fund-raising centres and programmes, analogous to those for spending centres and programmes, is proposed in row 8, Figure 5.1(c).

The improvement suggested in Figure 5.1(c), row 12, to the year-end reporting of information to all internal and external stakeholders corresponds to the proposed improvements at the budgeting and monitoring stages. There is, however, one proposed change at the retrospective stage in Figure 5.1(c) which builds directly on these proposed improvements but was not seen by any of the users during the interviews as necessary. External validation (closing the accountability loop) of information produced by EDs and boards for funders and other external users is currently limited to an attest audit of financial statements. The proposal in Figure 5.1(c), row 14, to extend external validation through a value-for-money audit process reflects the need of external stakeholders, particularly funders and accreditation or regulatory bodies, to close the accountability loop on performance information.

As a cross-check on the normative set of performance information generated on the basis of perceived or inferred respondent needs, the researchers then turned to the approach proposed by the CCAF/FCVI.[5] This approach defines effectiveness comprehensively in terms of a set of 12 attributes as follows: Management Direction – the extent to which organizational objectives are clearly stated and understood; Relevance – the extent to which a programme continues to make sense with respect to the problems or conditions to which it is intended to respond; Appropriateness – the extent to which the design of a programme and the level of effort are logical in relation to organizational objectives; Achievement of Intended Results – the extent to which the goals and objectives of a programme have been achieved; Acceptance – the extent to which the stakeholders for whom a programme is designed judge it to be satisfactory; Secondary Impacts – the extent to which significant consequences, either intended or unintended and either positive or negative, have occurred; Costs and Productivity – the relationship between costs, inputs and outputs; Responsiveness – an organization's ability to adapt to changes in such factors as markets, competition, available funding, or technology; Financial Results – accounting for revenues and expenditures, and assets and liabilities; Working Environment – the extent to which an organization provides an appropriate work environment for its staff, and staff have the information, capacities, and disposition to serve organizational objectives; Protection of Assets – the extent to which the various assets entrusted to an organization are safeguarded; and, Monitoring and Reporting – the extent to which key matters pertaining to performance and organizational strength are identified, reported, and carefully monitored.

There would appear to be two distinct groupings of attributes in the CCAF/FCVI set: those relating to performance and those relating to management systems. The former set includes four attributes: financial results, which are already produced in sufficient quantity and quality in the four organizations; the achievement of intended performance or service results; client acceptance; and costs and productivity – all three of which have been specified in Figures 5.1(b) and 5.1(c) as needed directly by users or normatively by the researchers. But it also includes secondary impacts, and this insight into the importance of 'spillover' relationships among NPOs and among NPOs and government programmes is a useful addition to the set of information requirements.

Three of the attributes relating to management systems have already been included in the information set developed (Figures 5.1(a)–(c)): management direction (systems for strategic planning, programming and budgeting); working environment (human resource management systems); and monitoring and reporting (systems for internal and external accountability reporting). The attribute relating to the protection of organizational assets is, however, a useful addition for NPOs that are typically quite casual about tracking human and physical assets. There are also some novel and important insights in the other management system attributes: appropriateness; relevance; and responsiveness.

At first glance appropriateness would seem to be just an interesting elaboration of the proposed emphasis on efficiency – are there management systems in place to ensure due care for resource utilization? But the early practice in the use of the attributes[6] stresses the examination of alternative and innovative methods of service delivery, including alternative technologies, under the head of appropriateness, and this attribute is a useful addition for NPOs where the incentives for such an emphasis are limited. The attribute of responsiveness – systems to identify and anticipate or respond to changes in the organizational environment – is closely linked to systems for strategic planning, but is worth adding on its own merits for NPOs where fiscal exigencies and incentives tend to make for reactive management. The relevance attribute – systems to determine that NPOs' programmes continue to make sense with respect to the problems or conditions to which they were intended to respond – is also linked to strategic planning, but stresses the usefulness of monitoring *why* programmes are carried out and whether they are still meeting social needs.

Appropriateness, responsiveness and relevance combine to provide a useful perspective at both agency and programme levels on the need for flexibility in applying the traditional 'rational' management model which forms the core of the reporting framework developed above. They also remind NPOs of the need to detect and adapt to changing technologies, demands, needs, attitudes, values and other circumstances, indeed, to sense and adapt to paradigm shifts in the organizational environment at a system-wide level. In the highly uncertain and competitive world in which NPOs operate, the inclusion of the appropriateness, responsiveness and relevance attributes provides, in effect, for the ongoing monitoring of the changing meaning of the dynamic concepts of efficiency and effectiveness.

# IV General standards for reporting performance information in NPOs

## *Introduction*

The additional insights from the CCAF/FCVI attributes complete the normative proposals, and in combination with the stated needs of the various users, provide a proposed set of general standards for reporting internal and external accountability information across the management cycle in NPOs on a consistent and comparable basis.

The reporting of performance or 'success' in NPOs is necessarily complex and multi-dimensional, reflecting the range of different types of information across the management cycle required by different groups of internal and external users. Performance information can be seen in a descriptive matrix relating types of information across the cycle to various users, illustrated in Figures 5.1(b) and 5.1(c). The obvious question is whether this matrix is relevant only for the four organizations in question, or whether generalization to other NPOs is appropriate. An attempt at generalization among human service NPOs can perhaps be ventured on the basis of the very similar responses in the four organizations investigated in Victoria, BC. Further, the remarkable homogeneity in perceived core needs among the primary users in the four organizations may also permit the prescription of a set of standards for what core information should be presented to these primary users across the cycle. Particular primary users may, of course, choose to focus on selected parts of the information set – their own 'critical success factors' – and it would fall to EDs to tailor, clarify, and, if necessary, negotiate the resolution of conflicts among primary users. Other users may use all or part of the general information set, but are also likely to have organization-specific, or even programme-specific, information needs – ' satellites' of information around the general set – which EDs would be responsible for identifying and addressing.

The general standards, it should be stressed, are standards for what performance information should be reported across the cycle. They are standards *for* performance reporting, but they are not standards *of* performance. The development of such criteria or benchmarks of success for each kind of performance information would be the next logical step in the analysis of performance in NPOs. Given the acceptance of some sort of information set of the sort proposed here, primary users, including funders, could move to negotiate a set of general performance criteria for each of the component parts of the information framework for similar NPOs. Such general criteria, which would serve the purpose of organizational comparison, could be supplemented by organization-specific and programme-specific criteria, and by organization-specific or programme-specific weighting or prioritization of the various components of performance, both of which EDs would be responsible for negotiating with primary and other users in each NPO.

## A proposal for a set of general information reporting standards

The information set is conceptualized as a model of organizational activity in NPOs, and is illustrated in Figure 5.2(a). Management organizes itself in various ways, i.e. establishes management systems and practices, to provide information at two levels of accountability (procedural and consequential) for decisions which occur across the management cycle. The information produced by management systems is further classified into two categories. First, information about internal operations deals with such matters as the strategic plan developed by the strategic planning management system, or the information on staff morale produced by the human resource management system. Information about internal operations is intermediate in that it serves to support the external operations of the organization. The second category of information produced by management systems relates to the external operations of the organization in the various external markets, client service and fund-raising, in which it operates. This information includes matters such as the actual programme and activity targets achieved relative to targets, or an external evaluation/audit report on organizational achievements compared to targets. Some information, such as an internal audit report on both internal and external operations, falls into both categories.

It should be stressed that the distinction between internal and external operations is different from the distinction between internal and external users of information. For instance, funding bodies are external information users, but are likely to want information on some aspects of internal operations, such as assurance that a strategic plan is in place, and also information on external operations such as actual achievements compared to targets. Staff members are obviously internal users, but are likely to want information on external operations as well as on such internal operations matters as staff morale and turnover.

The first set of management systems at the prospective stage (Figure 5.2(a)) deals with the strategic context of the organization, covering three of the 12 attributes proposed by the CCAF/FCVI – relevance (are we doing the right thing?); appropriateness (are we doing the thing right?); and responsiveness (are we adaptive in relation to changing needs?). The information here would take the form of a statement by the ED on the nature and functioning of the management systems put in place to assess this strategic context, and an actual statement on 'organizational positioning and flexibility' generated through those systems. Figure 5.2(a) shows that this initial statement is monitored and reported over the course of the year and at the end of the year as part of the annual report.

The strategic context leads directly to management direction. This includes a statement on the nature and functioning of the management direction system (including quality assurance), and a statement of

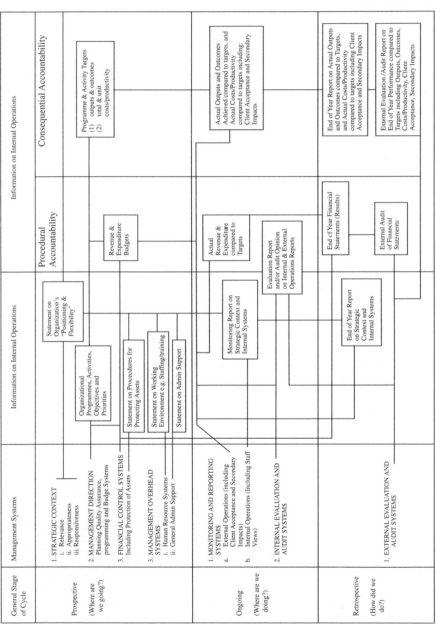

*Figure 5.2 (a)* General information standards (spending programmes).

organizational programmes, activities, objectives and priorities, and corresponding information within the consequential accountability column on programme and activity targets for outputs and outcomes, and costs and productivity. Still within the set of prospective management systems, the financial control system provides for a statement on the nature and functioning of the system, a statement on procedures for protecting assets, a statement of budgeted revenue and expenditure, and, possibly, some financial ratio analysis. Financial statements and any associated financial analysis are defined for spending programmes within the procedural accountability column, since, by definition, they include no information on the (non-monetary) service achievements of the organization. Finally, management overhead systems provide for a statement on the nature and functioning of the systems, and a statement on support system targets for the year, for instance, with respect to staffing and training. The targets and statements from the management direction, financial control, and management overhead systems are monitored and reported over the course of the year and in the annual report.

Management systems for ongoing information are shown in two categories in Figure 5.2(a). First, monitoring and reporting systems are shown in relation to both external and internal operations. For external operations, this requires a report (in the procedural accountability column) on actual revenue and expenditure compared to targets, and a report (in the consequential accountability column) on actual outputs and outcomes achieved compared to targets, including information on client acceptance and secondary impacts. For internal operations, the necessary information includes a statement on the nature and functioning of the monitoring and reporting systems, and a report monitoring the strategic context and performance targets in internal systems including the protection of assets, human resource systems, and general administrative systems. Second, internal evaluation and audit systems are designed to 'complete the accountability loop' internally, and require a statement on the nature and functioning of the management systems and an evaluation report and/or internal audit opinion on the results of internal and external operations. This independent opinion provides assurance to boards on the information provided by management. Since an internal evaluation/audit report may deal with information about both internal and external operations, it is shown in Figure 5.2(a) as straddling the line dividing internal and external operations.

Monitoring and reporting systems continue to operate to the end of the year, and produce the material that makes up the annual report of the organization. This is shown in Figure 5.2(a) to include the end-of-year report on the strategic context and internal systems, the end-of-year financial results, and an end-of-year report on outputs, outcomes, costs and productivity corresponding to that produced over the course of the year. The annual report thus contains reference to all 12 attributes of effec-

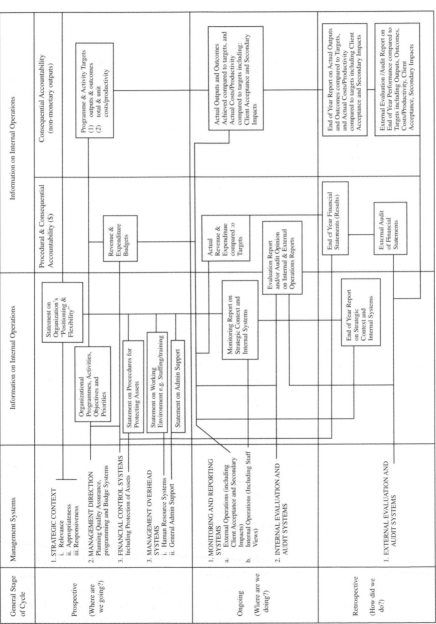

*Figure 5.2 (b)* General information standards (fund-raising programmes).

tiveness proposed by the CCAF/FCVI, includes information on both internal and external operations, and serves both internal and external users of information.

The retrospective stage also adds explicitly external evaluation and audit management systems, intended to complete the accountability loop between the ED and the board within the NPO and external users of information (particularly funders), just as internal audit/evaluation systems complete the loop internally between the ED and the board. A formal external audit of the financial statements is universal in NPOs, and this audit report is shown in the procedural accountability column as a component of the set of information on external operations. The accountability loop is thus always completed at the procedural level. Much less common, but just as important, is the completion of the loop at the consequential level, and this is shown in Figure 5.2(a) as an external evaluation/audit report on the performance of the NPO with respect to performance in relation to targets for outputs, outcomes (including client acceptance and secondary impacts), and costs and productivity. This evaluation/audit may be based on a direct examination and report by the evaluator/auditor, or may take the form of an attestation by the evaluator/auditor to the completeness and accuracy of the annual performance report prepared by the management of the NPO.

The proposed information reporting standards are intended to capture the comprehensive view of effectiveness proposed by the CCAF, but to develop that framework as an 'organic' model of information needs over the annual management cycle in NPOs. The standards also include several additions to the CCAF proposals. First, the working environment attribute is extended to include a broader set of overhead support systems. Second, the monitoring and reporting attribute is broken down explicitly into its ongoing and end-of-year components. Third, internal audit/evaluation has been added to close the internal accountability loop. And, finally, external audit/evaluation is added explicitly to the set of information requirements; in the CCAF/FCVI proposals, it is left as an appropriate sequel.

The information standards proposed in Figure 5.2(a) are focused on the internal and external spending programmes of NPOs. Revenue is included in the form of budgetary revenue targets and actual revenue obtained, as an input to the non-monetary service objectives of the organization. This would be a complete representation for NPOs that receive an annual grant from a government agency to carry on client service programmes, and do not have any formal fund-raising programmes. Where NPOs do have formal fund-raising programmes for all or a significant proportion of their revenue, the accountability representation of revenue information must be modified (see Figure 5.2(b)). For such fund-raising programmes, the primary consequential measure of accountability relates to dollars raised compared to targets and the dollar costs of the fund-raising activities compared to targets. In short, the performance measure is analogous to commercial profit. Monetary information thus serves the purposes of both procedural and consequential accountability, and may be supplemented by additional performance information relating, say, to market shares, in non-dollar terms. Figure 5.2(b) illustrates the changed headings in the two account-ability columns under Information on External Operations. All other parts of Figure 5.2(a) continue to apply to fund-raising programmes, and are repeated in Figure 5.2(b).

## V  Conclusion

In the absence of performance reporting standards, human service NPOs face difficulties in accommodating the varied and changing information requirements of public and private funders, and other users of perfor-mance information such as clients, volunteers, management and staff. This paper draws on the views of the various information users in four human service NPOs in Victoria, BC, Canada, and reporting attributes proposed by the CCAF/FCVI, to develop a proposal for a set of general reporting standards for the primary information users – EDs, boards, staff and funders – in human service NPOs; the generalization from the findings in Victoria is ventured on the basis of the remarkable homogeneity among primary users in the four organizations. The proposed standards are stan-dards for what performance information should be reported across the management cycle, from planning and budgeting through to external reporting and auditing. They are not standards of performance; the devel-opment of such criteria or benchmarks of success for each kind of performance information would be the next logical step in the analysis of performance in human service NPOs.

Consistent reporting standards do offer a place to start, and the research reported in this chapter suggests that accountability to primary users of performance information may be well served by a comprehensive frame-work of the sort developed here for human service NPOs.

A gratifying consequence of the more cautious and consultative approach used in this part of the research project was that the HSNPOs directly involved, as well as the other agencies in the cultural and human service sectors in Victoria and Toronto, were generally persuaded that a general approach of the sort suggested in this paper would be useful to them both for internal governance and management control and for external account-ability, and indeed marketing. We were encouraged to take the next steps of demonstrating the practical applicability of the accountability frame-work, particularly with respect to methods of evaluation, and to key components of consequential accountability such as service costing, defining service outputs and outcomes, and providing guidance about organization and focus in the universal circumstance of multiple outputs and outcomes. So we turned from general standards to methods of evaluation and to generating information about the costs and results. These steps are described in the next four chapters.

## Notes

1   R.N. Anthony, J. Dearden and V. Govindarajan, *Management Control Systems* (Homewood, Ill., Richard D. Irwin, 1992).
    R.N. Anthony, and D.W. Young, *Management Control in Non-profit Organizations* (6th edn, Boston, Mass., Irwin/McGraw-Hill, 1999).
2   P. Kolter and A.R. Adreason, *Strategic Marketing for Non-profit Organizations*, 3rd edn (Englewood Cliffs, NJ, Prentice Hall, 1987).
    C.H. Lovelock and C.B. Weinberg *Public and Non-profit Marketing*, 2nd edn (Redwood City, CA, The Scientific Press, 1989).
3   CCAF/FCVI, *Effectiveness Reporting and Auditing in the Public Sector* (Ottawa, CCAF, 1987).
4   H. Mintzberg *The Rise and Fall of Strategic Planning* (New York, Free Press and Prentice Hall International, 1994).
5   CCAF/FCVI, *Effectiveness Reporting*.
6   W.D. Moynagh *Reporting and Auditing Effectiveness: Putting Theory Into Practice* (Ottawa, Canadian Comprehensive Auditing Foundation, 1993).

# 6  Grappling with the dilemmas of evaluation

## A review of existing evaluation tools for non-profit organizations

In Chapters 1 and 2, it was pointed out that non-profit organizations in most Western countries are under pressure from funders, government contractors and clients to show that they are 'making a difference'. They eagerly seek valid and reliable measurements that will yield clear indicators of how well they are doing. Many also yearn for proven 'best practices' for managing their organizations which, when implemented, will ensure that they run as efficiently and effectively as they can. This way, if they are unable to show directly the impact of their efforts, at least they can assure concerned stakeholders that they are doing things the way they 'ought' to be done.

Chapter 2 looked at the questions: (1) Is there a set of performance indicators which can be easily applied by many different kinds of charitable organizations and which will yield the clear picture of impact that stakeholders want? and (2) Are there universally agreed-upon 'best practices' applicable to all non-profit organizations which have been proven to increase performance? The chapter provided an introductory look at the underlying theory and concept of evaluation, and in a nutshell, concluded that the answers to both questions are 'not yet'. But there are some promising leads in the form of *processes* that a non-profit organization and its stakeholders can adopt which could help improve the analysis of performance and, most importantly, lead to better decisions on needed changes that are right for it (if not for others).

## Problems with evaluation

To recap the argument presented in Chapter 2, there are two main sets of reasons why the impact of non-profit organizations and their programmes is so difficult to measure. One has to do with the basic technical and logic-related problems of all evaluation systems, and the other with common human foibles that arise when evaluation is undertaken.

### Technical and logic-related problems

It is often very difficult to directly measure the outcomes of an organization's or programme's activities. In many cases goals are too broad, diffuse and long-term to capture in measurable terms with a few indicators that will produce data for immediate use.

When outcomes cannot be measured with confidence, attempt is often made to measure inputs, processes, activities or outputs (the latter are summations of activities) on the assumption that showing improvements in these areas will cause outcomes to be achieved. Unfortunately, there are often no ways to prove that engaging in certain activities will produce particular outcomes.

Outcomes can also be affected by uncontrollable conditions. As well, activities may also create unanticipated negative 'side effects' which are not measured and may cause more problems than benefits.

When one raises the question of 'value for money' i.e. which organization or programme provides the best results for a given amount of money), there are even more problems because one ends up trying to compare 'apples and oranges'.

Once it is agreed upon *what* to measure, there is the problem of *how* to measure. There are many technical methods for getting information and the problem is that not all are equally appropriate, valid or reliable. As well, in the non-profit sector, in which something like 90 per cent of the Canada's 74,000 registered charities operate with fewer than three paid staff, many do not have the time, money or expertise for developing these methods.

When measurement has occurred, by whatever method, there is then the question of interpreting the data. One of the reasons interpretation is difficult is due to the lack of standards that will reveal if the measurements indicate success or failure: good, average or poor results. In the non-profit sector there is a general dearth of such standards. With few exceptions there are no 'industry norms' or even benchmarks for comparison with other organizations or programmes.

Similarly, a measurement is useless unless it can be used for making decisions. To do this, there must always be an effort to understand *why* the results are the way they are. Very often one cannot be sure. Many explanations are possible. They could be due to the poor design of the programme, inept staff, poor management, external conditions that could not be controlled or other variables and combinations of variables.

All these technical problems are very common and can cause evaluation efforts to fail in their ultimate aim of leading to better performance. In spite of this, many of the attempts made at evaluation do not reveal any awareness of these problems. This is why experts urge that every evaluation system contain explicit 'logic models' – statements that lay out why the evaluation is being undertaken, who is to be involved, what is to be measured, how the resultant data are to be interpreted and how the final results will be used in decision-making.

## Human problems

The other set of factors that create major problems when it comes to clearly showing how a programme or organization makes a difference have to do with certain very common psychological tendencies that arise frequently whenever evaluators attempt to measure the work of others.

The first of these tendencies is that those being measured usually want to present their work in as positive a light as possible, or, conversely, if things are not looking good, want to avoid being blamed for the situation. This was called the 'Look good, avoid blame' syndrome in Chapter 2. Once this mind set is operative, the chances of obtaining a successful evaluation drop dramatically.

The other human problem arises due to the almost inevitable ambiguity that occurs when it comes to interpreting the meaning of data. Just because there is ambiguity does not mean that no interpretation will occur. In fact it inevitably will in some fashion. People want answers and solutions, so every kind of subjective explanation can arise to provide them. But with no tested logic model in place (as is so often the case), these interpretations come from the evaluator's personal pre-existing beliefs, perceptions and experiences. When these subjective interpretations of reality (SIRs) differ, as they often do, conflict and political behaviour arises.

With this awareness of the inherent problems and pitfalls of the evaluation process in mind, sixteen existing evaluation systems are examined in detail in this chapter and two others, Chapters 10 and 11. Descriptions are provided of what they evaluate, the type of evaluation they provide, how it is carried out and how the results are to be used. The chapter concludes with a discussion of which evaluation systems show the more promise as useful tools for the non-profit sector.

## Review of existing performance evaluation systems for the non-profit sector

Attempts to assess performance in the non-profit sector have been numerous and varied. However, none have become widely adopted or used over long periods of time. The remainder of this chapter describes and reviews a number of evaluation systems that have been put forward explicitly for use in the non-profit sector or which have been designed for the commercial sector but are claimed by some to have applicability for the former. Based on the foregoing discussion, they can be categorized in a number of ways.

- What they evaluate: are they aimed at the level of the programme/ function, organization or system? (For our purposes we will not deal with individual performance appraisal systems here. Full discussion of these can be found in most textbooks on human resources management.)

- Type of evaluation: do they tend to focus primarily on outcomes, outputs/processes/activities, inputs, or some combination of these?
- How they evaluate: Data collection. Are the methods quantitative or qualitative? Formal or informal?; Interpretation. Are the standards absolute (targets or 'best practices') or relative (comparative benchmarks or time-periods)?; Logic models. Are there explicitly stated connections between two or more levels of evaluation (programmes, functions, organization, larger system) and/or between measurements (inputs, processes, outcomes)?
- Implementation: does the system specify who should design and carry out the evaluation, how it should be implemented, and how the results should be used and communicated?

An overview of evaluation systems is presented in Figure 6.1. The profile of each of the following evaluation systems contains basic descriptive information, references to additional published material, and an analysis of the system using the above criteria, including the extent to which it has been applied and whether these applications have themselves been assessed. Finally, some of the probable strengths and weaknesses of the system are discussed.

## Sector systems that evaluate programmes, units or functions within the organization

### Canadian Centre for Philanthropy: 'Ethical Fund-raising Accountability Code'

References: Canadian Centre for Philanthropy publication of same name as above (Toronto: 1998). Also available on the Internet at: www.ccp.ca

#### Purpose

This system was created by the Canadian Centre for Philanthropy in response to publicity in recent years about unethical fund-raising practices, such as large proportions of donations going to pay fund-raisers rather than to the cause for which the donations were given. Its purpose is to provide a set of standards to be followed by fund-raisers that will create an 'ethical' fund-raising programme. As such it is a system based on processes and aimed at the programme or function level of non-profit organizations.

#### How it works

The system comes in three parts. Part A, 'Donor's Rights', lists what donors are entitled to receive in the way of information and treatment when they are asked to give. For example, a charitable donation receipt

| WHAT IS EVALUATED | TYPE OF EVALUATION | | HOW IS EVALUATION CARRIED OUT | | | |
| Programmes, Units or Functions | Process | Outcome | Data Collection | Standards | Logic Models | Implementation Discussed |
|---|---|---|---|---|---|---|
| 1. Cdn. Centre for Philanthropy "Ethical Fundraising Standards" | ✓ | | Quantitative & Qualitative | Absolute | None | No |
| 2. *Outcome Funding* (Rensselaervill Institute) | | ✓ | Quantitative | Absolute | None | No |
| 3. *High Performance Non-profit Organizations* (Letts et al) | ✓ | | Quantitative & Qualitative | Relative | None | Yes |
| Whole Organizations | | | | | | |
| 4. Balanced Scorecard | ✓ | | Quantitative preferred | Relative | Measurement & Level | Yes |
| 5. Cdn. Comprehensive Auditing Foundation *Framework for Performance Reporting* | ✓ | | Quantitative preferred | Relative | Measurement & Level | Yes |
| 6. Drucker Foundation "Self Improvement Tool" | ✓ | | Not discussed | Relative | Level | Yes |
| 7. United Way of America Outcome Funding Approach | | ✓ | Quantitative & Qualitative | Relative | Measurement & Level | Yes |
| 8. Baldrige Award | ✓ | | Quantitative & Qualitative | Absolute & Relative | Level | No |
| 9. ISO 9000 | ✓ | | Quantitative | Absolute | Level | No |
| 10. National Standards Information Bureau "Standards in Philanthropy" | ✓ | | Quantitative | Absolute | None | No |
| 11. American Institute for Philanthropy *Charity Rating Guide* | ✓ | | Quantitative | Absolute | None | No |
| 12. Cdn. Council of Christian Charities *Standards for Organizational and Financial Integrity* | ✓ | | Quantitative | Absolute | None | No |
| 13. Charities Review Council of Minnesota | ✓ | | Quantitative | Absolute | None | No |
| 14. Guidestar Bulletin on Cost Ratios | ✓ | | Quantitative | Absolute | None | No |
| *Larger Systems:* | | | | | | |
| *Jurisdictional* | | | | | | |
| 15. Oregon Benchmarks | | ✓ | Quantitative preferred | Relative | None | No |
| *Sectional* | | | | | | |
| 16. Council on Accreditation | ✓ | | Quantitative & Qualitative | Absolute | None | No |
| 17. Cdn. Council on Social Development | | ✓ | Quantitative preferred | Relative | Measurement & Level | No |
| *Occupational* | | | | | | |
| 18. Professional Accreditation Bodies | ✓ | | Quantitative & Qualitative | Absolute | None | No |

*Figure 6.1* Framework for classifying evaluation systems in the non-profit sector.

(if applicable); full disclosure of the charity's name, registration number and purpose for which funds are requested; status of the individual soliciting the funds (volunteer or paid), donor privacy, etc. Part B, 'Fund-raising Practices', lists 5 sets of standards of behaviour for fund-raisers. They include being truthful and accurate in describing the charity's activities, not using harassment or undue pressure, and not being compensated on a contingency or commission basis (i.e. being paid a percentage of the funds raised). Part C, Financial Accountability, specifies that all donations must be used to support the charity's objects as registered with Revenue Canada, restricted or designated donations must be used for the purposes for which they were given, and publicly available financial reports must reveal such information as total funds raised, costs of fund-raising and sources of funds. All this is to be done using generally accepted accounting principles and standards established by the Canadian Institute of Chartered Accountants.

### Logic models

This system is based on the implicit assumption that a desirable outcome in fund-raising is ethical behaviour and that this will be achieved if the specified practices are followed. It does not try to make any connection between ethical practices and the outcomes of fund-raising or any other aspect of the organization's effectiveness in achieving its mission other than the implicit assumption that being seen to be unethical damages the organization.

### Evaluation methods

The adoption of this system is entirely voluntary. The organization's leaders (board, CEO) are the evaluators and it is their own fund-raising programme they are evaluating. The means to be used for assessing the degree of adherence to the code are unspecified. Organizations which subscribe to it are supposed to develop their own implementation and measurement procedures. It appears from the way the Code is worded that complaints initiated by the public are key sources of data.

### Evaluation standards used

The basis for judging ethicality in this system is adherence to pre-set, absolute, standards. Relative comparisons are not an option. These standards are the product of the judgements of a body of fundraising experts convened by the Canadian Centre for Philanthropy. They are similar to other ethical fund-raising codes that exist in the US and UK.

*Actual experience using the system*

Since the Code was introduced in 1997, fewer than 100 of Canada's 74,000 registered charities have officially adopted it. Its value or the degree of user satisfaction with it is not yet known

*Strengths*

The *Ethical Fund-raising Code* is a very useful limited-purpose tool for assessing the ethicality of a fund-raising function in non-profit organizations. There is a high degree of probability that adherence to the specified standards will result in few complaints about fund-raising practices. The CCP needs help in disseminating the Code to a larger number of non-profits and persuading them to adopt it.

*Weaknesses*

The greatest weakness of the Code is its lack of a measurement system for gathering valid data on the degree of adherence to the specified standards. Another problem is that self-generated public complaints seems to be the only source of data to be obtained. That fact that, at present, it is largely a self-evaluation system with no external checks on the degree of compliance would lower its value in the eyes of stakeholders outside the organization who are not completely comfortable with the validity of self-generated reports.

Finally, like most evaluation systems, there is no way it can avoid the LGAB and SIR phenomena if evaluatees believe that the result of applying the Code is likely to damage or benefit them substantially.

*Recommendation*

The CCP, or another external body might consider ways to apply the Code as an evaluative tool and offer endorsement to charities that apply it, provide evidence of their compliance to it, and are willing to submit to independent auditing of their compliance.

### Outcome funding: the Rensselaerville Institute approach

References: Book: Harold S. Williams, A.Y. Webb and W. J. Phillips *Outcome Funding: A New Approach to Targeted Grantmaking*, 2nd edn, (Rensselaerville, N.Y.: The Rensselaerville Institute, 1993); Internet: www.crisny.org/not-for-profit/thetute/INDEX.HTM

*Purpose*

This is a *programme-oriented* system for use primarily by government funders in deciding among applicants for the delivery of services or programmes. While it is a complete system detailing all the elements that a good programme proposal should contain, its heart is the process for planning around specific outcomes. It is not like the Balanced ScoreCard (see below) in that its focus in on developing outcomes, and how to measure them and how to use them in decision-making. It is less concerned with the processes leading to the results and more with measuring the results themselves.

*How it works*

The system begins with the evaluator or grant-maker deciding on the issues it wishes to see tackled and the goals it wishes to see achieved. Those seeking funding are then urged to submit a 'Target Plan' (in our terms the logic model that outlines the means to be taken to achieve the ends sought). A Target Plan comprises statements about the following:

- 'Customers' or 'market' to be served;
- The nature of the 'product' that will be created to achieve the targets;
- The key individuals that will be involved in delivering the product;
- The organizational support that will be provided to enable them to do their work;
- Projections of the finances needed to carry out the project;
- Performance targets to be reached and 'milestones', or mini-targets, to be reached along the way to the main target;
- 'Customer evidence' – indicators of how satisfied the 'customers' are with the services provided to them;
- How achievement of the targets will be verified.

Following the development of the target plan, a 'due diligence' process must be developed for reviewing and checking on the grant-seeker's ability to deliver what is in the plan. The guidelines for this process include:

- Independent verification of the grantseeker's claims;
- A focus on 4 key questions: How compelling are the performance target and the outcome it will yield? How high is the probability that implementers will achieve their target? What is the return on investment compared with others we might make? Where does this fit within portfolio needs and other investment objectives?

Once a target plan is approved and funding provided it is implemented. As it progresses and at the end of the effort, verification of progress occurs using the means presented in the Target Plan. In the light of these results, the process moves to a final 'learning phase'. The emphasis is not to place blame but use the data as the basis for solving problems and learning how to do things better next time.

## Logic model

The system insists that a complete measurement logic model be developed for each programme or project showing what means are to be used to achieve what ends. Level of focus logic models are not discussed. The focus is on the programme level only.

## Methods of evaluation

Though this system focuses primarily on outcome measurement, it does use 'milestones' as indicators of achievements along the way. This involves having to identify both process and output measures. The system varies from most of the others in that it recognizes the temptations of the LGAB phenomenon by demanding independent verification of results. Various methods are suggested for achieving this, e.g. independently conducted surveys of 'customer' satisfaction. Implementation processes are not discussed.

## Evaluation standards

The system insists that outcomes must be specified and numerical targets (absolute standards) must be set representing the level of achievement desired. Relative standards, such benchmarking and comparisons over time, are not discussed.

## Actual experience with the system

The Rensselaerville Institute says it has implemented this system in a number of government and non-profit organizations. It is used primarily to help governments decide whom to choose to deliver programmes they wish to have carried out by non-profit agencies or other governmental units. Publicly available research into how well the system works is not available.

## Strengths

This system benefits from insisting on the development of a full measurement logic model that connects goals with outcome indicators and outcomes with outputs/processes and these with inputs. The insistence on independent verification appears to be a way to directly confront the LGAB phenomenon.

*Weaknesses*

Independent verification systems other than those concerned with the use of money have to be very sophisticated to avoid being subverted by those wanting to avoid blame. It is much better if the system can run on trust with the evaluatee as a willing provider of data.

As well, the heavy emphasis on quantitative outcome indicators suggests that there could be a high possibility of goal displacement. 'Making the numbers' by whatever means are necessary could become the dominant aim of those being evaluated and, as noted previously, outcome indicators often miss the more complex ends suggested by the goals.

Using previously set absolute targets as the basis for evaluation rather than less rigid relative standards such as benchmarking and time comparisons could be a bad idea if there is no way of knowing what a reasonable target should be. To know this requires a lot of data from a lot of sources over a long period of time. This situation often does not prevail in the non-profit sector.

## High performance non-profit organizations: managing upstream for greater impact

References: Book of the same name by Christina W. Letts, William Ryan, and Allan Grossman (New York: John Wiley and Sons, 1999).

*Purpose*

This approach emphasizes the benchmarking of processes and activities as a way of evaluating programmes and functions within non-profit organizations. Benchmarking compares the evaluatee's practices with those of others doing the same kind of thing but who are deemed to be doing it better.

*How it works*

The book provides a good description of how a benchmarking evaluation system should be developed. It begins by identifying projects, programmes or functions that are important to the organization's success in that they cost a lot and/or their outcomes contribute heavily to the organization's overall mission. Examples from the book include a ballet company's fundraising programme and an international aid organization's water improvement projects in a number of countries.

The next step is the development of a range of indicators that will present a picture of the project's performance. These could be indicators of costs, service delivery times, complaints, client satisfaction surveys, etc. Organizations providing comparable services who are generally viewed as highly effective are then identified and effort is made to find out how well they perform on the selected indicators and, most importantly, what they do to achieve superior performance. (Note: the organizations selected do not have to have identical services for the same clients. Also, in large organizations with multiple units providing the same service, comparisons could be made internally between the units.) The 'best practices' of the better performing programmes, projects or functions are then adopted.

The book contains extensive discussions on how to identify the criteria for which benchmarks to choose, how to find high-performing comparison organizations and how to implement the findings of the benchmarking exercise.

### Logic models

The level of focus logic model implicit in this system is that effective programmes and functions lead to success at the organization level. The measurement logic model – that processes and activities determine outcomes – is implicit.

### Evaluation methods

Both qualitative and quantitative methods are encouraged. It is also recognized that some of the key determinants of the success of a better performing programme might be intangible, such as the organization's culture or management attitudes. Attention is paid to the process for implementing benchmarking, especially the need to involve the evaluatees.

### Evaluation standards

The use of benchmarks (relative standards) is the distinguishing feature of this system.

### Actual experience with this system

The book on the system describes a number of cases in which benchmarking was used by non-profits. There is no independent published research assessing the value of this system.

### Strengths

This benchmarking approach shows a lot of promise in that it is practical and outward oriented. Adoption of it would force non-profit managers to look beyond their boundaries for organizations that perform certain functions and programmes better. Eventually, if enough organizations in a given sector adopt this system it could lead to shared 'standards' or 'best practices' comparable to those called for by the Baldrige and ISO 9000 systems described below.

*Weaknesses*

Successful benchmarking is dependent on first identifying indicators that will measure the critical aspects of a programme or function. However, as we have seen, coming up with the 'right' indicators and preventing indicators from displacing real goals is often difficult.

Another problem is finding higher performing organizations to benchmark against. Unlike many sectors in the business world, most non-profit sectors do not gather and share information that could be used for this purpose. Widespread use of the benchmarking system will be difficult until non-profits create stronger intermediate levels of infrastructure at the sector level similar to the industry level in business.

Finally, once benchmark data are gathered on the practices of higher performing organizations, there is no way of knowing if the 'best practices' of these others is the *real* reason they are more successful. It is also possible that what 'works' for another organization will *not* work for one's own due to unique situational characteristics of history, culture, personalities, economic conditions, etc.

## Systems that evaluate the whole organization

*Note: Two evaluation systems of particular importance are the Balanced Scorecard and the Canadian Comprehensive Auditing Foundation's Framework for Performance Reporting. These are given special treatment in Chapters 10 and 11.*

### The Drucker Foundation self-assessment tool for non-profit organizations

References: Peter Drucker and Constance Rossum, *How to Assess Your Non-profit Organization: User Guide* and *Participant's Workbook* (San Francisco: Jossey-Bass, 1993).

*Purpose*

This tool is primarily intended to assist non-profit organizations in developing strategic and operational plans in a more rational manner. Evaluations of results are a part of the tool. It is focused at the organizational level and deals with both activities and outcomes. In is meant to be a *self*-evaluation tool for formative purposes rather than one to be used by external evaluators for summative purposes.

*How it works*

Those involved in developing plans are led through a process that involves answering 'The Five Drucker Questions':

1  What is our business (mission)?
2  Who is our customer?
3  What does the customer consider value?
4  What have been our results?
5  What is our plan?

Each question contains several sub-questions, the answers to which will lead to the answer to the larger question. In the case of the results question (4), the planners are asked: What are the results you want? To what extent have you achieved them? What are the major activities or programmes that have helped, or hindered, the achievement of these results? How well is the organization using its human and financial resources? What have been the results of the organization's effort to attract and keep donors?

### *Logic models*

The Drucker tool does ask its users to develop an explicit measurement logic model that starts with mission, leads to specific organizational goals, and identifies which programmes will lead to the achievement of those goals and what human and financial inputs are needed to implement the programmes. Evaluation is embedded in the larger planning process.

### *Methods of evaluation*

Unfortunately, the Drucker tool does not provide any details on how it should be implemented other than a brief guide for facilitators who are expected to lead the planners in a retreat setting. In particular the 'results measurement' part of the tool does not suggest how to go about answering the key questions it asks.

### *Evaluation standards*

The tool does not discuss the kinds of standards that should be used to interpret the results obtained. The only basis for judgement mentioned is benchmarking. Organizations are asked to identify other similar organizations doing a better job of using their human and financial resources, attracting and satisfying donors and using their board of directors. How to do this is not discussed.

### *Actual experience with applying this system*

Many copies of the published material on the Drucker tool have been sold and The Drucker Foundation in New York offers occasional courses on its use. To date there are no published accounts on the extent to which it has been put into practice or which assess its value for users.

*Strengths*

The Drucker tool has value in being part of a complete logic model and aid in strategic and operational planning. In this sense it is similar to the Balanced Scorecard and the CCAF system though it is far less well developed.

*Weaknesses*

The chief weaknesses of the tool are that it provides no detail on how to develop measures of performance or how to interpret results and no awareness of the difficulties created by the LGAB and SIR mindsets.

## Programme outcomes: the United Way approach

References: Current United Way of America Approaches to Measuring Programme Outcomes and Community Change (1995); *Focusing on Programme Outcomes: A Guide for United Ways* (1996); *Measuring Programme Outcomes: A Practical Approach for Agencies* (1996); *Measuring Programme Outcomes Training Kit* (1996); Internet: http://www.unitedway.org/outcomes

*Purpose*

This evaluation system focuses on the identification and measurement of programme outcomes for the United Way and its funded agencies in the US. The purpose of the outcome measurement system is to demonstrate that charitable donations to the United Way can improve the quality of life of people and communities through the activities of United Way-funded programmes.

While the system evaluates results at the programme level, the results are aggregated at the organizational level by member agencies to report on their effectiveness in meeting United Way priorities (particularly when those agencies are funded primarily by the United Way). The United Way, in turn, aggregates the results of member agencies to report on its effectiveness in achieving community-wide change.

The outcome information is used by the United Way to help member agencies to improve programme performance (agency reviews), to identify and achieve United Way priorities (funding allocations) and to broaden the base of financial and volunteer support (fund-raising). The United Way also uses the outcome information to help address community issues, specifically through leveraging other sources of funding, influencing public policy, and mobilizing citizens.

*How it works*

The system begins with a member agency submitting a plan to the United Way describing its programme outcomes, indicators, and data collection methods. The United Way defines the outcome information that the agency should provide on an annual or multi-year basis and develops a reporting format for the agency. For each outcome indicator, this information usually includes results, annual targets, breakdown of data by key client characteristics, and explanatory information. The agency then begins to collect and report the outcome data. The United Way periodically monitors and reviews the agency's measurement system to ensure the reliability and validity of the data.

## Logic model

The outcome measurement system requires that programme inputs be linked to activities or outputs, and outputs to outcomes (short, medium and longer-term benefits for participants), and outcomes to agency goals (strategic and operational). It also asks the agency to identify constraints or factors beyond its control that will likely affect the production of outputs and the achievement of outcomes.

## Method

Implementation of the outcome measurement system is divided into six stages: building agency commitment and clarifying expectations; building agency capacity to measure outcomes; identifying outcomes, indicators, and data collection methods; collecting and analysing outcome data; improving the outcome measurement system; and using and communicating outcome information.

The United Way has developed a set of guiding principles and specific steps to help the member agencies complete each stage of the implementation process. Rather than advocate one particular way to develop outcomes or to collect outcome data, the United Way uses a checklist approach to encourage agencies to think more broadly and critically about its measurement process. For example, agencies are asked about the validity, reliability, sensitivity to client characteristics, and ability to capture longer-term results of their proposed data collection methods, not which ones to use.

## Evaluation standards

The outcome measurement system does not specify the type of evaluation standards to be used but does suggest that target-based absolute standards, and time-based relative standards are best. Agencies are not expected to establish targets until they have at least one year of baseline data. The system discourages the use of benchmark-based relative standards, or those that involve comparison with similar programmes that are considered exemplary, until such times as accurate outcome data is available. It is generally understood that in the first few years of an outcome measurement system, the data often say more about what is wrong with the system than what is taking place in the programmes.

### Actual experience with the system

As of August 1998, approximately 279 United Ways in the US were involved in, or considering implementation of, outcome measurement systems for their member agencies. Of those United Ways that are collecting outcome information, most are using it to establish baseline performance and to improve programme effectiveness of their member agencies. It is generally understood that outcome information will only be useful in making funding decisions after the measurement system has been in place for three to five years. At present, some United Ways are linking allocations to the effort of member agencies to increase their capacity to measure programme outcomes, rather than to the achievement of results.

### Strengths

This system builds public confidence and support by enhancing United Way and agency accountability for results. As agency capacity to measure results increases, the United Way is better able to link programme outcomes to individual and overall community change. The outcome measurement system encourages member agencies to improve their services to clients and helps the United Way to rationalize its allocations process.

### Weaknesses

Perhaps the biggest challenge in an outcome measurement system is developing meaningful outcomes for vague, general and/or poorly conceived programme goals. A related difficulty is defining outcomes for activities that are hard to measure, such as outreach to a highly transient population or services that promise anonymity for participants.

The measurement of programme outcomes does not in itself lead to broad social change, although it does help to 'unbundle' the specific results needed to influence complex community issues. Similarly, the measurement of outcomes does not indicate that a particular programme caused the result, although it can provide reliable information on the benefit of that programme for its participants.

Critics argue that an outcome orientation should not be seen as a substitute for needs assessment or the evaluation of programme design and delivery. Also, a focus on outcomes invites greater public and political scrutiny, which may result in unrealistic expectations for improved performance.

An outcome measurement system requires significant resources to implement and maintain. The United Way will need to provide member agencies with training, support and technical assistance on an ongoing basis.

## Malcolm Baldrige National Quality Award

References: Malcolm Baldrige National Quality Improvement Act (1987); *Technology Administration Act* (1998); Foundation for the Malcolm Baldrige National Quality Award; Internet: http://www.quality.nist.gov – web site of the Malcolm Baldrige Quality Award Programme, US Commerce Department National Institute of Standards and Technology (NIST).

*Purpose*

The Baldrige Award was established in 1987 to enhance US competitiveness by promoting quality awareness, recognizing quality achievements of US companies, and publicizing successful performance strategies.

The purpose of the award is to promote an understanding of the requirements for performance excellence and to share best practices. Winners are expected to educate other companies about the benefits of using the Baldrige criteria and to share their own performance strategies and methods.

Two awards are given annually in each of three categories: manufacturing, service, and small business. Any for-profit businesses with headquarters in the US including US sub-units of foreign companies, is eligible to apply for the award. In 1999, the award was extended to include profit and non-profit education and healthcare organizations.

*How it works*

The award evaluates management processes at the departmental or subunit level, which are aggregated at the organizational level. There are seven performance excellence criteria that are used to measure how an organization manages its products and services, human resources, and customer relations.

Taken together, these criteria become a framework to improve overall performance, including employee relations, productivity, customer satisfaction, market share, and profitability. These criteria are:

- *Leadership* – examines how senior executives guide the company and how the company addresses its responsibilities to the public and practices good citizenship;
- *Strategic planning* – examines how the company sets strategic directions and how it determines key action plans;
- *Customer and market focus* – examines how the company determines requirements and expectations of customers and markets;

- *Information and analysis* – examines the management, effective use and analysis of data and information to support key company processes and the company's performance management system;
- *Human resources development and management* – examines how the company enables its workforce to develop its full potential and how the workforce is aligned with the company's objectives;
- *Process management* – examines aspects of how key production/delivery and support processes are designed, managed, and improved;
- *Business results* – examines the company's performance and improvement in key business areas: customer satisfaction, financial and market-place performance, human resources, supplier and partner performance, and operational performance.

### Logic model

The implied logic is that quality is necessary to compete successfully in a world market. The Baldrige Award operates on the assumption that an investment in quality will lead to significantly better returns in the form of increased productivity, satisfied employees and customers, and improved profitability.

### Method

Applicants are evaluated by an independent Board of Examiners comprised of leading experts in quality and organizational management practices from industry, professional and trade organizations, government agencies, and the non-profit sector. Examiners are selected each year and receive training in the performance criteria, scoring system, and examination process.

Companies submit a written application that addresses a number of attributes or items under each performance criteria. Emphasis is placed on the use of quantitative data to substantiate claims of a 'world-class' management system, and to demonstrate continuous improvement by the applicant.

The Board of Examiners reviews each application. The examiners look for achievements and improvements over time in all seven performance criteria. High-scoring applicants are selected for site visits by a subset of the Board, referred to as the Panel of Judges. During the site visit, the judges verify the information contained in the application. The judges then recommend award recipients from among the sites visited. All applicants receive a written summary of strengths and weaknesses for each performance criteria.

### Evaluation standards

The Baldrige Award appears to use mostly time-based and benchmark-based relative evaluation standards. The Award's web site states that 'there are no secret answers or even *right or wrong answers* [our italics] to the Baldrige application.' While this would seem to suggest that winning the award is based, in large part, on the strength of the other applicants, the web site also notes that fewer than two awards may be given in each category if the high standards of the award programme are not met. This, then, would suggest the use of target-based absolute evaluation standards.

*Experience with this system*

Since its inception, 32 awards have been presented to US companies. More than 40 US states have quality award programmes for business based on the Baldrige criteria. Thirty-five of the 40 states recognize non-profit education and healthcare organizations in their award programmes. Many companies apply for these awards instead of the Baldrige Award. Internationally, there are approximately 25 quality-award programmes modelled on the Baldrige Award.

*Strengths*

The Baldrige Award focuses on results and continuous improvement. It provides a framework for designing, implementing and assessing a process for managing all business operations. Even if a company decides not to apply for the award, the Baldrige criteria can be used for self-assessment and training. The primary benefit of the award is its emphasis on sharing of information and actively disseminating best practices in quality management.

*Weaknesses*

The Baldrige Award has been criticized for its focus on finding the 'best of the best' through a competitive selection process, rather than building capacity to assess and improve performance. This has led some companies to apply the concepts of quality management simply to win the award. In the non-profit sector, this could result in an organization diverting very limited resources away from direct service to clients.

Given the uniqueness and rich diversity of non-profit organizations, it is not yet clear if the original Baldrige criteria and their standards of excellence are sufficiently relevant to the voluntary sector. Some of the key differences between profit and non-profit organizations, which are *not* reflected in the performance criteria, include: governance and the relationship between CEOs and boards, limits of statutory authority, legal liability, use of volunteers in service provision, client satisfaction within a highly regulated environment, and dependency on external funding sources.

## ISO 9000 standards

References: Internet: http://www.iso.ch – Website of the International Organization for Standardization, Geneva, Switzerland; James G. Patterson, *ISO 9000: Worldwide Quality Standard* (Menlo Park, CA: Crisp Publications Inc. 1995); David Hoyle, *ISO 9000 Quality Systems Handbook, 2nd edn* (Oxford: Butterworths-Heinemann Ltd., 1994).

### Purpose

The ISO 9000 standards is a series of five, generic standards to help establish and maintain an effective quality management system (9000–9004). The purpose of the ISO 9000 series is to provide organizations with guidelines on what constitutes an effective quality management system, which in turn can serve as a framework for continuous improvement.

### How it works

The ISO 9000 series of standards represents an international consensus on good quality management practice. The standards are primarily concerned with what an organization should do to ensure that its products and services conform to the stated or implied needs of the customer. The ISO 9000 series of standards evaluates the processes that influence quality at the departmental or sub-unit level, which are aggregated at the organizational level.

The first standard, ISO 9000, enumerates the basic rules governing a quality system. ISO 9001, 9002 and 9003 define three quality assurance models against which the quality system can be assessed. ISO 9001 refers to quality assurance in the areas of design and development, production, installation and servicing of products and services. ISO 9002 is limited to quality assurance in production and installation only. ISO 9003 covers quality assurance in the areas of final inspection and testing. ISO 9004 is a comprehensive set of 20 elements from which an organization can choose to customize its quality management and quality assurance system.

### Logic model

The implied logic is that improved quality leads to greater customer satisfaction which, in turn, leads to increased demand, lower costs and higher profits. The ISO 9000 standards operate on the assumption that the way an organization manages its processes (activities) will affect the quality of its products or services (outputs) which, in turn, will affect its productivity and long term profitability (outcomes).

### Method

ISO 9000 is based entirely on the measurement of processes.

*Evaluation standards*

The ISO 9000 standards function as a set of predetermined targets for those organizational processes that influence quality. An organization is measured on the extent to which its processes achieve the targets by conforming to the requirements of the ISO 9000 standards.

*Experience with this system*

The ISO 9000 series of standards was first published in 1987. It has been adopted in more than 90 countries and is being implemented by thousands of manufacturing and service organizations in both public and private sectors.

*Strengths*

The ISO 9000 series of standards help to establish a level international playing field for quality management. Compliance with the standards allows for comparability between international organizations in the manufacturing and service sectors. The two standards, ISO 9000 and 9004, provide a framework for continuous improvement that can be adapted by non-profit organizations for the purposes of self-assessment and training.

*Weaknesses*

The ISO 9000 series of standards apply mainly to private sector organizations that have a relatively homogeneous customer base with specific and consistent needs, and where cost is the primary constraint in responding to customer needs. In contrast, non-profit organizations have multiple customers or stakeholders with complex, changing, and often conflicting needs. The ability to respond to these needs can be limited by reasons beyond the organization's control, including legislative authority, regulatory responsibility, shifting priorities of external funders, and sharp, unpredictable fluctuations in demand for service.

## National Charities Information Bureau standards in philanthropy

Reference: Internet: www.give.org; various NCIB publications similar to what is available on the web site.

*Purpose*

The NCIB, along with the American Institute of Philanthropy and the Canadian Council of Christian Charities are organizations devoted to increasing the public accountability of charities by rating them in terms of their effectiveness and efficiency. Those that pass their tests are certified as acceptable. A major aim of these systems is to provide information for potential donors who want independent assurance that an organization they might give to is well run. Thus, the focus of the system is the organization.

## How it works

The NCIB publishes a list of criteria which they believe a well-run charity should meet. The standards applied are 'the result of a study in the late 1980s by a distinguished national panel'. They claim the application of these standards is useful for all charities though 'for organizations less that 3 years old or with annual budgets of less than $100,000, greater flexibility in applying some of the standards may be appropriate'. The standards are called 'Governance, Policy and Programme Fundamentals' and cover nine areas:

1    *Board governance.* For example, boards should be independent and voluntary, have a minimum of five voting members, possess an attendance policy that eliminates non-attendees, specify fixed terms of office for members, and possess policies that prevent conflicts of interest and encourage pluralism and diversity.
2    *Purpose.* The organization must have a formally stated purpose approved by the board.
3    *Programmes.* The organization's activities should be consistent with its statement of purpose.
4    *Information.* Promotion, fund-raising and public information should describe accurately the organization's identity, purpose, programmes, and financial needs.
5    *Financial support and related activities.* Guidelines aim at ethical fund-raising and full disclosure of how funds are obtained and spent.
6    *Use of funds.* The organization's use of funds should reflect considerations of current and future needs and resources in planning for programme continuity. Several more specific standards are provided. For example: 60 per cent of annual expenses should be for direct programme-related activities, i.e. *not* for covering general administration or fund-raising costs).
7    *Annual reporting.* Annual reports should be available on request and contain a narrative of the organization's activities and a list of board members and audited financial statements.
8    *Accountability.* The organization should supply on request such information as: complete financial statements which are prepared in accordance with Generally Accepted Accounting Principles, all economic resources and obligations and how expenses are allocated.

9    *Budget.* The organization should prepare a detailed annual budget consistent with the major classifications in the audited financial statements.

## Logic models

No explicit logic models are provided to explain why the 9 criteria were selected as the critical indicators for revealing an organization's performance. The implicit measurement logic model is that organizations that meet the standards (all of which are process-based), will be efficient and effective in achieving their mission.

## Methods of evaluation

Charities are ranked as 'meeting all NCIB standards' or not meeting them, based on documents relating to the 9 criteria which are sent to the NCIB office by organizations seeking its certification. The NCIB looks them over and may seek clarification of the submitted information, then issues its judgement on whether the organization passes or fails its tests.

## Evaluation standards used

The standards for assessing the data provided by the organization are all of the absolute target variety. Either the organization does what the standard requires or does not. A few terms in the criteria are vague such as 'reasonable', 'adequate', 'suitable', etc. but it is assumed that the NCIB has strict definitions of these terms for the judges who assess the organization.

## Actual experience using the system

So far, the NCIB has evaluated 400 national non-profit organizations in the US in the areas of cancer research and treatment, international relief and environmental protection. The choice of which specific charities to evaluate within these categories is based mainly on inquiries from the public.

## Weaknesses

While the intent of the NCIB programme is to provide a 'seal of approval' for charities which are well run, in its present form it is liable to result in many misleading judgements of two kinds: approving organizations that are not effective and not approving some that are. While it may be possible that those who fail on all or most of the 9 standards are ineffective, it is far from certain that they are. Conversely, it would be quite possible to meet all 9 of the standards and still be doing a poor job in terms of both efficiency and effectiveness in achieving the organization's mission. This is because there is, as yet, no research that supports the claim that meeting the nine standards is actually related to outcome performance. In fact, it is highly probable that some of them do not.

### American Institute for Philanthropy 'Charity Rating Guide'

References: Internet: www.charitywatch.org; the AIP's print publications: *Charity Rating Guide* and *Charity Watchdog Report*.

#### Purpose

Similar to the National Charities Information Bureau. Stated mission: 'To maximize the effectiveness of every dollar contributed to charity by providing donors with the information they need to make more informed giving decisions. Among its goals are: 'to research the efficiency, account-ability and governance of non-profit organizations'.

#### How it works

Like the NCIB, the AIP focuses only on large national charities. The rating system appears to be based on how well the charity meets certain ratios:

1   Percentage spent on charitable purpose (as opposed to money spent on administrative overhead). '60 per cent or greater is reasonable for most charities.'
2   Cost to raise $100. '$35 or less to raise $100 is reasonable for most charities.' (This is calculated on the basis of the expenses incurred in raising funds by specified methods divided by the amount of income raised by those same methods.)
3   Years of available assets. An estimate of how long a charity could continue to operate at current levels using available reserves. Less than 3 years is deemed to be acceptable.

#### Logic models

There are no explicit measurement or level logic models stated, however, the implicit level of focus logic model is that organizations that meet the 3 main standards noted above will be deemed to be effective and efficient.

#### Methods of evaluation

Charities are asked to submit the following documents: their US govern-ment tax form (990), their annual report, and complete audited financial statements. Specific charities may be chosen for more intense investigation if they are suspected of mismanagement as a result of complaints from the public. The criteria applied and methods used in these special investigations are not stated in the AIP publications.

## Evaluation standards

For what they are worth, AIP does specify absolute standards for assessing non-profits (though some exceptions and qualifications are noted in their literature). Each charity that is assessed receives a grade, from 'A' for Excellent through 'B' (Good), 'C' (Satisfactory), 'D' (Unsatisfactory) to 'F' (Poor).

## Actual experience with the system

So far AIP has rated 360 national charities. There are no published independent assessments of the value or validity of the AIP ratings.

## Weaknesses

The AIP system suffers from the same problems as those noted for the NCIB described above except their criteria are fewer and even more focused on financial and fund-raising matters. It is equally unable to estimate the organization's effectiveness or efficiency in achieving its mission and makes no attempt to assess management processes like the Balanced Scorecard or the CCAF/FCVI guidelines.

## Canadian Council of Christian Charities' 'Standards for Organizational and Financial Integrity'

Reference: Web site: www.cccc.org

## Purpose

'To assist Christian ministries of all types and sizes to conduct themselves in keeping with the Lord they serve ... In order to be an attractive testimony to a watching world a Christian organization must give appropriate account of its finances and activities to governments and to the public at large' (from the CCCC document 'Standards for Organizational and Financial Integrity'). To do this they must meet 7 'Standards':

1   *An independent active board* of at least 5 members that meets at least twice a year. A majority of it must reside in Canada, be unpaid and unrelated to paid staff members.
2   *An independent audit* using Generally Accepted Accounting Principles.

3    *Public financial disclosure.* Full financial statements and the auditors report must be provided to anyone on request.
4    *An Audit Committee* of at least 3 board members meeting at least twice a year must 'review internal controls and the audit programme of the auditor, review the financial statements of the organizations and make recommendations to the board on financial reporting procedures'.
5    *Pursuit of integrity.* This standard in essence says that the organization must use its resources solely to advance the achievement of its mission. It must act responsibly and not violate the spirit or letter of any laws applying to it.
6    *A declared doctrinal position.* Board members and officers must affirm their 'commitment to the Christian faith'.
7    *A declared stewardship policy.* The organization must have policies respecting the remuneration of paid staff and consultants and fund-raising guidelines similar to those advocated by the Canadian Centre for Philanthropy.

## Logic models

Neither measurement or level of focus logic models are explicitly articulated but implicitly the belief is that adherence to the 7 standards will ensure financial accountability and perhaps effectiveness and efficiency in achieving the organization's mission.

## Methods of evaluation

Organizations must pay a fee and submit documentation showing that they meet the 7 standards.

## Evaluation standards

The first four standards are absolute targets. The latter three are very vague and unspecified as to the bases by which an organization will be judged as passing or failing.

## Actual experience with the system

To date, the CCCC has 'certified' 60 charities

## Strengths and weaknesses

Same as for the NCIB and AIP systems discussed above.

## Charities Review Council of Minnesota 'Standards"

References: Internet: www.crcmn.org Booklet: *Charities Review Council of Minnesota Standards*, rev. January 1998 (Minneapolis, Minn.)

*Purpose*

The purpose of the Charities Review Council of Minnesota (a private non-profit organization) is to promote informed giving by Minnesota donors. In this respect it resembles the National Standards Information Bureau, the American Institute for Philanthropy, and the Canadian Council of Christian Charities. It focuses on organizations and has established 16 standards which they believe 'indicate effective, ethical and accountable management practices'.

*How it works*

Charities may apply to be certified by the Council or members of the public may request that a charity be investigated. The results of the subsequent evaluation are published in the Council's 'Giving Guide'. They are certified as 'meeting all accountability standards' or, if not, the particular standards they fail to meet are noted. The standards are grouped into four categories: (1) Public Disclosure, (2) Governance, (3) Financial Activity, and (4) Fund-raising. An abbreviated version of the 16 standards is as follows.

1A The charity has not violated any state or federal laws pertaining to it for 3 years
1B An annual report and annual financial statement will be provided on request
1C Specific and objective information on the organization's mission and accomplishments will be provided
1D There is a consistency between programme names, activities, and financial information across all published statements and materials

2A The governing board meets at least three times a year and maintains minutes of meetings
2B There is a clear conflict of interest policy for the board
2C Board members are not compensated
2D Only one paid staff person may sit on the board and s/he may not be its chair or treasurer
2E Board members must not serve more than 5 years without standing for re-election.

3A At least 70 per cent of annual expenditures must be for programme activity and not more than 30 per cent should be spent for management and fund-raising

3B Unrestricted net assets available for current use are not more than twice the current or next year's operating expenses

3C There is no persistent or increasing operating deficit

3D The board approves the budget at the beginning of the year and receives quarterly financial reports comparing actual to budgeted expenses

4A Donors are provided with full information on the organization

4B Solicitations do not cause donors to feel threatened or intimidated

4C Professional fund-raisers not directly employed by the charity should identify themselves as such.

### Logic model

The implicit logic model is focus based and assumes that following certain processes will lead to an effective organization.

### Evaluation method

Evaluation is based on self-report data from the organization in response to a list of information items required by the Council.

### Evaluation standards

Absolute standards as established. The basis for these is not made known in the published literature.

### Actual experience with the system

The Council has reviewed hundreds of charities seeking to raise funds in Minnesota. No published assessment of the impact of the system is available.

### Strengths

Like the other systems of the same type already reviewed, the Minnesota Council standards provide a minimum level of accountability and doubtless help reveal the more extreme cases of mismanagement and unethical behaviour by charities, especially in the fund-raising and financial management areas.

*Weaknesses*

Again, like the others, this system is unable to say anything about outcomes, depends on self-report data and covers only those who apply for certification or who respond to a request for information from the Council.

## Guidestar database on non-profit organizations and performance ratios

Reference: Internet: www.guidestar.org

*Purpose*

Donors to non-profit organizations would like assurances that the money they donate will 'make a difference' for the cause they support. They fear that it may end up paying for excessive 'administrative overhead' such as abnormally large salaries for managers, overstaffing, costly accommodation, fat expense accounts, etc. A number of the tools often suggested for evaluating the efficiency of non-profits involve the calculation of a variety of financial 'ratios' such as the ratio of expenditures that go directly to its 'programmes', 'overhead' costs such as general administration, and costly fund-raising activities. What follows is a discussion of the nature of several ratios, and how the Guidestar database of 669,000 US non-profit tax returns (IRS form 990) can be used in calculating these ratios for any given organization.

*How it works*

The Guidestar web site discusses 6 ratios and indicators:

1   *Programme ratio.* This is a ratio of programme service expenses to total expenses. It measures the relationship between programme expenses (funds devoted to the direct mission-related work of the organization) and funds spent for administration and fund-raising.
2   *Contributions and grants ratio.* This is the ratio of the amount of income derived from contributions and grants to total revenue. It indicates the extent of the organization's dependence on voluntary support.
3   *Debt ratio.* This is a ratio of total liabilities to total assets. It indicates the organization's financial solvency.
4   *Savings ratio.* This divides fund balances (other than effectively frozen endowment and land, building and equipment funds) by an average month's expenses to yield an indicator, in months, of the organization's operating liquidity. These are the financial resources an organization may legally and reasonably draw down. A high liquid funds indicator could indicate low cash funding urgency or excessive savings.

5   *Accounts payable aging indicator.* This figure may shed light upon the credit-worthiness of the organization. The lower the indicator, the faster the organization pays its bills.
6   *Fund-raising ratio.* This is the ratio of the cost of raising funds to the total funds raised.

Detailed descriptions of how to calculate these ratios are not provided but there is some discussion of how valid and reliable they are as indicators of the area of performance they attempt to address.

### Logic models

There are no explicit level of focus or method logic models presented. Implicitly, the assumption is that these financial indicators reveal the efficiency of the way the organization uses its financial resources. No inferences are drawn as to effectiveness in achieving outcomes.

### Evaluation method

The claim is made that the financial data for calculating the 6 ratios can be obtained from the organization's IRS form 990 (in the US). On the other hand they point out how erroneous and incomplete many of these submissions are. (A new reporting form has recently been introduced which might improve this situation.)

### Evaluation standards

No specific standards of any kind are discussed.

### Strengths

If calculated in the same way consistently and over time, the ratios may be of some use in producing trends that are worth discussing. Major shifts could indicate problems or show improvements.

### Weaknesses

The problem with most of the ratios presented is that there are no standardized and widely accepted methods for calculating them and many organizations do not even gather the base data needed. For example the method of allocating costs to 'programmes' as opposed to 'overhead' is completely unstandardized as are the rules for calculating fund-raising costs. It also turns out that there are many reasons that most of the ratios might show the results they do so interpreting what they mean becomes highly problematic.

The bottom line on these ratios is that funders seeking to compare the efficiency of various non-profit organizations should not emphasize them. They may have some value for non-profit managers if used over time to generate trend indicators. The immediate need is to have experts in financial and cost accounting attempt to develop broad standards for allocating costs to programmes and overhead as well as to fund-raising.

After this it could be possible to generate benchmarks for specific groups of non-profits in a given jurisdiction or sector, e.g. the environmental protection sector, international aid, etc. Even here, however, the dangers posed by the LGAB phenomenon are large since the ease of 'fudging' the base data by the evaluatee is so great.

## Evaluation systems that evaluate larger systems: jurisdictionally-based

### Oregon Benchmarks

References: *Oregon Benchmark Reports* (1991, 1993, 1995, 1997, 1999); Internet: http://www.econ.state.or.us/opb – web site of the Oregon Progress Board.

*Purpose*

The Oregon Benchmarks are a set of 259 measurable indicators that Oregon uses at the statewide level to assess its progress toward broad strategic goals. The benchmarks serve as signs of Oregon's social, economic and environmental well being.

The benchmarks are divided into three categories: people, quality of life, and the economy. They emphasize results and measure outcomes where possible, although in some areas the benchmarks also measure inputs and activities. The benchmarks track progress on specific elements of the strategic vision as well as critical or emerging trends in society. Urgent benchmarks that require immediate attention to keep the state focused on its vision are flagged for action.

*How it works*

In 1989, the people and government of Oregon produced *Oregon Shines*, a 20-year strategic plan for the state. The overall goals of the plan are to achieve sustained economic prosperity and to enhance Oregon's quality of life through quality jobs for everyone, safe, caring and engaged communities and healthy, sustainable surroundings.

The Oregon Progress Board was established to implement and monitor the strategic plan. The Progress Board is an independent state planning and oversight agency comprised of leading citizens and chaired by the Governor. In 1990, the Board created the Oregon Benchmarks to translate the recommendations in the strategic plan into specific objectives, or indicators of progress.

The Progress Board worked with over 200 organizations and individuals statewide to develop, refine, and adopt the first set of 160 benchmarks which it recommended to the legislature in 1991. The Progress Board revisits the benchmarks every two years and, based on public input, refines and modifies the measures.

### Logic model

The logic model used in the Oregon Benchmarks explicitly links state expenditures, legislation and policies (inputs) to programmes and services in the public, private, and non-profit sector (activities/outputs) to desired results in the social, economic and environmental domains (outcomes) to a shared vision of the future (strategic goals).

### Method

Oregon's public, private, and non-profit organizations periodically measure their performance on each of the benchmarks using both quantitative and qualitative data. The Progress Board conducts the Oregon Population Survey, a biennial telephone survey of Oregon households. The survey is designed to provide a regularly gathered source of statewide and regional data on a broad range of population characteristics. It is used as the primary data source for over 30 benchmarks. The benchmark data is then collected by the Progress Board, compiled into biennial reports, and tabled in the legislature. The benchmark data is used by legislators and community and business leaders to reset priorities and to adapt or modify programmes and services.

For example, the state government uses the benchmark data to establish budget priorities. Public sector institutions use them for community planning, work force preparation, education reform, health planning and economic development. The private sector uses the benchmark data for strategic business planning. Community foundations use them to help focus grant-making priorities and non-profit organizations use benchmark measures and targets to develop agency-level performance measures.

### Evaluation standards

The Oregon Benchmarks use target-based evaluation standards. Historical data is used to establish a baseline for each benchmark and to set an appropriate target for the future. Depending on the benchmark, the target may be a new level of performance or a level that has already been achieved and needs to be maintained. In some cases, there are no targets because of insufficient baseline data or because the benchmark needs to be monitored to see if it merits further attention.

### *Experience with this system*

The Oregon Benchmarks planning system has been recognized nationally in the US and won several prestigious awards for innovation in government, community development and performance evaluation. Oregon has developed a workbook to help other states develop their own benchmark system.

The Oregon Option (1995) was the first attempt to use benchmarks in the delivery of federally funded public services through state and local governments. Under this programme, federal, state and local governments work together to define the outcomes (in the form of benchmarks) that they want to achieve with federal dollars. In exchange for latitude in determining how best to achieve the outcomes, service providers agree to measure progress towards the benchmarks and to be held accountable for results.

### *Strengths*

With its focus on results-based accountability, the Oregon Benchmarks attempt to demonstrate that public, private, and non-profit institutions can accomplish their intended purpose. Outcome information is used to assure the public that investments are producing results and to determine whether allocated resources are adequate to achieve significant improvement.

The benchmarks emphasize shared responsibility for outcomes. This facilitates cross sector collaboration and minimizes investment in activities that do not contribute to improved results. Outcome information enhances the capacity of communities and organizations to judge the effectiveness of their efforts and to modify their activities as needed to achieve the desired results.

The benchmarks also diminish the need for centralized management and detailed regulation of inputs and activities. Management by results allows for a significant degree of local variation and front-line discretion to meet a wide range of community needs.

### *Weaknesses*

The degree of effort needed to coordinate the activities of multiple agencies and systems to achieve statewide outcomes is not always appreciated by the public or political leaders. Similarly, the amount of time required to achieve significant improvement in outcomes is often underestimated

In order to generate results, individual organizations may feel pressured to distort their activities to emphasize those that show measurable and rapid results. Some organizations may avoid activities which are harder to quantify, take longer to have an impact, or are one of many related interventions designed to produce a cumulative future benefit.

The demand for documented results may be a hardship for those organizations without the infrastructure to collect outcome data. In the short term, they must allocate limited resources to the development of measurement systems, which for some could mean diverting time, money and/or energy away from the provision of direct services to clients.

An ongoing challenge for the evaluators is ensuring the validity and reliability of outcome data collected from diverse sources, using various methods and units of measurement, over different time periods. At issue is the ability to aggregate or 'roll up' outcome data from the agency, system, and sectoral level to report effectively and meaningfully on the achievement of statewide outcomes.

Some critics argue that the shift towards results-based accountability at the societal level can minimize the importance of procedural protections against fraud, abuse of power, poor services and inequalities based on factors such as ethnicity, gender, sexual orientation, ability, or income. Others believe that an outcome orientation risks being misinterpreted as a panacea or guarantee against ineffective service design and delivery.

## Evaluation systems that evaluate larger systems: sector-based

### Council on Accreditation

References: Internet: http://www.coanet.org.

#### Purpose

The Council on Accreditation of Services for Families and Children (COA) is an international non-profit organization that accredits behavioural health care and social service organizations. COA accreditation is a system of measuring the compliance of organizations in these sectors with national performance standards. The standards are divided into generic organizational and service specific standards, which represent a consensus of professional and consumer opinion on best practices.

#### How it works

COA accreditation is a sequential process through which an organization seeking accreditation is given a series of opportunities to demonstrate compliance with the standards. Organizations must comply with both generic organizational standards and service specific standards. There are eleven generic standards that encompass those aspects of performance that apply to all organizations regardless of the services provided. All organizations must comply with generic standards identified as G1–G7. Organizations that provide a behavioural health service must also comply with G8 and G9, and organizations that provide a community support and education service must also comply with G10 and G11. Each organization must then comply with the relevant service specific standards.

The generic organizational standards are as follows:

G1   Organizational purpose and relationship to the community
G2   Continuous quality improvement processes
G3   Organizational stability
G4   Management of human resources
G5   Quality of the service environment
G6   Financial and risk management
G7   Professional practices
G8   Person/family-centred assessment and planning (Behavioural Health Care)
G9   Person/family-centred service delivery processes (Behavioural Health Care)
G10  Person/family-centred assessment and planning (Community Support/ Education)
G11  Person/family-centred service delivery processes (Community Support/ Education)

*Logic model*

The implied measurement logic of an accreditation system is that compliance with specified industry, national and/or international standards of best practice contributes to improved service quality which, in turn, results in the achievement of better outcomes for consumers.

*Method*

There are 16 steps in the accreditation process divided into four broad categories: application, self-study, site visit, and final decision. The COA estimates that most organizations will be able to complete the accreditation process in 12 months, from application to decision. An organization can be accredited for a maximum of 4 years at which time it must be re-accredited.

The COA accreditation process includes the basic elements found in most accreditation systems:

•   Self-study completed by the organization
•   On-site evaluation by an accreditation team (peer reviewers), professionally qualified to evaluate compliance with the standards

- Accreditation report on the organization's compliance with COA standards
- Opportunity for the organization to review and comment on the report
- Objective evaluation of the report by the Accreditation Commission
- Decision to accredit the organization, to seek additional information, to require remedial action, or to deny or withdraw accreditation
- Appeals process for organizations denied accreditation
- Public disclosure about the status of accredited organizations
- Process for monitoring accredited organizations to ensure continued compliance

*Evaluation standards*

The evaluation standards used in an accreditation system are target-based absolute standards in that organizations must demonstrate the extent to which their activities meet or exceed predetermined levels of performance. These levels of performance are established and regularly reviewed by an advisory group of service providers, regulators and consumers.

*Actual experience with the system*

As of 1 April 1998, nearly 900 organizations were accredited by the COA in the US and Canada. These organizations deliver approximately 1,000 behavioural healthcare programmes and 3,000 social service programmes. The COA works in partnership with 23 national membership organizations to maintain the public trust for individuals and families served by organizations across North America. The Child Welfare League of Canada/Ligue pour le bien-etre de l'enfants du Canada was the COA's first Canadian affiliate. The COA is one of two accreditation bodies recently chosen by the British Columbia government to accredit contracted child and family service providers with total annual contracts over $350,000. There appears to be no published research on the performance of COA-accredited organizations as compared with non-accredited organizations.

*Strengths*

Accreditation is a process that compares an organization's level of competence in certain areas to that of other organizations accredited by the same body. It also identifies areas in need of improvement and provides suggestions on how those improvements could be made.

There are presumed benefits associated with accreditation that accrue to consumers or clients and the public, to the organizations being surveyed, and to funding bodies. Consumers and the public are more likely to receive good services from an accredited provider than from a non-accredited provider. They can expect service quality to meet or exceed industry standards and they can expect the same level of service quality in all accredited services within the same jurisdiction.

For an organization, accreditation legitimizes the good work it is doing and provides a systematic and participatory process for continuous improvement. It helps an organization to identify its level of performance on processes in relation to other service providers and other jurisdictions. Accreditation helps an organization to meet the measurement and reporting requirements of funders and regulators. It also strengthens an organization's case for financial support.

For a funding body, accreditation provides a reasonable level of assurance that an organization is well run. It also reduces or eliminates the need for regular practice or programme audits by the funder.

*Weaknesses*

The primary weakness of this type of evaluation is that accreditation does not link the effective design and delivery of programmes and management systems with the fulfilment of an organization's mission, or the achieve ment of outcomes. Although it is hoped that good practice will lead to good results for the consumer or the taxpayer, this connection is not necessarily established by a successful accreditation process.

Accreditation sets the minimum level of competence in critical functions, below which an organization cannot fall. However, it does not guarantee a certain level of competence or that problems of an urgent nature will not arise. Accreditation bodies differ in many ways, such as philosophy, nature and scope of standards, development of standards, measuring compliance with standards, and recruitment and training of reviewers. Therefore, it is important to find the right fit between accreditor and accreditee.

Accreditation is a lengthy and costly process that requires significant investment of time, energy and resources by the organization. It takes one year from application to accreditation for most organizations. Fees can range from $2,000 (US), excluding site costs, to several thousands of dollars for organizations with large operating budgets. This can run the risk of diverting limited resources away from core service delivery. Also, some organizations may be more interested in 'winning' the designation than actually building capacity to improve services

## Progress of Canada's Children, Canadian Council on Social Development

References: *Progress of Canada's Children* (1996, 1997, 1998); Internet: http://www.ccsd.ca – web site of the Canadian Council on Social Development.

*Purpose*

The purpose of this evaluation system is to monitor and report on the well being of children, youth, and families in Canada on an annual basis. The Canadian Council on Social Development (CCSD) uses this information to motivate public and private decision-makers to take action that will improve the life chances of children and youth.

*How it works*

The *Progress of Canada's Children* is a national report card on the health and well-being of children and youth in Canada. It is modeled on the United Nations' *Progress of Nations* report.

The *Progress of Canada's Children* tracks a series of objective social and economic indicators that reflect the challenges facing children and youth. The indicators are selected and reviewed by an advisory group and a national panel of experts. The first report (1996) established the baseline against which future progress will be assessed. The baseline data describes how Canadian children, youth, and families were faring in 1994.

The report is divided into two sections: environmental indicators and progress indicators. The first section, environmental indicators, assesses inputs into child and youth well-being. These include indicators of family life, economic security, physical safety, community resources, and civic vitality. In the area of family life, for example, the report looks at indicators of family structure, work and family, and family dynamics.

The second section, progress indicators, assesses child and youth outcomes. These include indicators of health status, social engagement, learning, and labour market status of youth. In the area of social engagement, for example, the report looks at indicators of family relationships, peer relationships, and community relationships. The progress indicators are organized into five age groups: young children (pre-birth to age 3), school-age children (ages 4–9), young teens (ages 10–14), teens (ages 15–19), and young adults (ages 20–24).

The primary data for *Progress of Canada's Children* is calculated using microdata from Statistics Canada surveys, such as the National Longitudinal Survey of Children and Youth, National Population Health Survey, Survey of Consumer Finances, and Survey of Family Expenditures.

*Logic model*

*The Progress of Canada's Children* uses a measurement-based logic model. It explicitly links input indicators to outcome indicators in the social and economic domains.

The CCSD has organized its indicators into a three-tiered model. The first tier is comprised of 'simple' indicators that represent data that are measured over time against a base period to indicate a direction of change. The simple indicators are grouped under a second tier of 'intermediate' indicators that represent key determinants of child and youth well-being. The intermediate indicators are grouped under a third tier of 'composite' indicators that assess both the environment for child development and children's progress through specific developmental stages. The indicators roll up from simple to intermediate to composite.

### Evaluation standards

The *Progress of Canada's Children* uses time-based relative evaluation standards. Every year, the performance on each indicator is compared to the previous year and to the baseline established in 1996 (using 1994 data). The report measures the extent to which performance on environmental indicators has improved or deteriorated, and how these changes are affecting performance on the progress indicators. The report does not establish targets for future performance or compare Canada's performance to that of other jurisdictions.

### Experience with the system

The *Progress of Canada's Children* is in its third year of publication. The CCSD intends that the report will be used to inform and stimulate debate among Canadians and decision-makers about what kind of social and economic policies are needed to improve the well-being of children and youth.

### Strengths

The *Progress of Canada's Children* provides a snapshot of the health and well-being of Canada's children, youth, and families. The use of baseline information allows for meaningful comparison of performance over time. As a form of self-assessment, the report evaluates performance within Canada rather than between jurisdictions. This prevents comparison with less developed countries that would make Canadian children and youth appear to be better off. Instead, the report reveals the extent to which Canadian children and youth are experiencing the best possible health and well-being in their own homes and communities.

### Weaknesses

Aside from technical problems with the availability of certain data, the primary limitation of this evaluation system is that it is not formally linked to any national or provincial planning, policy-making or service delivery function. It monitors the status of the health and well-being of children, youth and families, not the activities of the various organizations and programmes involved in this sector. As there is no obligation to act on the evidence contained in the report, it can be easily ignored by legislators, key decision-makers and service providers.

### Professional accreditation bodies relevant to the non-profit sector (Examples of such bodies are those covering nurses, psychologists, teachers, social workers, lawyers, and doctors)

#### Purpose

Many professions create governing bodies to certify their members as competent. Their purpose is to assure the public that persons claiming the professional designation are able to perform at a certain standard established by the governing body.

#### How they work

Professional accreditation is primarily an input-based form of evaluation. Persons entering the profession are checked to ascertain the amount and kind of education they have obtained and usually given qualifying examinations that must be passed at a certain standard. A few professions also measure 'competency' – the ability of the professional to actually carry out various activities in practice. A few also insist on re-qualification at regular intervals so as to ensure the professional keeps up to date with new knowledge and techniques.

#### Logic model

The implicit level-based logic model is that properly prepared and certified professionals will perform according to established standards and therefore the outcomes of their actions will lead to the achievement of the goals of that profession.

#### Evaluation methods

Evaluation is, as noted, largely based on measuring inputs and activities. Measurement is usually by examinations of various kinds. Competency measurement is based on checks that the evaluatee actually carried out certain activities.

*Evaluation standards*

Absolute standards are set that the evaluatee must meet, e.g. examination grades. One of the problems with competency based criteria is that there are often no standards against which to measure the level of competency achieved.

*Actual experience with these systems*

The evaluation of a professional by a body of their peers has been widely practised for centuries. Much less common is research into which professional standards lead to acceptable outcomes. The usual basis for testing this connection is the complaints of the profession's clients. Even then, there is some tendency for the professional body to blame the individual practitioner or discount the client's complaint rather than look at the bigger picture of the effectiveness of the profession's knowledge or training methods.

*Strengths*

At its best, professional accreditation provides assurance that a certain basic set of standards of preparation have been met. In the non-profit sector where the users of the services provided are not themselves able to check the competence of those who serve them, this is an important safeguard.

*Weaknesses*

There is a tendency for professional accreditation bodies to suggest that those who have passed their evaluation system will achieve the outcomes sought by the client. All too often, however, the links between the treatments provided and the outcomes obtained have not been well established and the professional body is slow to change in response to ineffective practices.

## Summary: the state of evaluation tools and systems for non-profit organizations

### Who is being evaluated?

Most of the systems reviewed in this chapter are aimed at evaluating the organization as a whole, closely followed by those that focus on programmes. There are many fewer efforts directed at assessing the state of larger systems either within geographical areas (such as the Oregon Benchmarks) or sectors (such as the *Progress of Canada's Children*). One of the major needs facing the non-profit world as a whole is that for more and better information on how the various parts of it are performing.

If we get more 'report cards' on how communities are faring (jurisdictional-based) and on the state of various key sectors, we will then be better able to assess how well the organizations that make up these larger systems are doing. To decide whether specific organizations make a difference or not requires information on the state of the field they are in.

## What is being evaluated?

As is clear from Figure 6.1, the majority of evaluation systems focus on measuring processes, activities, or outputs rather than outcomes. They make the implicit assumption that if the processes are performed well the outcomes will follow. Part of the reason for this is that outcomes are often difficult to define, only imperfectly represent the goals they are intended to reflect, and are difficult and costly to measure. Also, when one has measured them there are usually many explanations for why the results came out as they did. It seems so much easier to track processes and hope they lead to the desired outcomes.

The problem is that evaluation systems so seldom put forward a clear logic model which reveals the details of the hypothesized links between the processes and outcomes. They also fail to identify the non-controllable contingencies that can intervene to distort these relationships. As a result there are too many fads and fashions in management processes or treatment modalities which evaluations only serve to perpetuate rather than reveal as ineffective.

It seems clear from our analysis that more work needs to be done on developing outcome indicators at all levels (programmes, organizations, and larger systems) and more effort devoted to testing the assumed links between processes/activities/outputs and outcomes. At the very least evaluation systems need to be more aware of the common logical fallacies that can distort their results and explicitly show how they intend to minimize them.

## How is evaluation being carried out?

While most of the evaluation systems reviewed in this report make a considerable effort to specify *what* it is that should be evaluated (e.g. '12 attributes', '4 areas', '259 indicators', etc.) they are much less specific about *how* to implement the measurement of them. They say little about how to design and carry out specific measurements, who to involve and how the results should be interpreted and used.

## Evaluation methods

There is a tendency to prefer quantitative indicators of performance in the systems reviewed though some admit that they are often difficult to obtain so will settle for qualitative data. The various strengths and weaknesses of each of these kinds of data are rarely mentioned. Usually over-dependence on only one method is unwise.

The general failure of most evaluation systems to provide detailed guidance on how they should be implemented is a major problem. This is because research shows that both evaluators and evaluatees often reject formalizing the process so there is very slow growth in systematic evaluation and a low level of retention of those systems that are adopted. In order for evaluation systems to work, there must be a 'culture of accountability' among both evaluators and evaluatees. In this culture *both* accept responsibility for seeking to improve the programme, organization or larger system of which they are a part. The problem of how to create this culture is part of the 'how to implement' aspect of system design and the part that is largely ignored.[1] Among the systems reviewed, that of Letts et al. and the Balanced Scorecard (discussed in Chapter 11) offer the most detail on implementation processes that will build positive attitudes.

### Evaluation standards

Probably the most interesting difference among the evaluation tools reviewed is that between those that apply absolute standards for interpreting measurement data and those that prefer relative standards. The chief characteristic of absolute standard-oriented systems is that they specify a set of specified targets, goals or practices that the evaluatee should meet. If the standard is met, the programme, organization or larger system is judged as effective, at least in terms of what was measured. Examples of absolute standards are: at least 60 per cent of a charitable organization's income should be spent directly on its programmes; boards of directors should consist of at least 5 members and meet at least twice a year; nonprofit organizations should produce a strategic plan; and the costs of fund-raising should not exceed 20 per cent of the amount collected.

The chief characteristic of systems that are relative standard-oriented is that they may specify *what* to evaluate, and *how* to do the evaluation but do not specify any absolute standard or practice for the organization to meet. Rather they suggest comparing results to those of other organizations or programmes (benchmarks) or comparing changes over time.

The evaluation systems reviewed in this report that are absolute standard-oriented are: The Canadian Centre for Philanthropy, the Rensselaerville Institute, the National Charities Information Bureau, the American Institute for Philanthropy, the Canadian Council of Christian Charities, ISO 9000, Baldrige, Guidestar, Oregon, the Council on Accreditation, the Canadian Council on Social Development and the Nursing Profession. The standards they put forward relate to both processes and outcomes and apply to programmes, organizations and larger systems. It is not always clear how the specified standards were reached but some refer to a 'panel of experts' or 'prior research'.

If a target or standard is agreed to as something that is worth aiming at by both the evaluator and evaluatee, and if it is, in fact, achievable, it can be a powerful motivator. Absolute standards are also very useful for external evaluators who simply want to know if a programme or organization is worthy of support (such as the ethical fund-raising guidelines of the Centre for Philanthropy). On the other hand, if standards are set arbitrarily by the evaluator or are not based on valid research that shows that the target is feasible, they are likely to be rejected or a 'make the numbers at any cost' attitude is likely to prevail.

The relative standard-oriented systems reviewed in this report are: the Balanced Scorecard, the CCAF attributes (see Chapter 11), the Drucker tool and the benchmark system of Letts et al. These systems take the position that there are no absolute cut-off points that differentiate the successful from the unsuccessful. Rather they specify the activities or outcomes to be measured and suggest comparing the results to similar others or changes over time. The process of evaluation is meant to act primarily as a trigger for considering the need for change.

By not imposing absolute standards from outside there is less tendency for evaluatees to play the 'look good, avoid blame' game. Differences from benchmarks or over time can be threatening but, if handled simply as indicators of problems to be solved, are more likely to provoke a constructive learning approach. Finally, this approach avoids the tendency to become committed to a 'one best way' approach emphasizing certain best practices that may not be appropriate to the circumstances of a given organization.

On the other hand, the systems that emphasize relative standards do specify what should be evaluated. While the areas highlighted in this way are generally agreed by most theorists to be important in determining the success of the organization, in the final analysis they are not yet proven to be so. Some of the areas identified by the Balanced Scorecard, the CCAF/FCVI and the benchmarking system of Letts et al. may eventually prove to be unimportant, though there is a much greater chance that the absolute standards of the other systems will be found to be invalid.

### Bottom line: Which evaluation systems show the most promise?

As we have already noted, there is no such thing as a perfect evaluation system that will unambiguously reveal how well a programme, organization or larger system in the non-profit world is performing and why. There are no equivalents to profits, return on investment or share of market. In the final analysis all evaluation systems are subjective. The aim of any system can only be to put the discourse about performance into a more rational, data-based format. To do this a system should meet three basic criteria:

1   Both the evaluator and evaluatees must be involved in deciding what is to be evaluated, how the evaluation will be done, what standards are to be applied and how the results will be interpreted and used. This is the only way to reduce the 'Look good, avoid blame' effect and increase the chances of producing shared interpretations of the results.

2   The system should be an integral part of a larger planning process that looks to the future as well as the past and fully analyses the impact of the external environment on the programme or organization.

3   The system should require the development, before being implemented, of full logic models that attempt to specify the links between processes/activities/outputs on the one hand and outcomes on the other. Also, the link between outcome indicators and the goals they are meant to measure should be specified. Existing evidence supporting these assumed relationships needs to be identified and non-controllable external factors that can affect the relationships should be recognized. Finally, there should be an effort to think about 'side effects' – secondary impacts of the programme or the organization's operations that could occur.

Of the evaluation systems that have been reviewed in this chapter and elsewhere the following are the ones that come closest to meeting these three criteria, though all need more work to develop them for all parts of the non-profit sector and more research into their use when they are applied. The top-rated evaluation systems are: (1) the Balanced Scorecard and the Canadian Comprehensive Auditing Foundation systems in a combined format (see Chapter 11); (2) the 'High Performance Non-profit Organizations ' system of Letts et al.; (3) the 'Outcome Funding' system of the Rensselaerville Institute; and the United Way Outcome Funding Approach.

## Conclusions and recommendations

For those who seek improved performance in the non-profit sector, evaluation is one part of the tool kit that is needed. Progress requires looking back to find out about past performance. It also requires looking ahead in order to assess future conditions that will require change from past practices. Evaluation represents the tools for looking back. Other tools are needed for looking ahead. Most importantly, both sets of tools must be integrated into a conscious strategic direction-setting process.

Research into current evaluation practices reveals that it is still more talked about than practiced, and that, when it is carried out, it is often sporadic, short-lived and flawed. Evaluators draw their conclusions about performance from inadequate data, informally gleaned impressions and pre-existing beliefs. Evaluatees often try to avoid blame rather than accept responsibility for those matters for which they are accountable. Many games are played with evaluation systems to ensure positive conclusions.

In spite of all the problems with evaluation, decisions still must be made about funding and the continuation or change of programmes, organizational strategies or policies governing larger systems in the non-profit sector. Without some kind of formal evaluation process these decisions will be entirely based on impressions, ideological beliefs, personalities, historical precedent and the like. So, in spite of all its flaws, it is worth pursuing the goal of improving this process. How can this be done?

## Recommendations

The introduction to this chapter pointed out that the problems with evaluation systems could be clustered under two headings: 'technical' and 'psycho-social'. To improve the process requires work in both areas.

### Fixing the technical problems

It is necessary to realize that the logical fallacies that plague the evaluation process can never be overcome, only minimized. The 'perfect fix' requires knowing the causes of things and, in the realm of human behaviour, there is far too little known about causes. Indeed, many argue that deterministic theories of behaviour are not possible. So, at best, one can only hope to make the evaluation process somewhat more conscious, transparent and rational. How can that be done?

- It is probably too soon to promulgate absolute standards of performance and 'best practices' for non-profit programmes and organizations. Too little is known to warrant proclamations such as: 'organizations that spend less than 60 per cent of their income on direct programme costs are inefficient'; or 'all persons working in a counselling capacity must have a Master of Social Work degree'. Premature promulgation of best practice guidelines as the one best way to perform will likely end up supporting fads and fashions rather than achieving real improvement in performance.
- Rather than setting absolute standards, the emphasis should be on developing more and better kinds of relative standards – benchmark comparisons with others and trends over time.
- To develop better relative standards there should be more emphasis placed on building infrastructure within the non-profit sector – the equivalent of trade associations, Better Business Bureaus and Chambers of Commerce within the commercial sector. There are a few geographically oriented bodies concerned about local communities such as the United Way and various social planning councils. There are also some sector-oriented bodies such as the Association of Canadian Theatres

and the Canadian Council on Social Development. But many sectors have no intermediary body and those that exist have few resources for gathering information on performance effectiveness in their area of interest. New bodies need to be created and more support given to helping them create databases on the issues they deal with.

- These intermediary bodies should also take a lead in developing standardized methods for gathering information on the performance of organizations and programmes in their area and reach out to help them measure their own performance to compare with others.
- Much more work needs to be done by evaluators in addressing the logical fallacies that distort the value of most evaluation systems. This means more training in how to think through in advance the connections between programmes/functions and organization-wide mission and between organizations and results at larger system levels. It also means more research into how processes/activities connect to outcomes, how to establish the validity and reliability of measurement indicators, and how to predict and detect harmful side-effects.

### Fixing the psycho-social problems

The 'Look good, avoid blame' phenomenon will always be present when evaluatees believe the results will be used to make decisions affecting their lives. However, it may be reduced if evaluatees have influence in deciding the following critical elements of the evaluation process:

- What will be evaluated
- How it will be done
- What standards will be applied to the data
- How the final results will be interpreted and used

The latter element also addresses the 'Subjective Interpretation of Reality' (SIR) problem in that both evaluatee and evaluator agree beforehand on how to analyze and act on the results of the evaluation.

Finally, for evaluation to succeed, attention must be paid to creating an entire 'culture of accountability'[1] in which acceptance of responsibility is not something that is seen as threatening but is energizing and an incentive to learn and change. The *experiences* of all those connected with a programme, organization, or larger system must be based on mutual competence, trust, and respect between evaluators and evaluatees. These experiences then create *beliefs* that this atmosphere will exist in the future. These beliefs then drive *actions* aimed at constant improvement and the actions produce *results*.

## Note

1   See Roger Connors and Tom Smith, Journey to the Emerald City: Achieve a Competitive Edge by Creating a Culture of Accountability (Paramus, NJ, Prentice Hall, 1999).

# 7 From concepts to practice

Improving cost information for
decision-making in non-profit
organizations

## I Introduction

It is the normal state of affairs in human service non-profit organizations
(HSNPOs) that demand for services increases much more rapidly than the
resources needed to meet demand, and that managers and boards face a
constant problem of allocating scarce resources internally, on the one hand,
and competing for scarce public and voluntary resources externally, on
the other. Managers and boards should therefore have the answers to the
following basic costing questions at their fingertips: What do administrative support services cost in your organization? How do you respond to
the government's proposal that you take over a new clinical programme
with a grant covering only the salaries of the clinical staff? How much
does your prevention programme cost compared to your treatment
programme? How does the cost of treating a client in your rural office
compare with that in your downtown location? Do you use programme
cost information in your budgeting process internally, and do you use this
information in your funding requests to governments, federated charitable
associations, and other donors? Could you respond to a request from a
public auditor to demonstrate your efficiency in resource utilization
compared to other non-profit organizations and commercial alternatives?

As a step in focusing the broader research project on performance information, we asked managers and board members in the same four HSNPOs
in Victoria, BC, described in Chapter 5, whether they had cost information, and, if not, whether they would find it useful for making policy and
management decisions. This chapter demonstrates the development of a
relatively simple cost accounting model[1] for a hypothetical HSNPO –
Victoria Community Centre (VCC) – that was used to demonstrate and,
frankly, promote the case for costing in the four HSNPOs examined in
the research project.

## II Attitudes to cost information in HSNPOs

Without exception, managers and board members observed that their
major preoccupation was living within very tight budgets, and that detailed

financial information on actual line items of expenditure such as rent and salaries compared to budgeted information was available on a regular basis, often weekly to managers and board treasurers, and at least monthly to all board members and often all staff, as the most common bit of performance information. Given this tight control over budget totals and line items of expenditure, managers and board members assumed that they therefore had detailed cost information, and that living daily within a budget meant that efficiency – getting the most from limited resources – was optimized on a regular basis. In fact, this detailed financial information is only the first step in determining the full cost of the various programmes offered externally to clients, or indeed of the various internal support programmes (such as administration or building maintenance), and the average cost of units of service (such as the cost of a counselling visit).

Information on full and unit costs requires a cost-accounting system that includes specifying cost objectives, defining mission and support cost centres where information is accumulated, distinguishing direct and indirect costs for the group of cost centres, assigning indirect costs across centres, allocating the cost of support centres to mission centres, and using a process or job order system to arrive at the unit cost of outputs or activities. A basic cost accounting system using these components is illustrated for VCC in the next section of the chapter.

As interesting as the assumption that they already had cost information was the reaction of managers and board members to the usefulness of actually having regular information on the total cost of programmes serving clients and internal support programmes, as well as the average cost of units of the various services provided. In general, managers and board members regarded such information as of low priority relative to, say, better information on client satisfaction or staff morale. Some board members also went further to observe that additional information on the costs of programmes and units of output was unnecessary and even perhaps inappropriate in HSNPOs. The attitude of respondents to cost information clearly reflected, in part, some unfamiliarity with the specific nature of cost information. But the responses also reflected some other interesting perspectives on the concept of cost in HSNPOs.

Cost information was considered unnecessary because HSNPOs do not sell their products. Cost information is the first step to determining selling price, and is not necessary if no price is charged directly for the service. The only exception acknowledged by board and staff members was where HSNPOs receive all or part of their revenue based on a formal reimbursement formula; non-profit hospitals and nursing homes in both the US and Canada therefore generally pay close attention to costs. With this exception, however, it is clear that the major incentives to discovering cost information and to cost minimization in the commercial sector – appropriate pricing, competitive survival and profit maximization – do not apply in the HSNPO sector.

The question of appropriateness turned out to be subtler. Two different explanations emerged, the first political, the second philosophical. It was pointed out that such information as the total and unit costs of different services (such as acute and preventive health services), or the cost of administrative support, might be very sensitive and possibly politically embarrassing, both within the organization and between the organization and its funders, by explicitly matching declared priorities and actual resource allocation. It was argued that it would often be awkward to reveal the difference between rhetoric and reality, to show that the 'money did not go where the mouth was'. Like the pricing argument, this political argument also has substance; there is no question that total and unit cost information demonstrates actual rather than rhetorical resource allocation priorities, and might therefore be embarrassing if there is variance between rhetoric and reality. The philosophical argument is closely related to the political; cost information, it was argued, is actually inappropriate in HSNPOs since it connotes a philosophy of 'coping' rather than 'caring', and amounts to placing a monetary value, quite inappropriately, on human services. This argument is ill-founded in one respect; cost information does not place a monetary value on the services provided, but merely demonstrates how resources have been used in providing the whole programme or units of service. In another respect, however, the point is well taken. Cost information forces recognition of the nature of scarce resources and the consequences of choosing how to allocate them; if resources are used to provide one service, they are not available to provide another. This kind of information on 'doing as well as possible with limited resources' may be unwelcome to human service deliverers who believe in doing good as long as there is good to be done.

If cost information is less important because services are not sold and may also be politically and philosophically awkward, the question which clearly arises then is whether managers and board members in HSNPOs should bother with anything beyond the traditional line items of expenditure and the continuing chore of staying within budget. The response to that question can be framed in terms of the usefulness of cost information, despite the different set of incentives and political and philosophical reservations.

## III The usefulness of cost information in HSNPOs

Although managers and board members in HSNPOs are not concerned about pricing and profit maximization, they are or should be vitally concerned about the question of efficiency – about delivering services (at the programme level and at the unit of service level) at least cost. This information is important as one key component of performance accountability across the management cycle both internally and externally. The key is to discover how to make best use of scarce resources. Internally, managers and board members need cost information in the first instance at the planning or policy formulation stage to make strategic choices – to determine the least-cost way (by programme and by units of service) of pursuing organizational objectives through both programmes which provide direct services to clients and internal support programmes (such as administrative services). Such information at the 'front end' also makes possible the matching of actual priorities and resource allocation decisions manifested in budgetary decisions with respect to both financial and human resources. Cost information on what the organization is trying to do also serves as benchmarks by which the organization can determine on an ongoing basis how it is doing with respect to resource utilization, and retrospectively how it has done, and makes possible adjustments in the light of variances. Externally, the same accountability argument holds. At the front end, external funding proposals on organizational plans and budgets are likely to be much stronger and more persuasive if they contain careful costing of proposed programmes and demonstrated internal management systems to monitor efficiency. Funders are likely to require periodic reports over the cycle of funding, and more formal and comprehensive performance reports at the end of each cycle. Such reports, like those at the funding application stage, will be much more effective if sustained by costing information.

The case for internal and external accountability across the management cycle also puts the political argument against cost information in context. It is generally in the interests of all users of performance information – including external funders, evaluators and clients, and internal board and staff members – that performance information be valid, i.e. that it represent accurately what it is supposed to represent. Traditional line-item financial information simply does not provide a valid representation of resource allocation priorities, and possible occasional irritation on the part of one user, say, a board finance chairman, is a small price to pay for narrowing the gap between rhetoric and reality for other users. The philosophical argument provides an important reminder that the nature and use of cost information should be carefully explained to users, particularly staff and clients. But its extreme variant – that cost information is somehow improper and insensitive – simply reflects a misunderstanding of the concept of cost. Given the reality of scarce resources and the inevitability of choice, careful cost planning and monitoring help to ensure that resources are used to best effect in the pursuit of organizational goals. If resources are squandered in a costly or ineffective service, they are not available for other services; in short, knowing how well the organization is doing in allocating its scarce resources makes it possible for the organization to do as much good as possible. As usual, doing well and doing good are complementary rather than in conflict.

The argument then is that cost information is useful, interesting, and appropriate – perhaps, in the more or less normal situation of straitened resources, essential – for board members, staff and other constituencies in HSNPOs to have an 'approximately right' sense about such information as the following: the relative costs of their support activities (such as administration); the relative costs of their front-line services delivered to clients; and the costs of specific outputs (either in average terms, say, the average cost of a counselling visit versus that of a clinical visit, or the specific, perhaps reimbursable, cost of a package of services delivered to a particular client). The question is whether it is possible to go quite simply from basic line-item expenditure data to such information. If the necessary procedure is very complex or perhaps conceptually rather contrived, it may not be worth taking this extra step. The next section of the chapter attempts to demonstrate for VCC – the hypothetical HSNPO – that the steps are simple and defensible – that indeed they simply try to formalize what managers perceive intuitively in any event. The final section draws some conclusions on the use and attainability of cost information.

## IV Costing in the Victoria Community Centre (VCC)

### *The organization*

The Victoria Community Centre (VCC) is a non-profit agency dedicated to fostering the growth, development and well-being of individuals, groups and the community as a whole. The primary funding sources for its $459,000 budget are the federal, provincial and municipal levels of government, the local federated funding organization (the United Way), gaming revenue (from bingo and casinos), memberships, donations, course fees, and special events. VCC serves the communities of Victoria, Saanich (Central, and West), and Oak Bay, with its main clients being single parent, low-income families primarily headed by women and often receiving social assistance.

The mandate of VCC is to provide a friendly, supportive environment that encourages families and individuals by providing opportunities for community leadership and skill development. To meet this mandate, VCC offers such services as counselling, peer support, services to young children, a drop-in centre for parents and children, life skills, and employment preparation programmes. VCC's fiscal year runs from 1 September to 31 August, and the data analyzed are from 1 September 1991 to 31 August 1992. The first step in developing the cost-accounting for the VCC was to consolidate similar or duplicated items in its statement of expenditure (see Figure 7.1). This indicates that the largest category of expenditure of the VCC is wages and benefits ($342,191), followed distantly by such items as building rental ($18,200), overhead ($11,688), and photocopier rental ($10,300).

| ACCT# | LINE ITEM | TOTAL |
|---|---|---|
| 501 | ALARM | $598.00 |
| 502 | PUBLICITY/BROCHURES | $386.00 |
| 503 | ALMOST MUMS | $209.00 |
| 504 | BANK CHARGES | $36.00 |
| 505 | BOARD DEVELOPMENT | $506.00 |
| 506 | MISC. ADMINISTRATION | $597.00 |
| 507 | BOOKKEEPING | $9,757.00 |
| 508 | CLIENT CHILD MINDING | ($300.00) |
| 509 | CLIENT-TRAVEL | $1,233.00 |
| 510 | GROCERY SUPPLIES | $1,417.00 |
| 511 | HONORARIUMS | $1,380.00 |
| 512 | HYDRO | $1,586.00 |
| 513 | INSURANCE | $670.00 |
| 514 | GST EXPENSE | $4,190.00 |
| 515 | MISCELLANEOUS | $1,476.00 |
| 516 | OFFICE CLEANING | $457.00 |
| 517 | OFFICE EQUIPMENT | $1,565.00 |
| 518 | SUPPLIES/EXPENSE | $2,671.00 |
| 519 | PHOTOCOPIER SUPPLIES | $547.00 |
| 520 | PROGRAMME COSTS | $4,844.00 |
| 521 | SUBSCRIPTIONS | $414.00 |
| 522 | BUILDING RENTAL | $18,200.00 |
| 523 | STAFF DEVELOPMENT | $919.00 |
| 524 | POSTAGE | $1,734.00 |
| 525 | SUPPLEMENTS | $8,079.00 |
| 526 | PHOTOCOPIER RENTAL | $10,300.00 |
| 527 | TELEPHONE | $3,655.00 |
| 528 | TOY LIBRARY | $50.00 |
| 529 | TRAINING COSTS | $8,258.00 |
| 530 | TRAVEL/MILEAGE | $9,665.00 |
| 531 | UTILITIES | $600.00 |
| 532 | VOLUNTEER DEVELOPMENT | $70.00 |
| 533 | OVERHEAD | $11,688.00 |
| 534 | SPECIAL COSTS | $541.00 |
| 535 | TELEPHONE/COMPUTER | $3,919.00 |
| 536 | WAGES & BENEFITS | $342,191.00 |
| 537 | MEDICAL/DENTAL | $5,201.00 |
| | TOTAL | $459,309.00 |

*Figure 7.1* VCC consolidated statement of expenses.

## The cost model

*Cost objectives*

In the next step of model development, we obtained the agreement of the Administrator and board in VCC to provide information on the following cost objectives:

First, *to determine those activities that could be classified as organizational overhead, and calculate what proportion of total organizational cost could be attributed to them.* The point here is to arrive at an overhead proportion that is better than arbitrary or what the market will bear, and, further, to determine just what constitutes a defensible overhead proportion (in relation to similar organizations) in order to shed light on the consequences of slashing overhead activities in times of budget stringency and of accepting contracts that rule out any overhead support;

Second, *to go beyond an aggregative approach to overheads by determining what drives the use of overhead activities by client service programmes (funding programmes were excluded in the first instance) and then using that cost driver information to load overhead costs down onto client service programmes.* In this way, the *full cost* – including an appropriate share of organizational overhead costs – of each of the client service programmes could be determined. This information would make possible realistic negotiations with funders, and programme cost comparison with similar organizations. Further, this client service full programme cost information could be used in association with information on the number of clients (or a similar output measure) to determine *unit cost* – the average cost of a unit of service – and therefore, where necessary, what price to charge or reimbursement to request.

*Identifying the cost centres*

In light of the cost objectives, cost centres are the organizational units in which appropriate cost information is to be accumulated. The usual division is into two categories: mission centres which deliver services directly to clients, and support centres which support, that is, deliver services internally to, mission centre activities. The nature and number of overhead cost centres selected will reflect the cost objectives and the degree of detail needed in breaking down overhead costs, and the need to keep the model as simple and workable as possible. The mission centres developed from VCC's numerous programme functions are as follows: Youth and Family Counselling (YFC); Family Advancement Worker (FAW); Safe Home (SAFE); Peer Counselling (PEER); Work Orientation Workshop (WOW); Family Centre (F-CTR); Job Development (JOBDEV); Healthy Babies Programme (H-BABES); Job Activities (JOBACT); Community Kitchens (KITCH); and Nobody's Perfect (NOBODY).

Support centres were categorized by function as follows: Central Administration (ADMIN); Building and Maintenance Charges (BLD/MA);

Office Related Expenses (OFFICE); and Training and Development Costs (TR/DEV).

Figure 7.2 shows the line-items of expenditure and the set of mission and support centres; the task is to find some way of distributing the expenditure totals across the cost centres. The first part of this task was to make a decision about direct and indirect costs.

*Classifying direct and indirect costs and allocating indirect cost to cost centres*

The distinction between direct and indirect costs relates to the attribution or traceability of costs to the cost centre in question. Direct costs are those costs that can be clearly associated with, or physically traced to, particular cost centres; indirect costs apply to more than one centre. Both mission and support centres can therefore have direct as well as indirect costs; whereas direct costs can be assigned directly, indirect costs must be assigned indirectly, that is, using a formula (a 'first-stage' allocation base, as distinct from a 'second stage' allocation base which is used to allocate overhead cost centres to mission centres) to divide them as fairly as possible among the centres to which they relate. This is shown in Figure 7.3.

The allocation of indirect costs to their appropriate centres was an interesting exercise. Alarm, Hydro, Office Cleaning and Utilities, were allocated in total to BLD/MA. Bank Charges, Miscellaneous Administration, Bookkeeping, Honorariums, and Insurance were all allocated to ADMIN. Board Development, Staff Development and Volunteer Development were allocated fully to TR/DEV. Office Equipment, Telephone, and Photocopier Supplies were allocated fully to OFFICE. Publicity/Brochures was allocated among H-BABES, SAFE, and OFFICE on the basis of an estimate of the shares of specific and general promotion. GST (Goods and Services Tax) Expense was allocated on the basis of an estimate of purchasing activity in the various centres. Miscellaneous was allocated on the basis of relative usage between FAW and OFFICE. Building Rental presented an interesting allocation problem since VCC's programmes operate out of a central facility where floor space is not specifically divided among most of these programmes. Considering this, Building Rental was allocated in total to the BLD/MA support centre. Postage, Photocopier Rental, and Overhead were allocated among centres on the basis of an estimate of usage. The allocation of indirect costs is detailed in Figure 7.4.

The Administrator is now in a position to address the first part of the first cost objective. Summing the totals in the support centre columns, almost 25 per cent of the total expenditures in the VCC are accounted for by overhead costs. This information could sustain, for instance, an application for funding which included an analytically justified general overhead percentage.

But there is still much to be done. If the Administrator is to address the Board's interest in the full cost of Administration (now defined as a

|  | MISSION CENTRES | | | | | | | | | | | SUPPORT CENTRES | | | | |
|---|---|---|---|---|---|---|---|---|---|---|---|---|---|---|---|---|
| LINE ITEM | YFC | F-CTR | JOB DEV | H-BABES | KITCH | FAW | JOBACT | NOBODY | PEER | SAFE | WOW | ADMIN | OFFICE | BLD/MA | TR/DEV | TOTAL |
| ALARM |  |  |  |  |  |  |  |  |  |  |  |  |  |  |  | $598 |
| PUBLICITY/BROCHURES |  |  |  |  |  |  |  |  |  |  |  |  |  |  |  | $386 |
| ALMOST MUMS |  |  |  |  |  |  |  |  |  |  |  |  |  |  |  | $209 |
| BANK CHARGES |  |  |  |  |  |  |  |  |  |  |  |  |  |  |  | $36 |
| BOARD DEVELOPMENT |  |  |  |  |  |  |  |  |  |  |  |  |  |  |  | $506 |
| MISC. ADMINISTRATION |  |  |  |  |  |  |  |  |  |  |  |  |  |  |  | $597 |
| BOOKKEEPING |  |  |  |  |  |  |  |  |  |  |  |  |  |  |  | $9,757 |
| CLIENT-CHILD MINDING |  |  |  |  |  |  |  |  |  |  |  |  |  |  |  | ($300) |
| CLIENT-TRAVEL |  |  |  |  |  |  |  |  |  |  |  |  |  |  |  | $1,233 |
| GROCERY SUPPLIES |  |  |  |  |  |  |  |  |  |  |  |  |  |  |  | $1,417 |
| HONORARIUMS |  |  |  |  |  |  |  |  |  |  |  |  |  |  |  | $1,380 |
| HYDRO |  |  |  |  |  |  |  |  |  |  |  |  |  |  |  | $1,586 |
| INSURANCE |  |  |  |  |  |  |  |  |  |  |  |  |  |  |  | $670 |
| OST EXPENSE |  |  |  |  |  |  |  |  |  |  |  |  |  |  |  | $4,190 |
| MISCELLANEOUS |  |  |  |  |  |  |  |  |  |  |  |  |  |  |  | $1,476 |
| OFFICE CLEANING |  |  |  |  |  |  |  |  |  |  |  |  |  |  |  | $457 |
| OFFICE EQUIPMENT |  |  |  |  |  |  |  |  |  |  |  |  |  |  |  | $1,565 |
| SUPPLIES/EXPENSE |  |  |  |  |  |  |  |  |  |  |  |  |  |  |  | $2,671 |
| PHOTOCOPIER SUPPLIES |  |  |  |  |  |  |  |  |  |  |  |  |  |  |  | $2,147 |
| PROGRAMME COSTS |  |  |  |  |  |  |  |  |  |  |  |  |  |  |  | $4,988 |
| SUBSCRIPTIONS |  |  |  |  |  |  |  |  |  |  |  |  |  |  |  | $414 |
| BUILDING RENTAL |  |  |  |  |  |  |  |  |  |  |  |  |  |  |  | $18,200 |
| STAFF DEVELOPMENT |  |  |  |  |  |  |  |  |  |  |  |  |  |  |  | $919 |
| POSTAGE |  |  |  |  |  |  |  |  |  |  |  |  |  |  |  | $1,734 |
| SUPPLEMENTS |  |  |  |  |  |  |  |  |  |  |  |  |  |  |  | $8,079 |
| PHOTOCOPIER RENTA |  |  |  |  |  |  |  |  |  |  |  |  |  |  |  | $8,700 |
| TELEPHONE |  |  |  |  |  |  |  |  |  |  |  |  |  |  |  | $3,655 |
| TOY LIBRARY |  |  |  |  |  |  |  |  |  |  |  |  |  |  |  | $50 |
| TRAINING COSTS |  |  |  |  |  |  |  |  |  |  |  |  |  |  |  | $8,258 |
| TRAVEL/MILEAGE |  |  |  |  |  |  |  |  |  |  |  |  |  |  |  | $9,665 |
| UTILITIES |  |  |  |  |  |  |  |  |  |  |  |  |  |  |  | $600 |
| VOLUNTEER DEVELOPMENT |  |  |  |  |  |  |  |  |  |  |  |  |  |  |  | $70 |
| OVERHEAD |  |  |  |  |  |  |  |  |  |  |  |  |  |  |  | $11,688 |
| SPECIAL COSTS |  |  |  |  |  |  |  |  |  |  |  |  |  |  |  | $541 |
| TELEPHONE/COMPUTER |  |  |  |  |  |  |  |  |  |  |  |  |  |  |  | $3,191 |
| WAGES & BENEFITS |  |  |  |  |  |  |  |  |  |  |  |  |  |  |  | $347,248 |
| TOTAL |  |  |  |  |  |  |  |  |  |  |  |  |  |  |  | $459,309 |

*Figure 7.2* The cost model.

| LINE ITEM | YFC | F-CTR | JOB DEV | H-BABES | KITCH | FAW | JOBACT | NOBODY | PEER | SAFE | WOW | ADMIN | OFFICE | BLD/MA | TR/DEV | TOTAL |
|---|---|---|---|---|---|---|---|---|---|---|---|---|---|---|---|---|
| **DIRECT COSTS** | | | | | | | | | | | | | | | | |
| ALMOST MUMS | | | | $209 | | | | | | | | | | | | $209 |
| CLIENT-CHILD MINDING | | ($300) | | | | | | | | | | | | | | ($300) |
| CLIENT-TRAVEL | | | | | | | | $1,233 | | | | | | | | $1,233 |
| GROCERY SUPPLIES | | $587 | | | $504 | | | $326 | | | | | | | | $1,417 |
| SUPPLIES/EXPENSE | | | | $447 | $36 | | | | $1,808 | | $380 | | | | | $2,671 |
| PROGRAMME COSTS | $2,175 | $1,226 | | | $144 | $1,443 | | | | | | | | | | $4,988 |
| SUBSCRIPTIONS | | | | $414 | | | | | | | | | | | | $414 |
| SUPPLEMENTS | | | | $8,079 | | | | | | | | | | | | $8,079 |
| TOY LIBRARY | | $50 | | | | | $20 | | | | | | | | | $70 |
| TRAINING COSTS | $305 | $143 | $7,177 | $333 | | $300 | | | | | | | | | | $8,258 |
| TRAVEL/MILEAGE | $788 | | | | | $1,227 | | $105 | | $6,210 | $695 | $640 | | | | $9,665 |
| SPECIAL COSTS | | | $231 | $91 | | | | | | | $219 | | | | | $541 |
| TELEPHONE/COMPUTER | | | $1,755 | | | | | | $900 | | | | $1,264 | | | $3,919 |
| WAGES & BENEFITS | $57,253 | $25,355 | $75,970 | $46,492 | | $31,662 | $3,915 | $3,442 | $13,510 | $4,860 | $20,092 | $64,677 | | | | $347,228 |
| SUBTOTAL | $60,521 | $27,061 | $85,133 | $56,065 | $684 | $34,632 | $3,935 | $5,106 | $16,218 | $11,070 | £21,386 | $65,317 | $1,264 | | $50 | $388,392 |
| **INDIRECT COSTS** | | | | | | | | | | | | | | | | |
| ALARM | | | | | | | | | | | | | | | | $598 |
| PUBLICITY/BROCHURES | | | | | | | | | | | | | | | | $386 |
| BANK CHARGES | | | | | | | | | | | | | | | | $36 |
| BOARD DEVELOPMENT | | | | | | | | | | | | | | | | $506 |
| MISC. ASMINISTRATION | | | | | | | | | | | | | | | | $597 |
| BOOKKEEPING | | | | | | | | | | | | | | | | $9,597 |
| HONORARIUMS | | | | | | | | | | | | | | | | $3,757 |
| HYDRO | | | | | | | | | | | | | | | | $1,380 |
| INSURANCE | | | | | | | | | | | | | | | | $1,586 |
| GST EXPENSE | | | | | | | | | | | | | | | | $670 |
| MISCELLANEOUS | | | | | | | | | | | | | | | | $4,190 |
| OFFICE CLEANING | | | | | | | | | | | | | | | | $1,476 |
| OFFICE EQUIPMENT | | | | | | | | | | | | | | | | $457 |
| PHOTOCOPER SUPPLIES | | | | | | | | | | | | | | | | $1,565 |
| BUILDING RENTAL | | | | | | | | | | | | | | | | $2,147 |
| STAFF DEVELOPMENT | | | | | | | | | | | | | | | | $18,200 |
| POSTAGE | | | | | | | | | | | | | | | | $919 |
| PHOTOCOPIER RENTAL | | | | | | | | | | | | | | | | $1,734 |
| TELEPHONE | | | | | | | | | | | | | | | | $8,700 |
| UTILIIES | | | | | | | | | | | | | | | | $3,655 |
| VOLUNTEER DEVELOPMENT | | | | | | | | | | | | | | | | $600 |
| OVERHEAD | | | | | | | | | | | | | | | | $11,688 |
| SUB TOTAL | | | | | | | | | | | | | | | | $70,917 |
| TOTAL | | | | | | | | | | | | | | | | $459,309 |

*Figure 7.3* Classifying direct and indirect costs.

| LINE ITEM | MISSION CENTRES | | | | | | | | | | | SUPPORT CENTRES | | | | TOTAL |
|---|---|---|---|---|---|---|---|---|---|---|---|---|---|---|---|---|
| | YFC | F-CTR | JOB DEV | H-BABES | KITCH | FAW | JOBACT | NOBODY | PEER | SAFE | WOW | ADMIN | OFFICE | BLD/MA | TR/DEV | |
| **DIRECT COSTS** | | | | | | | | | | | | | | | | $209 |
| ALMOST MUMS | | ($300) | | $209 | | | | | | | | | | | | ($300) |
| CLIENT-CHILD MINDING | | | | | | | | | | | | | | | | $1,233 |
| CLIENT-TRAVEL | | | | | | | | $1,233 | | | | | | | | $1,417 |
| GROCERY SUPPLIES | | $587 | | | $504 | | | $326 | | | | | | | | $2,671 |
| SUPPLIES/EXPENSE | | | | $447 | $36 | | | | | | | | | | | $4,988 |
| PROGRAMME COSTS | $2,175 | $1,226 | | | $144 | $1,433 | | | $1,808 | | $380 | | | | | $414 |
| SUBSCRIPTIONS | | | | $414 | | | | | | | | | | | | $8,079 |
| SUPPLEMENTS | | | | $8,079 | | | | | | | | | | | | $50 |
| TOY LIBRARY | | $50 | | | | | | | | | | | | | | $8,258 |
| TRAINING COSTS | $305 | $143 | $7,177 | $533 | | $300 | | | | | | $640 | | | | $9,665 |
| TRAVEL/MILEAGE | $788 | | | | | $1,227 | | $105 | | $6,210 | $695 | | | | | $541 |
| SPECIAL COSTS | | | $231 | $91 | | | | | | | $219 | | | | | $3,919 |
| TELEPHONE/COMPUTER | | | $1,755 | $46,492 | | $31,662 | $3,915 | $3,442 | $900 | $4,860 | $20,092 | $64,677 | $1,264 | | | $947,248 |
| WAGES & BENEFITS | $57,253 | $25,355 | $75,970 | $56,065 | $684 | $34,632 | $3,935 | $5,106 | $13,510 | $11,070 | $21,386 | $65,317 | $1,264 | $50 | $50 | $388,392 |
| SUBTOTAL | $60,521 | $27,061 | $85,133 | $56,065 | $684 | $34,632 | $3,935 | $5,106 | $16,218 | $11,070 | $21,386 | $65,317 | $1,264 | | | |
| **INDIRECT COSTS** | | | | | | | | | | | | | | | | |
| ALARM | | | | $58 | | | | | | | | | | $598 | | $598 |
| PUBLICITY/BROCHURES | | | | | | | | | | | | | $298 | | | $386 |
| BANK CHARGES | | | | | | | | | | $43 | | $36 | | | | $36 |
| BOARD DEVELOPMENT | | | | | | | | | | | | | | | $506 | $506 |
| MISC. ASMINISTRATION | | | | | | | | | | | | $597 | | | | $597 |
| BOOKKEEPING | | | | | | | | | | | | $9,380 | | | | $9,597 |
| HONORARIUMS | | | | | | | | | | | | | | | | $3,757 |
| HYDRO | | | | | | | | | | | | | | $1,586 | | $1,380 |
| INSURANCE | | | | | | | | | | | | $670 | | | | $1,586 |
| GST EXPENSE | $180 | $1,003 | $841 | $157 | | | | $18 | $297 | $14 | $31 | | $1,649 | | | $670 |
| MISCELLANEOUS | | | | | | $129 | | | | | | | $1,347 | | | $4,190 |
| OFFICE CLEANING | | | | | | | | | | | | | | $457 | | $1,476 |
| OFFICE EQUIPMENT | | | | | | | | | | | | | $1,565 | | | $457 |
| PHOTOCOPER SUPPLIES | | | | | | | | | | | | | $2,147 | | | $1,565 |
| BUILDING RENTAL | | | | | | | | | | | | | | $18,200 | | $2,147 |
| STAFF DEVELOPMENT | | | | | | | | | | | | | | | $919 | $18,200 |
| POSTAGE | | | | $320 | | | | $31 | | | | | $1,383 | | | $919 |
| PHOTOCOPIER RENTAL | | | $7,950 | | | | $750 | | | | | | | | | $1,734 |
| TELEPHONE | | | | | | | | | | | | | $3,655 | | | $8,700 |
| UTILIIES | | | | | | | | | | | | | | $600 | | $3,655 |
| VOLUNTEER DEVELOPMENT | | | | | | | | | | | | | | | $70 | $600 |
| OVERHEAD | | | $10,938 | | | | $750 | | | | | | | | | $70 |
| SUB TOTAL | $180 | $1,000 | $19,729 | $535 | $0 | $129 | $1,500 | | | | $31 | $12,440 | $12,031 | $21,441 | $1,495 | $11,688 |
| TOTAL | $60,701 | $28,064 | $104,862 | $56,600 | $684 | $34,761 | $5,435 | $5,155 | $16,515 | $11,127 | $21,417 | $77,575 | $13,295 | $21,441 | $1,495 | $70,917 |
| | | | | | | | | | | | | | | | | $459,309 |

*Figure 7.4* Allocation of indirect costs.

support centre) and of front-line programmes (now classified as mission centres) and in the unit cost of dealing with clients, the support centre costs, or organizational overheads, must be allocated to the mission centres.

*The allocation of support centre costs (the step-down process)*

The second stage of cost allocation is the process of distributing support centre costs among mission centres in order to determine the full cost of each mission centre. Before overhead costs can actually be allocated however, the Administrator must determine, first, the allocation model, and second, the set of allocation bases.

The allocation model requires the conceptualization of how overhead costs actually work in the organization. Three alternatives are available.

The most basic, and least accurate, allocates the total costs of each support centre directly to the various mission centres. This approach is simple but least accurate because it ignores the services that support centres render to each other.

The most accurate, but most complex, recognizes the complete set of reciprocal relationships among interdependent support centres and solves a set of simultaneous equations to determine the reciprocal allocation of support centre costs before allocating support centre costs to the mission centres. For two support centres, this involves two equations in two unknowns and is relatively simple; but the process becomes more complex as the number of support centres increases. The increased computational complexity can be easily addressed by using a computer, but we found that the increased conceptual complexity makes this approach much more difficult to explain to users.

The compromise model which is always much more accurate than simple direct allocation and is usually acceptably close in accuracy to the reciprocal model is the step-down model. This approach recognizes that support centres serve other support centres as well as mission centres, but recognizes that service in a linear, approximate way rather than a fully reciprocal way. Essentially, the set of support centres is arranged in order from that which serves most other support centres to that serving least. Beginning with the support centre that serves most other support centres, the costs of that centre are stepped down, that is, allocated in a step-down or cascading way, onto all the other support centres and the mission centres. That completely allocated support centre plays no further part in the allocation process. The procedure is then repeated for each support centre, in turn, until the costs of all support centres are fully allocated to the set of mission centres. This method ignores reciprocity, but allows managers to reflect on the set of support centres in a functional way, as a working model of organizational activity. It emerged really as a model for the expression of management's assumptions about how the organization worked.

| | | | BLD/MA | OFFICE | TR/DEV | ADMIN | TOTAL |
|---|---|---|---|---|---|---|---|
| SUPPORT CENTRES | BLD/MA | $21,441 | – | – | – | | |
| | OFFICE | $13,295 | – | – | – | | |
| | TR/DEV | $1,495 | – | $47 | – | | |
| | ADMIN | $77,757 | $2,144 | $2,435 | $514 | | |
| MISSION CENTRES | YPC | $60,701 | $1,340 | $1,901 | $343 | $14,563 | $78,848 |
| | F/CTR | $28,064 | $4,288 | $879 | $171 | $6,733 | $40,135 |
| | JOB DEV | $104,862 | $2,144 | $3,284 | $171 | $25,159 | $135,620 |
| | H-BABES | $56,600 | $2,144 | $1,772 | $171 | $13,580 | $74,267 |
| | KITCH | $684 | $1,340 | $21 | | $164 | $2,210 |
| | FAW | $34,761 | $1,340 | $1,088 | $171 | $8,340 | $45,701 |
| | JOBACT | $5,435 | $1,340 | $170 | | $1,304 | $8,249 |
| | NOBODY | $5,155 | $1,340 | $161 | | $1,237 | $7,893 |
| | PEER | $16,515 | $1,340 | $517 | | $3,962 | $22,335 |
| | SAFE | $11,127 | $1,340 | $348 | | $2,670 | $15,485 |
| | WOW | $21,417 | $1,340 | $671 | | $5,138 | $28,566 |
| | SUBTOTAL | $345,321 | $1,340 | $10,813 | $1,028 | $2,850 | $459,309 |
| | TOTAL | $459,309 | $21,441 | $13,295 | $1,542 | $82,850 | $459,309 |

*Figure 7.5* VCC – step down process.

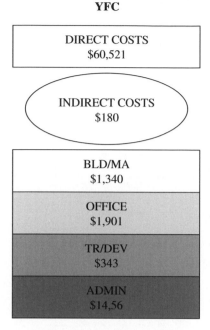

**YFC**

DIRECT COSTS
$60,521

INDIRECT COSTS
$180

BLD/MA
$1,340

OFFICE
$1,901

TR/DEV
$343

ADMIN
$14,56

TOTAL PROGRAMME COST
$78,848
NUMBER OF CLIENTS = 131
COST/CLIENT = $601,89

*Figure 7.6* Calculation of unit cost of client services (YFC).

The selection of allocation bases parallels the use of formulas to allocate indirect costs among mission and support centres; the most appropriate base is obviously that which most accurately reflects the use of support centres by mission centres. The allocation formulas have to recognize that support centres may serve other support centres as well as mission centres; the procedure for stepping down support centres into mission centres is detailed in Figure 7.5.

First, Building and Maintenance (BLD/MA) was charged across the remaining mission and support centers. This was accomplished through an estimate of floor space usage where possible. Family Centre (F-CTR) was allocated 20 per cent of BLD/MA, Healthy Babies (H-BABES) 10 per cent, Job Development (JOB DEV) 10 per cent, and Administration (ADMIN) 10 per cent. The remaining 50 per cent of costs were allocated evenly among the rest of the mission centres. The OFFICE and TR/DEV support centres were not allocated any BLD/MA costs.

Second, the OFFICE support centre was stepped-down across all of the remaining mission and support centres as a percentage of total expenditure.

**HEALTHY BABIES**

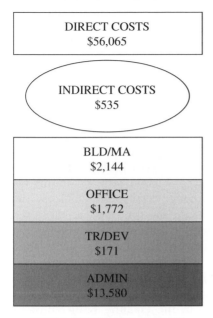

TOTAL PROGRAMME COST
$74,267
NUMBER OF CLIENTS = 110
COST/CLIENT = $675,15

*Figure 7.7* Calculation of unit cost of client services (Healthy Babies).

Third, Training and Development (TR/DEV) was allocated by the number of Full Time Equivalent (FTE) staff in each mission and support centre.

Finally, in the absence of data regarding how the Administrator, the Bookkeeper and other manager's spent their time on the mission centres, Administration (ADMIN) was allocated as a percentage of the total expenditure of each of the mission centres.

The Administrator is now in a position to address the second part of the first cost objective, and the second cost objective. Figure 5 shows that the full cost of the ADMIN support centre, including an allocated share of the other support centre costs, is $82,850, and also shows in the final column the full cost of each of the eleven mission centres. This bit of information could be used for comparison with like organizations, and in dealing with unsubstantiated assertions about how much is consumed by Administration.

How interesting the above figures are depends, of course, on comparable figures in similar organizations and on figures for previous years (if available) for VCC. Since interest in some unit cost figures has been expressed, the Administrator has to turn to a final step to provide this information.

*Determining the unit costs of client services*

The calculation of unit costs obviously requires a definition of 'unit'. The Administrator has two major choices in calculating cost per client: the process method and the job order method. The process method is used when all units of output are homogeneous, and it is also used in many manufacturing processes. The job order method is used when units of output are different, and would be used in situations such as an auto-mobile repair shop. Using the process method, full mission centre costs for the accounting period are calculated using the steps described above, and are then divided by the number of units of output to give unit cost. Using the job order method, all direct costs associated with a particular job are collected separately on a job order record, and indirect costs are assigned to each job using an overhead rate. Many cost accounting systems have features of both process and job order costing. In VCC, the mission centre full costs can be used to calculate the unit cost of client services (Figure 7.6 and Figure 7.7). For instance, to determine the cost of providing service for a client in Youth and Family Counselling (YFC), the total programme cost is divided, using the process costing model, by the total number of clients using this service. Since the programme cost was $78,848 and 131 clients used the programme, the cost per client was $601.89. Similarly, the cost of serving a client in the Healthy Babies programme averages $675.15 ($74,267 programme cost with 110 clients).

A much simplified job order costing system for clients can be illus-trated by postulating circumstances in which the funding agency for VCC proposes that additional counselling services be given to designated clients, and that the reimbursement price for each client be determined by adding to the YFC process-based unit cost of $601.89/client an amount to cover the additional hours of counselling at some negotiated rate per hour. If designated clients require 10 additional hours of counselling at a negotiated rate of $40/hour, the additional 'job order' charge would be $400, giving a cost/client for designated clients of $601.89 + $400 = $1,001.89.

*The achievement of cost objectives*

Using the relatively simple cost accounting model illustrated above, the Administrator is now in a position to provide to the board information on the specified cost objectives. Four broad areas of overhead or support activities have been classified – Administration, Office Expenses, Building and Maintenance, and Training and Development – and these over-head areas account for almost 25 per cent of total expenditures in VCC. Using one set of explicit allocation rules to allocate indirect costs to the various mission centres and support centres, and another explicit set to step-down the total costs of the support centres in a defined order to the remaining support centres and the mission centres, the Administrator can demonstrate the full costs, including an appropriate share of organizational overhead, of each mission centre. Further, the Administrator can divide the full cost of each mission centre by the number of clients served to arrive, using a simple process model, at the unit cost of a client, and can supplement that unit cost information, if required for reimbursement purposes, by specific job-order information for particular clients.

## V Conclusion

The concept of costs is not well understood in human service NPOs in British Columbia, either by internal decision-makers or by external funders. Line-item financial information, either as budgets or financial statements, is frequently, and erroneously, taken to convey useful information on programme costs. This chapter is specifically concerned with the importance of understanding, and including in cost calculations the cost of the support or overhead activities that are necessary to sustain direct client service activities. The work has attempted to demonstrate that information on the nature and role of overhead costs, and the derivative information on the full and unit costs of client service programmes can be generated using a relatively simple model which essentially invites managers to start with simple line-item budget information, and then to formalize the assumptions with which they are working intuitively, and to explore the implications of these assumptions. Further, it is argued that cost information is necessary for internal and external accountability in human service NPOs. Information on the relative costs of direct client service programmes, fund-raising programmes, and internal support programmes contributes to informed resource allocation decision-making by managers and boards internally and funders and evaluators/auditors externally, and is essential where funding is geared to formal reimbursement. Full cost information contributes to strategic planning, programming, and performance budgeting, and to associated performance monitoring and evaluation. The controllable costs component of cost centres also serves as the basis for responsibility centre budgeting and monitoring. Human service NPOs rightly concerned about effectiveness – about doing the right thing. This chapter has argued that they should also be concerned about efficiency – about doing the thing right – and that such information is within the reach of all managers and boards using their line-item budgets and a willingness to articulate and test their assumptions about how the organization functions.

The VCC example and associated argument were well received when presented to board and staff members in the agencies in the research project. Both board and staff members were reassured that the computational gymnastics were eminently manageable, and indeed that the model amounted really to a method of examining the implications of board and staff assumptions about how resources were used in the agency. They also recognized the various types of situations in which analytically justified information about total and unit costs would be useful for internal accountability and for reporting and contract negotiation externally. It seems fair to conclude that the elements of cost accounting can be, and hopefully will be, practised as one of the core components of management information systems in the various agencies.

## Note

1    R.N. Anthony and D.W. Young, *Management Control In Non-Profit Organizations*, 6th edn (Boston, Mass., Irwin/McGraw-Hill, 1999). James Cutt, et al., *From Financial Statements to Cost Information: Efficient Resource Utilization in Non-Profit Organizations* (Victoria, BC, Centre for Public Sector Studies, 1994). D.W. Young, *Financial Control in Health Care* (Homewood, Ill. Dow-Jones-Irwin, 1984).

# 8 Case studies in performance measurement

## 1 Capital Mental Health Association

## I Introduction

The Capital Mental Health Association (CMHA) is an umbrella organization of 12 psycho-social rehabilitation programmes. For forty years CMHA has been serving persons with mental illness in the Capital Regional District (CRD) on Vancouver Island, BC, Canada. Its mission is:

> To enhance and enrich the quality of life of persons with mental illness and to promote their integration in the communities of the capital region, through partnership with the individuals, their family members and the community.[1]

CMHA pursues its mission through 12 programmes, 5 vocational, 5 social-recreational, and 2 in the area of supported housing. In Chapter 4, we discussed our preliminary report to the CMHA Executive Director and Board. The experience was interesting and instructive, but not particularly productive. The agency did not find our first attempt persuasive, and we did not succeed in our objective of demonstrating that the development of a performance accountability framework was practically feasible and useful, even essential, to both management and the board for both internal governance and management control and external reporting and fund-raising. We continued to work with the agency and re-established a constructive relationship through the development, from the bottom up, of general reporting standards, and of specific approaches such as programme costing. The relationship progressed to the point where we were encouraged to offer assistance in addressing the very difficult area of performance measurement on the other side of the value-for-money equation – what is achieved by spending these resources. This chapter reports on this part of the research project.

Five of the 12 programmes are illustrated in this abridged version of the larger study of all 12 programmes which, as part of our research project, was completed as a graduate dissertation in 1997 at the University of Victoria.[2] The first two are vocational, the next two social-recreational, and the last comes within supported housing. The five programmes are as follows:

- The Therapeutic Volunteer Placement Programme works with approximately 30 adults referred each year by Mental Health Centres. Each volunteer has a mental illness, is considered unfit to prepare for competitive employment, but wishes to make a contribution through volunteer effort.
- The Job Search Consultant Programme promotes integration by assisting job-ready adults with mental illness to find employment in the community.
- Laurel House provides social, recreational, and pre-vocational activities and skill development to over 200 adults with serious mental illness. Some adults have attended for years, and use Laurel House as their main support in continuing to live in the community; other attend for shorter periods, as needed, before moving into other activities.
- The Alzheimer's Support Centre provides a day-respite programme for older persons with mild, moderate or severe dementia who continue to reside at home.
- The Supported Independent Living Programme provides a team of life skills workers and a nurse coordinator for a group of 30 seriously mentally ill clients. Clients are referred by Mental Health Services and highest priority is given to those who are without support in the community and are at high risk of hospitalization.

## II Purpose of the study

The purpose of the study was to design performance logic models, including outcome indicators, to enable CMHA to meet the requirements of public sector (primarily Ministry of Health) and federated funding agency (United Way in the CRD) funders for evidence of outcomes in both requests for funding and reports on performance. The Executive Director of CMHA requested that the study treat in detail only one strategic outcome in each programme. Although this request was made by the Director with a view to regarding the study as a pilot or experimental project which could set the stage for later development, it turned out to be entirely consistent with, indeed to foreshadow, our later argument – developed in Chapter 11 – that the effective design of programme logic models requires a focus on one strategic, long-term objective and associated outcome.

## III Organizational context

Consistent with the work reported in other chapters, this study was addressed to the programme level in CMHA. The 12 programmes all contribute, within the three broad functional groupings (vocational, social-recreational, and supported housing), to the organizational mission. So the logic of each programme should be seen within an overall organizational logic. This over-arching organizational logic is illustrated for CMHA in Figure 8.1, and a subsequent development of the performance measurement approach illustrated here for individual programmes would move to the comparison among programmes which the CMHA Board of Directors, and indeed external funders, must face, in deciding how best to achieve the organizational mission. At the level of comparable programmes, say, those focused on client employment, a common long-term strategic objective and outcome measure can be defined, and technical evidence using these commensurable performance measures can inform resource allocation and evaluation choices among programmes. For programmes which do not share a common long-term strategic objective, say, programmes relating to employment and programmes relating to housing, technical evidence cannot clearly inform decisions. But these decisions must still be made. To this problem of incommensurability and technical limits we turn our attention in Chapter 12.

## IV  Methodology

The methodology used in the study was primarily qualitative and informal. It included a review of CMHA's documentation (communications, statistics, annual reports, Constitution and By-laws), federated funding agency (United Way) documentation, and meetings with the Executive Director, programme managers, and board members. In the nature of CMHA's clients, formal client consultation presents some difficulties, and no such consultation was attempted in this study. But implementation of some of the proposed measurement and further development of the proposed framework would have to include the measurement of client satisfaction, perhaps through surrogates, and consultation with other external stakeholders.

The strong support of the CMHA Executive Director and programme managers was contingent on an approach that was not only consultative but also practical and useful. This included commitments, which we attempted to honour throughout the project, to the following:

1   A focus on *feasibility*. The focus was on tangible outcomes that would not have onerous measurement or reporting requirements.
2   A focus on the *primary rationale* for a programme. The central, strategic long-term objective for each programme was defined as the basis for outcome measurement.
3   A focus on *clarity and understandability*. Once general agreement on a programme's strategic outcome was achieved, the concept was then defined in a way that allowed clear measurement and understanding.

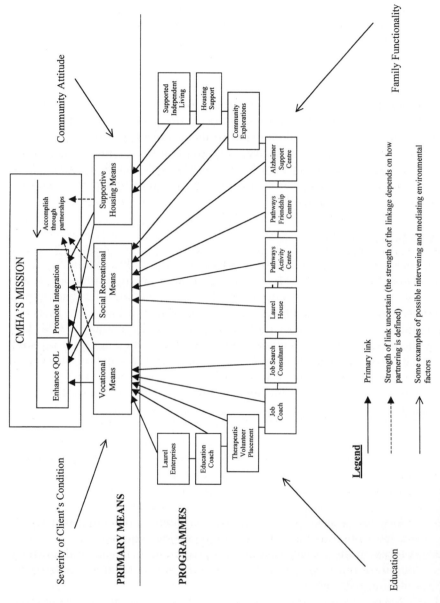

*Figure 8.1* CMHA's organizational logic model.

4   A focus on the *outcome rather than the outcome measurement tool*. Agreed outcomes were not manipulated to fit preferred measurement tools; rather agreed outcomes were protected, and the best possible measurement tool developed for these outcomes.

5   A focus on a *clearly specified set of indicators* to determine the presence or absence of the chosen outcome. An attempt was made for each programme to define a set of indicators, including the indicators for the various stages of outcomes, which was exhaustive and mutually exclusive.

During the study a number of outcome measures were created uniquely for CMHA's programmes. In other cases, however, the complexities of clients' mental illnesses suggested the adoption of established measurement tools. To this end, a variety of survey tools were investigated to determine the most valid, reliable and feasible for CMHA's purposes. Many of these tools are very thorough and sophisticated, but are simply too resource-intensive. The Bigelow Scale, for example, is a 263-item structured interview; the Lehman Quality of Life Scale involves a 45-minute interview; and the Global Assessment Function questionnaire requires a professional interviewer. After a review of the various survey tools available, the International Association of Psycho-social Rehabilitation Services (IAPSRS) *Toolkit for Measuring Psycho-social Outcomes*[2] was selected as the primary measurement instrument. The primary reasons for choosing this tool were its ease of administration, its supportive tool kit package, its application to many of the domains addressed by CMHA's programmes (e.g. residential, employment, education, quality of life, mastery, empowerment and programme satisfaction), and the comfort of CMHA programme managers with the instrument.

# V Establishing programme objectives and logic models

Two different but related tables were constructed for each programme. One table provides programme objective specifics, while the second provides the logic underlying the outcome model.

The first table provides the primary programme objective, assumptions underlying the programme, the stated target of the programme and its relevant indicators, and finally the programme evaluation method. Programme objectives, all derived from discussion with programme managers, state the primary, strategic objective of programmes. Programme assumptions describe the fundamental logic or implicit causal sequence of programmes – these are formalized in the second table. Targets define programme objectives in an operational way, that is, in a way that permits measurement; and associated indicators determine the presence or absence of the outcome defined by the target. Evaluation methods define the way in which programme measurement information will be collected and analyzed.

Once each programme's objective, target, and related information had been developed, the information was then recast in outcome terms and placed under the appropriate outcome heading (initial, intermediate, and long-term) of a logic model in the second table. The purpose of the logic model is to clarify the logic underlying the achievement of each programme's objective. It links the various stages implicit in each programme, from programme inputs and activities through initial, intermediate, and long-term outcomes. The detail in the subsequent illustrations is confined to outputs and outcomes – the 'value' side of value for money. The 'money' side was explored in Chapter 7.

Formally, the sequential stages of the model are defined as follows:

*   *Inputs* are the resources used by a programme to achieve the programme objective;
*   *Activities/processes* describe how a programme uses its inputs;
*   *Outputs* are described in physical units of some kind, and represent measures of the immediate products of a programme, such as the number of clients served. They can also be thought of as measures of 'busyness' or activity; and are the most frequently used measure of the 'value' produced by a programme in the unit cost calculations illustrated in Chapter 7;
*   *Initial outcomes* are the first post-programme changes seen in the participant following from, and attributable to, programme outputs. They are often represented as changes in understanding, knowledge or skills, and are seen as necessary preconditions for the attainment of later outcomes;
*   *Intermediate outcomes* provide the link between initial outcomes and long-term outcomes. They are usually described in terms of new behaviour that is attributable to the new knowledge and skills gained by clients; and
*   *Long-term outcomes* represent the ultimate long-term consequence for the client that is attributable to the programme, and are a measure of the long-term strategic objective of the programme. They are usually represented as changes in the condition or status of the client. Since they are furthest removed from the programme, the inferred causality is most difficult to define and defend.

The model allows the logic underlying each programme's long-term strategic objective to be clearly and consistently articulated. While this logic is largely a statement of the obvious for the Executive Director and programme managers, this is not the case for most of CMHA's stakeholders, including board members. Further, it is simply prudent business practice to articulate the logic in case, at some future date, the Executive

Director or a programme manager is unable to continue her role at CMHA. At such a juncture, the heretofore tacit knowledge could prove invaluable.

The causal theory implicit in the logic model is simple, if heroic. It assumes that if the output occurs, there is a significant probability that the initial outcome will occur, and so on. So the causation that is assumed is probabilistic in nature, but sustained by the expertise and experience of the professionals delivering the programme. For example, the initial outcome of a counselling programme for teenagers may to be increase the teenager's appreciation of the value of staying in school. The intermediate outcome would then involve the transfer of this knowledge into behaviour – the teen chooses to stay in school. The long-term intended outcome involves the translation of school completion into desired consequences such as higher education or employment. The causal link to the long-term outcome is clearly more difficult to sustain by good technical evidence than that for initial and intermediate outcomes, and the accountability of programme managers (credit or blame) would have to be formally limited to those consequences over which the manager had significant control or influence. This does not mean that managers should not try to collect such information by, say, longitudinal studies of clients.

Figure 8.2 (a) to (e) show the programme objective and logic models developed for five of CMHA's 12 programmes.

## VI Implementation

The proposed models were well received by the Executive Director, programme managers and board at CMHA, and preliminary implementation of the approach for all 12 programmes begun on 1 September 1997. CMHA's demonstrated commitment to measuring outcomes and developing better accountability information has made it a leader in the human service NPO sector in BC, and has certainly contributed to the organization's success in receiving accreditation from an international accreditation agency and to successful fund-raising.

## Notes

1   Capital Mental Health Association of Greater Victoria, Annual Report, 1966, p. 1.
2   G. Dinsdale, 'Enhancing performance at Capital Mental Health Association', MPA dissertation completed at the University of Victoria, reproduced in G. Dinsdale, J. Cutt and V. Murray, *Performance and Accountability in Non-Profit Organizations: Theory and Practice*, Victoria Papers in Public Policy, No.4 (Victoria, BC, Centre for Public Sector Studies, 1998).
2   International Association of Psycho-social Rehabilitation Services, *Toolkit for Measuring Psycho-social* Outcomes (Columbia, International Association of Psycho-social Services, 1995).

## Programme Description

Approximately 30 adults are referred each year by Mental Health Centres to this programme. Each has a mental illness and is unlikely at this time to be ready to prepare for competitive employment, but each wants to make a contribution through volunteer effort.

The staff assesses the individuals' abilities and strengths and assists each to choose an area of volunteer involvement. Staff helps each participant to approach the selected agency and offers support to the placement supervisor and the participant, as needed. Job coaching is also made available, and an honorarium is arranged for participants in recognition of the extra costs related to volunteering. If for some reason the placement is terminated, the staff assists the client in securing a new placement.

| Programme Objective | Definitions/Assumptions | Target | Indicator | Evaluation Method |
|---|---|---|---|---|
| Clients maintain or increase their quality and mastery of life. | "Mastery" (as per IAPSRS) indicates the member's belief regarding how much he/she is able to control and influence his/her life.<br><br>"Quality of life" (as per IAPSRS) indicates the members' overall perception of their well-being.<br><br>Assumption: being involved in a volunteer capacity at a nonprofit agency is an indicator of enhanced health, and a process that enhance wellness. | For 30% of clients to increase – and the remaining 70% to maintain – their mastery and quality of life. | Clients' responses to the Members Survey. | Using the Members Survey, baseline survey all continuing clients for mastery.<br><br>All new members will be baseline surveyed at programme entrance.<br><br>The survey will be re-administered at 6 month intervals from each client's respective baseline date. |

*Figure* 8.2 (*a*) (*i*) Therapeutic Volunteer Placement Programme.

| Inputs | Activities | Outputs | Outcomes | | | |
|---|---|---|---|---|---|---|
| | | | Initial | Intermediate | | Long-term |
| • funding: Capital Health Region<br><br>• 100 staff hrs/wk | work with clients to determine assessment, goal setting, and assist them to locate and maintain placement<br><br>provide support to clients at their work site, support their therapeutic plan, and their supervisor<br><br>liaise with case manager, therapist, etc. as needed | • # of clients<br><br>• length of attendance<br><br>• number of potential "employers" contacted<br><br>• number of successful placements | Volunteer (client) locates and maintains placement. | After 6 months, 30% of clients indicate an increased level of mastery, while the remaining clients maintain their present level of mastery.<br><br>Clients experience an increased sense of self identification, and connected affiliation. | After 6 months, 30% of clients indicate an increased quality of life, while the remaining clients maintain their quality of life. | The client is more integrated with the general community.<br><br>Clients' status as contributing members of society is strengthened and societal stigma is reduced. |

*Figure 8.2 (a) (ii)* Logic model.

To promote integration by assisting adults with mental illness to access employment in general community through assessments, resume assistance, job application assistance, etc.

| Programme Objective | Strategy/Assumptions | Target | Indicator | Evaluation Method |
|---|---|---|---|---|
| To assist job-ready clients with serious mental illnesses to gain employment. | It is assumed that clients entering the programme are already job-ready – e.g. they possess the required skills, capacity and confidence to gain employment.<br><br>This programme only applies to obtaining employment (job search, resume, interviewing, etc.); any additional support required to ensure continued employment will be provided by the "Job Coach" programme.<br><br>It is also important to recognize that in the general population unemployment rates are between 9% & 11&%, and, as a result, a 100% success rate would be an unrealistic goal. | 75% of clients achieve employment within 6 months of entering the programme. | Number and percentage of clients who indicate an improvement in employment status, as provided by IAPSRS employment domain. | Track clients using the IAPSRS continuum.<br><br>Improvements in employment status are expected within 6 months. |

*Figure 8.2 (b) (i)* Job Search Consultant Programme.

| Inputs | Activities | Outputs | Outcomes | | |
|---|---|---|---|---|---|
| | | | Initial | Intermediate | Long-term |
| • funding: Human Resources Canada Centre<br>• 35 staff hrs/wk<br>• computer & internet | • assess needs, aptitudes, skills and interests<br>• assess barriers to employment<br>• provide information on the labour and volunteer market<br>• advocate for the clients and liaise with other agencies<br>• teach job search techniques and assist in the preparation of resumes<br>• supporting individuals and making calls<br>• arranging volunteer work experiences<br>• transportation assistance | • # of clients served<br>• length of service provision<br>• interview practices<br>• prospective employers contacted<br>• volunteer work experiences developed<br>• referrals to other programmes | Clients gain job search knowledge, and get interview(s) | 75% of clients gain employment | The clients are more integrated with the general community.<br><br>Clients' status as contributing members of society is strengthened and societal stigma is reduced. |

*Figure 8.2 (b) (ii)* Logic model.

Programme Description

Laurel House provides social, recreational, and pre-vocational activities and skills development for over 200 adults with serious mental illness. Some individuals have attended for years, and for them Laurel House is their main support in continuing community living; others may attend for a much shorter period, as needed, before moving on to more mainstream "activities". About 60 people attend each day, many of whom attend 2-3 times a week and some every day. Laurel House iteself is a grand old building ideally located one mile from downtown and one mile from the hospital, with five bus routes less than a block away. The House activities are also carried out in the ground floor of an office building next door, which shares with the House a quiet shady garden. Some activities take place in the general community with Laurel House staff and members participating together.

| Programme Objective | Definition/Assumptions | Target | Indicator | Evaluation Method |
|---|---|---|---|---|
| To increase members' quality and mastery of life. | "Mastery" (as per IAPSRS) indicates the member's belief regarding how much he/she is able to control and influence his/her life.<br><br>"Quality of life" (as per IAPSRS) indicates the members' overall perception of their well being. | For 90% of sample of existing members and all new members to indicate a higher quality and mastery of life after attending the programme for 6 months. | Clients' answers to questions provided in the IAPSRS Members Survey under mastery and quality of life. | Using the Members Survey, baseline survey all continuing members (or as many as possible) for mastery and quality of life.<br><br>All new members will be baseline surveyed when they enter the programme.<br><br>Six months later, take a manageable random sample from members who have attended the programme an average of at least 5 times per month and resurvey them.<br><br>Conduct a comprehensive baseline survey annually. |

Figure 8.2 (c) (i) Laurel House Programme.

| Inputs | Activities | Outputs | Outcomes | | |
|---|---|---|---|---|---|
| | | | Initial | Intermediate | Long-term |
| • funding: $10 lunch charge, Capital Health Region, and United Way funding.<br>• 179 staff hrs/wk<br>• 25 volunteer hrs/wk | • various self or group determined activities (in and out of house)<br>• illness awareness<br>• life and coping skills.<br>• links to needed services and supports<br>• goal setting<br>• activities to enhance per support networks<br>• prevocational skills | • # of clients served<br>• # of life skill (e.g. cooking and medicine) related sessions<br>• # of referrals to supports<br>• duration and frequency of attendance<br>• # of meals | **Members indicate an increased mastery of life.**<br><br>They gain a greater understanding and awareness of their illness and how to cope with it. For example:<br><br>• life skills (cooking and hygiene)<br><br>• are more aware of available services and supports<br><br>Members gain a greater appreciation for the importance of developing a wider social network. | **Members develop stronger social networks and friendships, and employ coping and life skills.** | **Members indicate an increased quality of life.** |

*Figure 8.2 (c) (ii)* Logic model.

Programme Description

The Alzheimer's Support Centre provides a day programme for older persons with mild and moderate dementia, who live at home. Programme activities are designed for monitoring and stabilization of the elderly who are experiencing mild or moderate dementia, Alzheimer's disease, or other cognitive impairment. The programme hours are Monday through Thursday from 9:30 to 2:30 pm. Participants generally attend twice a week. Supplies and a hot lunch are provided at a nominal cost. Transportation can be arranged, if necessary. Programme activities include: leisure (e.g. music and story telling), recreation (e.g. games and various events), art and crafts, reminiscence and family support, and reality orientations. The programme also offers daily assessment of health and functioning levels, intervention strategies for problems, activities designed specifically for each person, continence training/behaviour management; respite, education and support for caregivers; and advocacy and liaison with other professionals.

| Programme Objectives | Definitions/ Assumptions | Target | Indicator | Evaluation Method |
|---|---|---|---|---|
| To delay admission to 24 hour care. | Clients without considerable support (beyond informal caregiving) will require admission to a care facility despite the wishes of the client and his caregiver.<br><br>It is assumed that clients will remain in the programme until it no longer meets their needs.<br><br>The intensive daycare allows clients to remain at home longer.<br><br>Improved functioning includes, for example, the ability to sleep through the night, thus reducing the load on caregivers. | That 100% of clients already assessed at Intermediate Care Level II and III attend the program for a period 25% longer than Alzheimer's patients referred to but not attending the programme (statistic provided by Continuing Care) | The time clients remain out of intensive 24 hour care. | Track clients on a continuous basis. |

*Figure 8.2 (d) (i)* Alzheimer's Support Centre Programme.

| Inputs | Activities | Outputs | Outcomes | | | |
| --- | --- | --- | --- | --- | --- | --- |
| | | | Initial | Intermediate | Long-term | |
| • funding: Capital Health Region, United Way, Municipality of Saanich, and a small family fee | • assessment of client functioning | • # of clients in programme | Caregivers become more aware and knowledgeable of alternative techniques. | Caregivers employ alternative techniques | Clients' admission to 24 hour care is delayed. |
| • 109 staff hrs/wk | • discussion of particular interventions and approaches with caregivers. | • # of communications with caregivers regarding effective interventions | Caregivers are provided breaks, and provide improved care to clients. | Measurable improvement in client functioning. | |
| • 9 volunteer hrs/wk | • highly structured interventions | • length of attendance and thus respite for caregivers | Clients develop a sense of comfort in Centre's environment. | | |
| | • various activities (e.g. discussions, games, handicrafts, outdoor events) | | | | |
| | • intensive day care | | | | |

*Figure 8.2 (d) (ii)* Logic model.

## Programme Description

This programme provides a team of life skills workers and nurse co-ordinator for a group of 30 seriously ill clients. The client group is referred by Mental Health Services and highest priority is given to people who are at high risk of hospitalization unless considerable support is available. Services are practical and offered after intensive assessment and goal setting with the client as well as consultation with the case manager and others. A plan of care is developed and implemented with ongoing feedback and responsive modification. Service is offered 365 days of the year. Monday to Friday the programme operates with 2 overlapping shifts of workers; on the weekends there are two staff members available. The purpose of the programme is to enable the clients to live as independently as possible in the most normal and least restrictive environment compatible with the illness each experiences.

| Programme Objective | Definitions/Assumptions | Target | Indicator | Evaluation Method |
|---|---|---|---|---|
| To reduce hospitalization due to acute psychiatric illness. | The programme involves stabilizing clients at high risk. It is assumed that given appropriate support by the programme team, each client's need for hospitalization will by reduced.<br><br>For clients who have already been in the programme for a length of time, the programme's effect is assumed to be cumulative – each year hospitalization rates should decrease. | An average of 50% reduction in each client's psychiatric bed days when compared to the previous 2 years. | Clients' rate of hospitalization. | Compare hospitalization days for the previous 2 years to the present year.<br><br>Baseline survey present clients and all new clients at programme entry.<br><br>Statistics will be collected on a monthly basis. |

*Figure 8.2 (e) (i)* Supported Independent Living Programme.

| Inputs | Activities | Outputs | Outcomes | | |
| --- | --- | --- | --- | --- | --- |
| | | | Initial | Intermediate | Long-term |
| • funding: Capital Health Region, United Way<br><br>• 199 staff hrs/wk<br><br>• 4 volunteer hrs/wk | • assessment of functioning<br><br>• provide support<br><br>• restore, maintain and enhance skills (e.g. life and coping skills) that enable clients to participate in community living<br><br>• limited social recreation opportunities | • amount of one-to-one support provided<br><br>• time spent with clients to develop stress coping techniques. | Clients receive support and their knowledge of life skills and coping techniques increases. | Clients employ life and stabilizing skills | Clients' use of hospitalization is reduced. |

*Figure 8.2 (e) (ii)* Logic model.

# 9 Case studies in performance measurement

## 2 The Art Gallery of Greater Victoria

Chapter 4 described an effort to engage in action research involving evaluation systems in a non-profit art gallery. The initial research attempted to discover existing organization-wide processes for assessing how well the gallery was faring in achieving its mission of 'enlivening and enriching the human spirit through the visual arts'. As revealed in the earlier chapters, this first attempt at action research did not succeed. However, subsequent discussions with the gallery's Director revealed that she had several concerns that could be tied to the researcher's interests in evaluation. These concerns had to do with how she 'told the art gallery story' to funders and the public. Believing that the organization was well run and effective, she also believed that it could do a better job of showing this to critical external stakeholders. In particular, she wanted to tell the story about specific *programmes* within the gallery rather than attempting to make generalizations about the gallery as a whole. This chapter is an abridged version of a study of the gallery's programmes which, as part of the research project, was completed as a graduate dissertation in 1999 at the University of Victoria.[1]

## Background

The Art Gallery of Greater Victoria (AGGV or the Gallery) is one of Canada's finest mid-sized art museums and the only not-for-profit public collecting art museum in its geographic area. It comprises a permanent collection of 15,000 objets d'art. The collection features art from Asia, Europe, and North America with primary emphasis placed on Canada and Japan. The Gallery commits to about thirty exhibitions per year, covering historical, Asian, and contemporary curatorial themes in approximately equal proportions. AGGV public programmes are designed to provide individual contemplative viewing of art, information about the art and artists, and interactive and hands-on participation. Programmes delivery occurs in the Gallery itself, in the community of Victoria, throughout the province, and on the Internet. The Gallery also runs a gift shop and an art rental and sales service with works by local contemporary artists. Funding comes from the municipal, provincial, and federal levels of government, school boards, charitable foundations, corporate sponsorships, fund-raising campaigns, and members. Recognizing that almost 67 per cent of revenues now come from the private sector, the Gallery has recently reaffirmed its commitment to seek new and growing audiences.

The Gallery's mission, adopted in 1995, is enlivening and enriching the human spirit through the visual arts. 'This mission is achieved through collecting, caring for, and presenting visual art and by facilitating the interaction of artists and their works with the public' (AGGV *Five-Year Plan*, 1996).

The AGGV is mandated, through its constitution, to do the following:

- establish and preserve collections of the arts and crafts which are to be held in trust for the benefit of current and future generations;
- display those collections;
- create a receptive field for the artist and his/her work;
- provide, in addition to the primary emphasis on the collection and presentation of the visual arts, public programmes such as lectures, recitals of artistic, musical and other works of cultural merit;
- provide and manage facilities for the appreciation and study of the fine arts; and
- operate such artistic and other sales outlets as are deemed advisable from time to time.[2]

## The AGGV organizational structure

The AGGV has a Board of Trustees which consists of a chair, an executive, and a number of working committees, such as Finance and Administration, Works of Art, and Volunteer. The Board works with the Gallery staff primarily through the director, whose duties include ensuring that information flows between the staff and the Board. In the 1997/8 year, there were 17 full-time staff and 14 part-time. Also that year, the Gallery had a list of some 375 volunteers and approximately 5,400 members.[3]

The Gallery's programmes structure has been defined in different ways; for example, what is called Public Programmes in a submission to funders may not include the same functions as the area named Public Programmes in the *Five-Year Plan*.[4] For the purposes of this study, the *Five-Year Plan* programmes definitions were adopted. Figure 9.1 illustrates the Programmes structure as it was described in the Plan. It takes the structure further and relates the programmes to the broad strategic areas that show what issues the Gallery must address to achieve its mission. The Gallery's strategy must respond to the questions: what can we do, how will we do it, for whom are we doing it, and what means or resources do we need?

The Gallery programmes do not actually relate to each other in a linear fashion, as the two-dimensional Figure 9.1 would seem to indicate.

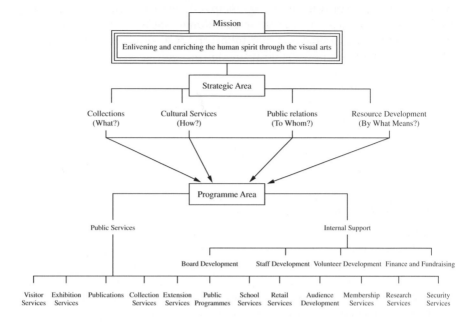

*Figure 9.1* Organizational chart: Art Gallery of Greater Victoria.

Programming at the Gallery is flexible and interdependent; even a three-dimensional chart would have to be very complicated to show how the programmes interact with each other. Programmes are often complementary, with some relating hierarchically while no programmes operate in isolation.

## Research purpose

The Director of the AGGV had made constant efforts over the years to improve accountability information reporting. At the time of the research, this goal had assumed even greater importance. The Gallery had a deficit as a result of major and unexpected federal government funding cuts a few years ago. Staff were working heroically to reduce it and at that time were doing better than budgeted, but more funding cuts were expected.

The Director believed funders were looking for evidence of value that goes beyond numbers and dollars – the enriching of the human spirit. She asked, 'How do I show that? How can the qualitative experience be measured and shown in a meaningful way for funders?'

There was a level of Programmes information – between the overview perspective that exists at the director's level and the day-to-day detailed information that is collected for each part of each programme – that would help the Gallery tell its story in a useful way. With very little additional information collection, the Gallery could create logic models of its programmes.

This method of reporting on programmes shows not only what planning and resources have gone into the programmes but also what benefits are accruing to participants. The information could be presented in a way that allows the reader to make the connections between programme inputs and programme results.

The major funders – federal, provincial, and municipal governments – all required that the Gallery collects and presents accountability information in submissions for funding. While there were differences in the way they wanted information presented, their Programmes reporting needs could be met by using some or all of the material collected and shown in the logic models.

## Research goal and objectives

The goal of second phase of the research project, undertaken in 1998–9, *was to help the Gallery tell it's story*. That is, to help the AGGV show funders and others that the Gallery is well-managed by: illustrating the benefits of AGGV programming, relating programme activities to budgets and resources, and showing how programme results contribute to the mission.

More specifically the project objectives were:

- to examine current AGGV information systems and accountability reporting mechanisms.
- to develop an accountability information framework for AGGV programmes reporting;
- to illustrate the framework by presenting logic models of selected programmes;
- to demonstrate an improved method of programme reporting using information already collected;
- to suggest specific changes the Gallery could make to improve programme planning, information collecting, and reporting;
- to provide guidelines for the development of programme logic models; and
- to make recommendations regarding AGGV systems and procedures for collecting and presenting accountability information.

## Research approach

A qualitative, iterative approach was used to develop and illustrate techniques that would help the Art Gallery of Greater Victoria tell its story. The focus was on finding a method that would show outcomes at a programmes level; a method that could relate programme results to the mission, budget, and the strategic plan of the Gallery. An outcome reporting structure was adopted then developed into an Accountability

Information Framework that could be used for all AGGV programmes. The framework was illustrated by constructing logic models of selected Gallery programmes.

It was important that the Accountability Information Framework be easy to use yet comprehensive and that the process of translating programme information into logic models be readily understood. Completed models should be transparent: anyone should be able to follow the logic of a programme model to see how the goals relate to the Gallery's mission and to trace the programme from its inputs through activities to outputs and beyond. To show that this was feasible with Gallery programmes, actual AGGV information was used to construct the illustrative logic models.

Data on programmes were gathered from both the formal and informal AGGV information systems. An extensive review of Gallery documents was conducted including: Policy and Procedures Manual, financial statements, funding submissions (Canada Council, Museum Assistance Programme, Cultural Services Branch, Inter-Municipal Committee), Gallery Facility Programmes, exhibition schedules, annual reports to the Board, the Five-Year Strategic Plan, programmes budgets, newsletters, and brochures.

The data collected, reviewed, and analysed from internal sources included monthly and yearly programmes reports, the General Ledger, PR clippings, attendance records, membership and donation records, participant evaluations, and visitors' books. Ordinarily, programmes would be reported on an annual basis, but to broaden the perspective of this review, two years of documents and data were reviewed. Some data from external sources were reviewed for comparative information on art museums in Canada.

The AGGV informal information system was explored through a series of interviews with Gallery staff, volunteers and exhibiting artists. In deference to the scope of the project and to the time constraints on Gallery staff, only those people directly involved with the selected programmes were interviewed. Material from these interviews was indispensable for the construction of the logic models.

In this chapter only one of the programmes will be presented as an illustration of the process and its results.

## Accountability Information Framework

The graphic representation of the Accountability Information Framework in Figure 9.2 shows the two sides of the programmes reporting process: describing what was planned and what actually occurred. In the real world, these sections overlap considerably. Ideally, everything about a programme should be planned in advance, including inputs, activities, and even outputs; however, once the programme is underway, activities may not go as

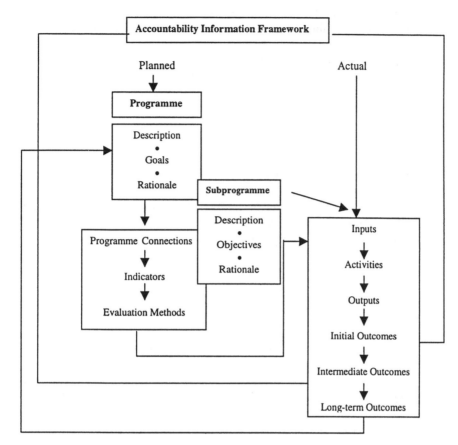

*Figure 9.2* AGGV Accountability Information Framework: Art Gallery of
Greater Victoria.

planned, objectives may have to change, and then the indicators and evaluation methods will change, and so on. Whether the programme occurs
exactly as planned or not, the measuring and reporting of outcomes should
be used to inform planning.

## Definitions

For the purpose of applying the Accountability Information Framework
to the AGGV programmes, the elements of the Framework are defined
in the following ways:

- *Programme description*: a brief description of what the Programme is
  or what it does and a list of the elements or sub-programmes
  included.

- *Programme goals*: statements that describe the intent of the programme. When looking at the programme as a whole, it is appropriate to talk about 'goals' rather than using the term 'objectives'. Goals are broad and over-arching, while objectives should be specific and tied to a period of time.

- *Rationale*: this answers the question, Why do this programme? Here is where the connection to the mission of the Gallery is made; that is, the rationale describes how this programme helps the Gallery to achieve its mission.

- *Programme connections*: this category was added to show how interconnected Gallery programmes are – it is difficult to talk about one programme without involving another.

- *Indicators*: brief descriptions of what will be measured to 'indicate' success or failure (that is, the achievement of objectives). Traditionally, indicators have been expressed quantitatively, with comparative numbers, rates, and so on.

- *Evaluation methods*: within the context of this framework, evaluation methods refers to all of the ways the Gallery can collect information on its programmes: tracking and monitoring, recording feedback, surveying users, soliciting assessments, etc.

- *Sub-programmes*: or programme elements, share the overall programme goals, but have their own objectives. The accountability information that follows the sub-programmes in the logic models (Inputs, Activities, Outputs, and Outcomes) refers to that specific programme element.

- *Objectives*: should be specific, measurable, and related to a time-period, usually the reporting period. In the logic models, they are used for the sub-programmes only.

- *Rationale*: relates the sub-programmes to the programme goals and, ultimately, to the mission. For Exhibitions, this is usually the curatorial thesis.

- *Inputs*: the financial and human resources used for the sub-programmes (or programmes if this is used in an aggregated report). This includes the staff needed and their hours, the volunteers and the number of hours, facilities, equipment, supplies, and money. In the end, all of the inputs can be expressed in dollars. For the Gallery's logic models, the money that is given by a funder or sponsor for a specific exhibition or programme is considered an input to that programme.

- *Activities*: the steps taken to present the programmes or sub-programmes to the public. The Activities show how the outputs are related to the inputs and what was done with the inputs to carry out the goals of the programmes. A detailed activity list can be a useful planning tool.

- *Outputs*: the direct quantitative results of programme activities; they usually include measures like the number of classes held, the number of presentations made, and so on. Outputs should also include attendance or numbers served, particularly if the Gallery exercises some control over that number. For example, the Gallery has control over the number of students who see Gallery through the Schools programme because it decides the number of presentations that will be made (although that number is usually limited by the availability of volunteers).

- *Outcomes*: the benefits accruing to visitors and participants as a consequence of interacting with an AGGV programme; a result not under the Gallery's direct control. The term outcome is used when referring to actual information; for planning purposes, an intended outcome is an objective.
- *Initial outcomes*: the immediate benefits or results of a programme. If only one reporting period's worth of data is available, the assumption must be made that the outcomes noted are initial ones.
- *Intermediate outcomes*: the changes in behaviour exhibited by visitors and participants as a result of accrued benefits; these outcomes are only visible and measurable over time.
- *Long-term outcomes*: the results of a programme over long periods of time, as demonstrated by a wider audience or the impacts on society.

## Logic model and discussion

What follows is one illustration of the Accountability Information Framework. A logic model is developed for the Exhibitions programme. The discussion that follows offers explanations of certain choices made for the logic models and suggestions on how the Gallery data collection and reporting could move closer to the ideal. The comments refer to specific sections in the logic model – the same labels are used to make reference back to the original easier.

### Programme description

The Art Gallery of Greater Victoria realizes its mission to enliven and enrich the human spirit through the visual arts in its presentation of an active exhibition programme which highlights the Gallery's collection and the work of contemporary artists, primarily those of this region. Some 30 exhibitions are presented during a programme year, in three curatorial contexts: Historical, Asian, and Contemporary.[5]

### Programme goals

For Historical exhibitions:

- to use the permanent collection, as much as possible, in thoughtful, focused presentations;

- to provide a balance of presentations that will include those of broad public interest and those of greater interest to scholars, collectors, and other special interest groups;
- to increase the public's knowledge of the unique richness that is found in the permanent collection.

For Asian exhibitions:

- to promote learning and understanding of other cultures;
- to demonstrate the similarities and differences in the cultures of the East and West;
- Where possible, to show the fruitful exchange of artistic ideas and techniques that flowed between East and West;
- To document the history of art of the Asian world, both past and present.

For Contemporary exhibitions:

- to develop an expanded network within the contemporary visual arts community of British Columbia, and beyond, through thoughtful curatorial proposals that develop on a continuing basis;
- to address such areas as post-colonial identity, physical/spiritual health, environmental and formalist concerns and other issues as they arise;
- to contextualize contemporary art through a balance of exhibitions comprising significant current art, modern art exhibitions drawn from the AGGV collection, and an annual presentation of accessible popular art.[6]

### Rationale

- The Gallery's mission is achieved through collecting, caring for, and presenting visual art, and by facilitating the interaction of artists and their work with the public. The Exhibitions Programme is a fundamental activity that generates continuing vitality for the Gallery and its ability to maintain the public's interest and support.
- The Historical exhibitions serve as a mirror of human thought, experimentation, and emotion through the centuries. Using the permanent collection to illustrate these enduring truths about the human condition is part of an ongoing effort to foster a sense of community ownership of the Gallery and its collections.
- The Asian exhibitions endeavour to attract the attention and imagination of viewers, especially young visitors and visitors from the growing Asian community. Again, the AGGV collections are used, as well as special private and other public collections.
- The Contemporary exhibitions serve to stimulate, enrich, enliven, inform, and entertain the visiting public.

## Programme connections

- Public Programmes follow the exhibitions, i.e. the exhibitions and their curatorial theses inform programming. The programmes are designed to enhance the exhibition experience.
- School Services are, in a sense, part of public programming and usually follow the exhibitions as well.
- Under Audience Development, the Gallery's web site is being used for virtual exhibitions. This area handles advertising and PR, which are both essential components of an exhibition.

## Indicators

- number of people viewing the exhibition and increases over time;
- admissions revenue and increases over time;
- number of members and increases over time;
- number of Asian visitors and increases over time;
- public response to selections from the collection (survey);
- number and type of unsolicited public comments;
- contacts with the BC arts community and increases over time;
- number of regional artists involved and dollars paid to artists;
- number of scholars and special interest groups accessing collection and increases over time;
- number and content of unsolicited media reports and articles;
- number of web site hits;
- number of donations of articles resulting from an exhibit;
- decision by a corporate or other sponsor to fund another exhibit;

## Evaluation methods

- regular tracking of admissions (see Discussion);
- regular analysis of the visitors' books;
- recording of unsolicited feedback (at the visitors' desk, by phone, correspondence);
- tracking unsolicited media reports (to gauge public reaction and as a proxy for peer review);
- tracking donations of articles related to an exhibit;
- tracking membership growth and renewals (especially if a membership campaign is related to a specific exhibition)/comparison with other campaigns;
- tracking fund-raising returns (if a fund-raising campaign was conducted in conjunction with a specific exhibit)/comparison with other campaigns;
- exit surveys;
- membership surveys.

# Discussion of model

## *Programme goals*

The Exhibition Programme's goals, which were quoted from an application for municipal funding, appear in all funding submissions, usually under the three categories Historical, Asian, and Contemporary. However, goals are presented differently in different submissions. For example, while the municipal and provincial submissions generally use formatting and goal statements similar to those quoted in the model, the February 1997 Museums Assistance Programme application has nine fairly specific goals or objectives listed under the Asian category alone. The *Policy and Procedures* manual uses a very different approach for describing exhibition goals and the *Five-Year Plan* is different again, listing a few broader goals for exhibitions. While recognizing that different submissions and reports require different perspectives, I believe that the collection of accountability information would be easier if goals and objectives were rationalized, and all staff were working with the same set.

The Exhibition Programme's goals do not address the desired impact on the audience, except vaguely or by implication. As they are currently stated, it appears that it would be possible for the Gallery to meet most of the Historical, Asian, and Contemporary goals without any visitors.

## *Objectives*

> There are no stated Programme objectives. When I say that, what I mean is that at no point do I sit down with some committee or get input from other professional staff at the Gallery and establish programme objectives. That doesn't happen. I understand that that would be a very good thing to do, but I recognize too, that in the pragmatic day-to-day operation, there is no time to do that.[7]

Objectives are needed – this is the missing link between the goals of the programme and the activities. It is important to spell out – in specific, concrete terms – how the activities of the programme relate to the goals and, through them, to the mission of the Gallery. Objectives can be linked to a period of time, usually, although not necessarily, to the reporting period. Without objectives it is difficult to know what to measure, to determine if the Gallery is actually meeting its goals.

The objectives listed in the model for each exhibition, or sub-programme, were all from informal information sources (staff interviews). They should be formalized: developed and written down in the planning stages of each project. Everyone involved in the programme should be familiar with the current objectives and all programme reporting should address them.

Objectives should be developed for each programme as well as for the sub-programmes.

Targets (defined as very specific objectives, which are intended to follow the development of objectives) are not used by the Gallery; therefore this category has not been included in the Accountability Information Framework. The Gallery needs to work first on its development of objectives. Once the practice of setting and measuring objectives has been established and data have been gathered for several years, there will be a realistic basis for setting targets. Expecting staff to use targets effectively in the near future is not realistic.

### Rationale

For the exhibition programme as a whole, this is where the connection to the Gallery's mission is spelled out. For each exhibition, the Rationale becomes the curatorial thesis, which is important to inform not only the specific exhibition but also all of the programming that is connected to it.

### Programme connections

This section in the Framework was added to illustrate the interconnectedness of Gallery programmes. Exhibitions, particularly, interacts with many other programmes and understanding this is the key to understanding the logic of the programme. In practice, a model of one programme should include all the possible connections to other programmes, not just the ones illustrated here, which refer only to the four programmes examined in this study.

### Indicators

This is an area that needs to be developed. The selection of indicators should follow the generation and acceptance of objectives for each programme or programme element. The indicators listed in the model correspond to many of the goals described by the Gallery under Historical, Asian, and Contemporary; however, the information to measure all of those indicators systematically over time is not being collected.

In addition to those listed in the model, there could be a set of indicators that respond to objectives derived from the goals concerned with documenting history, addressing specific issues, contextualizing contemporary art, etc. Measuring these goals would probably require the judgements of qualified artists, art historians, and other scholars.

### Evaluation methods

Admissions are recorded daily and in several categories; however, the categories recorded do not correspond to the goals of this programme. It may be virtually impossible to track attendance accurately at a particular exhibition, nevertheless, to assess the relative popularity of exhibitions, some count should be made. Unfortunately, this activity may be unrealizable in the current Gallery venue. Likewise, it may be too difficult to record audience characteristics, such as ethnic background, to assess the growth in Asian audiences, for example.

Since the visitors' book is currently the only source of visitor feedback that is collected on an ongoing and regular basis, it should be improved and maintained.

Regular recording of unsolicited feedback is not done, although some records are kept. Tracked over time, this record could be a useful measure.

The Gallery should plan to do the following occasionally (and systematically) as funding permits:

- Exit surveys – Ask about specific exhibitions, as well as general impressions.
- Membership surveys – Administer a similar survey each year, so comparisons can be made over time – to reduce the work involved, the survey could be done with a sample of 100, or even fewer, members.
- Longitudinal studies – To gather data to measure longer-term outcomes, the Gallery could, for example, follow a visitor or family from initial contact into the future by interviewing them at regular intervals, years apart, or survey similar groups of visitors, years apart. An easier way to start looking at long-term effects of gallery going would be to ask current visitors about their attendance as children and their participation through the intervening years.

To assess the merit of exhibitions, the Gallery might consider soliciting peer assessments (other than those conducted by funding agencies when reviewing submissions). Perhaps a reciprocal arrangement could be made with other galleries. In addition, the Gallery's curators could do regular assessments of each exhibition. It could be brief, but as long as it is done regularly and systematically – using a consistent format – a useful record can be built up that will allow some tracking of improvement and trends.

### Inputs

The Gallery should have cost allocations for each exhibit that include all the direct and indirect costs. At this point, some direct costs and revenues are available in the General Ledger, but these records are new and not yet consistent among exhibitions.

The staff time involved in preparing exhibitions was considerable, although not tracked for every member of the staff involved. Volunteer time is recorded in the Education Department but not allocated to specific exhibitions.

The allocation of staff hours to programmes and programme elements could offer valuable information for planning and reporting, however, the collection of these data might prove very difficult. The Gallery will have to decide if this information is worth the effort it takes to collect it.

### Activities

This section could be used as planning guide for future exhibitions, particularly if it were done in more detail. Listing everything that needs to occur to get an exhibition in place will help with estimating the resources and time needed, as well as being a useful checklist. If each step was recorded with an estimate of the resources required and the direct results expected any deficiencies in inputs or unrealistic expectations would become evident, that is, 'activities' provides the logical connection between the inputs and the outputs in the model.

### Outputs

This section lists what the Gallery produced, based on what was intended (objectives), what resources were used (inputs), and what was done (activities). Here is where the reader can start examining the logic of the programme by asking the questions: Given the objectives, inputs, and activities, do these outputs make sense? Does one thing follow logically from another?

Again, because of the interconnectedness of Gallery programming, the outputs are shown with the outputs in other programme areas that are directly related.

### Initial outcomes

This model includes initial outcomes only, since it was not possible to compare Gallery performance over time. For the purposes of the logic model, the two-year period examined was treated as one period. Information must be gathered and reported systematically over time to begin to build a case for the achievement of longer-term goals.

By definition, an outcome refers to the benefits that accrue to a visitor as a result of viewing and interacting with an exhibition. Although attendance figures cannot show what benefit accrues, the Gallery does not have direct control over numbers of visitors, and for Exhibitions at least, attendance should probably be considered an outcome. The assumption can be made that since most attendees are not first-time or one-time visitors their presence is evidence that they believe they are benefiting from the experience.

The number of admissions is one measure of public reaction that can be illustrated graphically. Although attendance at individual exhibitions is not measured, aggregate attendance can be graphed then compared with the exhibition schedule, using the dates of a particular exhibition as a guide. Of course, conclusions cannot be drawn about attendance at a particular exhibition unless it is possible to discount the effects of other exhibitions or programmes on attendance. Mapping attendance data over time, with the periods of various exhibits indicated, would help clarify the probable impact of any given exhibition.

While the Gallery recognizes the importance of recording these numbers, its need to look beyond numbers to measure the qualitative experience of interacting with art means that both quantitative and qualitative data are included in Outcomes. In some cases, most of the outcomes measured were qualitative. For example, in the case of an exhibition of art produced by inmates of a nearby jail, the staff reported that the numbers of people who viewed this exhibition were limited. However, for those who did take the trouble to get involved with the photos or the carving, the impact was profound. Anecdotes were used as outcome measures in the model to attempt to convey some idea of the impact of this exhibition.

### Intermediate outcomes

Intermediate outcomes are not available from the two-year period of data studied; however, over a longer term, comparisons could be made of data collected systematically at the Gallery. Some additional efforts could be made to find funding for longitudinal studies. Also, AGGV could be compared with other galleries, using information from the National Association of Art Galleries, for example.

When information can be compared year-to-year, over time a picture will gradually emerge, showing how the Gallery is actually doing and whether it is meeting its longer-term goals or not.

### Long-term outcomes

It is not likely that long-term outcomes or impacts will be measured. It is not feasible for the Gallery to try to measure the societal impacts of its existence over the long-term. However, some inferences can be made, based on systematic, continual, and long-term collection of data.

## Logic models in context

One of the results of using an accountability information framework is more consistent and thorough reporting. The programme logic model provides information at levels that fall between the high-level Gallery over-sight and the detailed information that is collected day-to-day. It is this sometimes neglected level that is essential for programme decisions.

There is an advantage to using the same accountability information framework for each programme (or sub-programme) at the Gallery. Each staff person asks essentially the same questions to guide information collection, as the model is constructed:

- What is the programme? Give a succinct description.
- What are the goals? Keep in mind the benefit to the visitor or participant. Also ask: What are the objectives? They should be SMART: specific, measurable, achievable, relevant, and time-bound.
- What is the rationale for the programme? Show how it relates to the mission.
  Also ask: How does this sub-programme relate to the programme goals? If an exhibition: What is the curatorial thesis?
- How does it connect to other Gallery programmes?
- What needs to be measured to show if the goals are being met?
- What evaluation methods are needed or used?
- What human and financial resources are needed or used?
- What are the activities of the programme? List the steps taken from inception to completion of the programme.
- What are the products of the programme activities? List exhibitions presented, or classes held, or events arranged, and so on. Include visitor numbers when they are numbers controlled by the Gallery. Also, show the outputs that involve connections with other programme areas.
- What are the results? Report the indicator measurements; that is, the results of the monitoring and evaluation procedures. Include longer-term outcomes, if available.

Note that answering questions for a programme area will involve people from different functional areas: finances, PR, programming, and exhibition are all intertwined. For example, a curator could not prepare an exhibition logic model in isolation; information from many different areas is required: public programming, finance and fund-raising, public relations, and so on.

When a logic model is constructed using both sides of the Accountability Information Framework, it becomes a planning as well as a reporting tool. The first section of the resulting model, from Programmes Description to Evaluation Methods, should represent what was planned, while the Inputs to Outputs side is actual information, gathered and reported after the fact. The reported information feeds into the planning side for decision-making. Accurate and consistent information on outcomes means better planning, which leads to better programmes.

## Relating models to reporting requirements

The AGGV is accountable to its members and donors, its sponsors, and the three levels of government that provide funding. Each stakeholder has different reporting requirements. At the top of the list is the Gallery's membership – reporting is done primarily at the Annual General Meeting, where both the president and the director make their annual reports. Reporting to corporate sponsors is done as required, usually after the event (exhibition, programme, or other) has ended. Most onerous are the requirements of the submissions that are made to funders: the Gallery is required not only to report on completed events but also to project its plans for exhibitions, public programmes, and so on, for the approaching funding year.

While each report or submission requires different levels and types of information, Gallery staff would benefit from having a single framework to guide data collection. Once the material is gathered and the logic models of the programmes are created some or all of the information can be used as needed: for submissions to funders, for annual reports, etc. For example, when both 'planned' and 'actual' information are consistently and concisely recorded in a logic model, the results can be used to improve the submissions for funding: projections will be more accurate and it will be easier to 'tell the story'. Further, having a model with all of the information recorded under standard headings makes it easier to summarize a programme. For example, here is the programme (description), this is why we did it (rationale), what we intended (objectives), what we did (inputs, activities, outputs), and here are the results (outcomes).

Information from the models could also be used to help prepare activity reports for the newsletters – perhaps drawing from description, activities, outputs, and outcomes – or to write brochures for new programmes – using description, rationale, and objectives from the 'planned' side of the model. While aggregated data for a whole programme area are probably the most useful in a funding submission, the full details of sub-programmes can aid internal decision-making, especially when it comes to deciding which programmes to continue and which to cut.

## Notes

1   Marti Lea Thib, 'Accountability Information At The Art Gallery of Greater Victoria', MPA dissertation completed at the University of Victoria, BC, April 1999.
2   Material on mission and mandate quoted from the AGGV *Policy and Procedures* manual.
3   These figures are from the September 1998 submission to the Greater Victoria Intermunicipal Committee.
4   The Plan's full title is, *To the New Millennium: The Art Gallery of Greater Victoria Five-Year Plan: 1996–2001.*
5   Source: Submission to Municipality 1997.
6   Source: Submission to Municipality 1997.
7   From staff interviews.

# 10 Making sense of multiple measures of performance

## An assessment of the CCAF/FCVI approach to annual performance reporting

## I Introduction

The next stage in the research project responded to concerns expressed in all agencies about how to best present their accountability information externally at the end of the funding year – in the form of an annual report directed within the core model of accountability to their primary constituencies but also designed within the more general model of accountability to reflect the interests of a broader set of constituencies. In essence, agencies wanted to know how best to 'tell their story', recognizing that effective accountability is effective marketing and that they all functioned in a competitive environment for resources, financial and human, and clients. The approach developed by the CCAF/FCVI[1] in Canada had been designed primarily as an annual reporting framework, and agencies had expressed interest in the insights from that framework used in the approach to general standards of accountability information across the cycle discussed in Chapter 5, and in the development of some of the specific components of the framework in dealing with costing and outputs/outcomes. So we undertook to offer a brief history of the approach, to offer a critique of the approach including the development of criteria for its use in annual reporting, and, finally, to make a proposal for using the approach in the light of the critique as a means of preparing annual reports.

## II A framework for assessment of reports based on the 12 attributes

### The origins of the CCAF/FCVI approach

The approach to performance reporting using 12 attributes proposed by the CCAF/FCVI in 1987 represented a creative and quite radical response to general frustration with limited progress in responding to the calls in the 1970s by the Auditor General of Canada for improved public sector accountability. The Auditor General's concerns related primarily to the non-commercial, that is, non-profit part of the public sector (public departments and publicly financed 'arms-length' institutions such as hospitals and universities) and thus apply equally to the private non-profit sector. The Auditor General insisted on a scope of accountability that called for improvements in traditional financial accountability and went further to include both accountability for compliance with authorities of various kinds, and accountability for value for money defined to include economy in the acquisition of resources, efficiency in the use of resources, and effectiveness in the achievement of objectives. The primary actors in determining and reporting on this broader accountability were to be legislative auditors, and the statutory mandates of legislative auditors in the federal and most provincial governments were appropriately broadened in the late 1970s.

Some significant progress had been made by the mid-1980s. Using standards promulgated by the Public Sector Accounting and Auditing Committee (PSAAC) – now the Public Sector Accounting and Auditing Board – of the Canadian Institute of Chartered Accountants (CICA), legislative auditors regularly conducted and reported on audits of compliance with authorities. Progress had also been made – again with PSAAC as the primary agent – on moving toward generally accepted accounting principles for use in financial reporting by governments, and clean audit opinions by legislative auditors had come to require the use of these principles in financial reporting by government managers. But it was also recognized that financial information, even accrual-based financial information, in the public and private non-profit sector where products and services are not sold, provided necessary information on the sources and uses of funds but was silent, by definition, on questions of value for money.

Reports by managers on value for money were limited to occasional annual reports that were generally, at best, anecdotal and unsystematic, and, at worst, little more than a glossy smokescreen. This gap on accountability for value for money had been addressed in three ways, none satisfactory.

First, departments and agencies set up internal evaluation groups of various kinds – reflecting the range of disciplines and techniques that profess evaluation methodology – and used these groups to provide internal diagnostic information on specific value-for-money questions. Quite apart from the absence of consistent methodology, and therefore comparability, this approach did not address external or public accountability and generally was not subject to verification.

Second, federal and provincial central agencies – usually offices of the Comptroller General – began to move with more methodological consistency to internal (management) audit of value-for-money questions, using value-for-money auditing standards promulgated by PSAAC in Canada and the Institute of Internal Auditors (I IA) in the US; but again this information did not address external accountability.

Third, using their broadened statutory mandates, federal and provincial legislative auditors in Canada used the value-for-money auditing standards promulgated by PSAAC to conduct and report publicly on value-for-money audits of non-profit agencies. These audits were conducted in the absence of any management reports or representations on value for money, and thus required the collection and analysis of evidence and the preparation of value-for-money reports by legislative auditors. Auditors were therefore not attesting to representations by management, as they were for financial statements, but were themselves assembling and analysing evidence, and preparing audit reports on value for money; managers were silent and usually reluctant partners. While this third approach to addressing the accountability gap on value for money was by far the most successful, and indeed can be credited with changing the perceptions of non-profit sector managers and the public on value for money, it suffered from several flaws.

The first flaw relates to the mandates of legislative audit offices. Audit mandates varied across Canada, but, with the single exception of Prince Edward Island, precluded direct audits of effectiveness – the achievement of objectives. Auditors were typically limited to investigating and reporting on whether departments and agencies had systems in place for monitoring effectiveness and, if so, whether these systems were working properly. Auditors were therefore obliged to ignore effectiveness or treat it indirectly; and where they did try to venture into the area, they frequently ran into accusations that they were going beyond their mandate and were intruding on the political domain.

The second flaw relates to the skills of legislative auditors. These offices had traditionally been staffed by accountants and financial auditors, and even when they broadened their range of skills – as proposed in the PSAAC standards – to include other disciplines such as engineering and economics, and functional area skills for particular government departments, the traditional accounting and auditing skills drove the value-for-money auditing exercise. Legislative audit offices were therefore limited in their capacity and/or willingness to bring to bear the expertise necessary to investigate and draw conclusions on value for money, and their general response was to play safe by concentrating on management systems in place rather than direct operational information on value for money.

The third flaw builds on the second and relates to the role of auditors in the absence of representations by management. In the development of value-for-money auditing standards by PSAAC, there was considerable and heated debate within the CICA on the appropriateness of using the term 'audit' to describe activities by auditors which did not involve attesting to management representations of some kind. Non-profit sector managers were generally given an opportunity to have their responses to value-for-money audits published with the audit report, but stressed consistently that the expertise to make informed judgements about value for money in non-profit programmes rested with managers themselves. Managers did not, of course, stress that auditors were assuming a 'default' role in the absence of demonstrated general willingness by managers to meet public concerns for accountability by providing valid and reliable reports on value for money.

A fourth flaw relates to methodological consistency. The definitions of economy, efficiency and effectiveness in the PSAAC standards were far too general to constitute useful standards for what sorts of information should be included in a report on value for money, and published audit reports varied widely in form and substance, and therefore in comparability and usefulness.

In sum, the forays of legislative auditors into value-for-money auditing did raise public awareness, and therefore the awareness of politicians, about accountability for value for money. But the achievement was limited for the reasons suggested above. The scope of audits was limited by statutory mandates and by auditor skills, both of which excluded serious consideration of effectiveness, and the comparability and usefulness of audits was limited by the absence of specific standards for what sorts of information should be examined and reported. Politicians in governing parties, supported by academic commentators, railed against perceived intrusion into policy and political prerogative, and managers generally resented and resisted the process on the grounds that auditors lacked the expertise necessary to deal with value for money across the range of non-profit sector activities. Perhaps only opposition politicians and journalists were happy, and the credibility of the improved public accountability brought about by the initiative of legislative audit offices was jeopardized by a focus on the trivial and the negative, and, it must be said, by occasional attempts by the Auditor General of Canada to assume the role of Leader of the Opposition.

## The CCAF/FCVI alternative

The proposal by the CCAF/FCVI in 1987 was designed to overcome the major deficiencies of the previous approaches. There are several key strengths to the proposal.

First, the 12 attributes provide an eclectic, comprehensive definition of the concept of effectiveness, reflecting the perspectives of the varied constituencies of public and private non-profit programmes. In effect, the 12 attributes constitute a proposal for a broad set of standards for what sorts of information should be included in public and private non-profit performance reports. The attributes are not, of course, standards *of* performance, but rather standards *for* reporting performance information.

For any non-profit programme, the 12 attributes in summary include: *Management direction* – the extent to which programmatic objectives are clearly stated and understood; *Relevance* – the extent to which the programme continues to make sense with respect to the problems or conditions to which it was intended to respond; *Appropriateness* – the extent to which the design of the programme and the level of effort are logical in relation to programmatic objectives; *Achievement of Intended Results* – the extent to which the goals and objectives of the programme have been achieved; *Acceptance* –

the extent to which the stakeholders for whom the programme is designed judge it to be satisfactory; *Secondary Impacts* – the extent to which significant consequences, either intended or unintended and either positive or negative, have occurred; *Costs and Productivity* – the relationship between costs, inputs, and outputs; *Responsiveness* – the capacity of the programme organization to adapt to changes in such factors as markets, competition, available funding, and technology; *Financial Results* – accounting for revenues and expenditures, and for assets and liabilities; *Working Environment* – the extent to which the programme organization provides an appropriate work environment for its staff, and staff have the information, capacities, and disposition to serve programme objectives; *Protection of Assets* – the extent to which the various assets entrusted to the programme organization are safeguarded; and *Monitoring and Reporting* – the extent to which key matters pertaining to performance and programme organizational strength are identified, reported, and monitored. The 12 attributes constitute by implication a broad set of standards for what sorts of information should be collected and reported on public sector performance.

The 12 attributes subsume financial accountability (Financial Results and Protection of Assets) and accountability for the efficiency component of value for money (Costs and Productivity and, more broadly, Appropriateness), and broaden the effectiveness component of value for money from its traditional focus on the achievement of objectives (Achievement of Intended Results) to include external perspectives such as customer satisfaction (Acceptance) and external effects (Secondary Impacts), and internal perspectives such as the quality of the workplace (Working Environment). Further, the comprehensive picture not only includes attributes that speak to a strategic perspective (Relevance and Responsiveness), but also captures the span of the cycle of management control from intentions (Management Direction) to results (Achievement of Intended Results) and associated attributes. Finally, the comprehensive picture includes both management systems and practices (such as Monitoring and Reporting) – the traditional implicit focus, by default, of value-for-money auditing, and operating results (such as Costs and Productivity and Achievement of Intended Results).

Second, accountability from managers to senior managers and boards, and, again by implication, through boards to the general public, is served by the preparation by managers of performance representations across the standard set of 12 attributes. Internal and external accountability is therefore served, and managers as acknowledged experts are required to produce representations on their performance in standard form.

Third, verification of the completeness and accuracy of management representations is provided by external auditors who therefore bring their skills to bear most appropriately in their traditional attestor role. Accountability thus requires auditability, and formal audit assurance completes the accountability loop to boards and, with an audit report in the public domain, to the various external constituencies and the general public.

Since its unveiling in 1987, strong interest, and even some excitement and a sense of discovery of a way of cutting the Gordian knot of accountability, have been expressed at annual CCAF/FCVI conferences. The papers and discussions at these conferences have provided evidence of experimentation in a variety of non-profit agencies in Canada and abroad, with particular emphasis on the use of the reporting framework as a tool of management diagnostics. On balance, however, there has been a slower rate of acceptance and utilization than might have been expected, given the potential contributions of the approach outlined above, and the increasing interest in Canada and elsewhere in non-profit accountability frameworks; the set of attributes have certainly not yet reached the stage of being 'generally accepted'.

## The 12 attributes: challenges, and criteria for assessment of management representations

The 12 attributes offer a broad and rich picture of programme performance that is potentially synergistic. The question is whether that potential can be realized from the attributes as they stand, or whether modifications might help to bring the attributes to the point of general acceptance in the public sector. The question is important because of the significant potential contribution, and the risk that, without wider acceptance and practice, the approach could slip into compliance in form rather than substance, and ultimately into misuse and disuse, like so many other approaches to accountability information.

The generic question is whether the attributes as they stand provide sufficient, appropriate evidence – enough evidence of the right kind – for the various constituencies of non-profit programmes. This question can be broken down into a series of parts – first, completeness; second, clarity; third, the nature and perspective of the information presented – including three sub-questions (whether the attributes are descriptive or implicitly theoretical; whether general prioritization among the attributes is useful and appropriate; and whether the attributes should be presented in such a way as to reflect the management cycle); and, fourth, the nature of the evidence, including four sub-questions (measurability; causality; operationality; and objectivity and verifiability). These four areas are dealt with in turn, and, under each head, criteria are suggested for the assessment of management reports based on the 12 attributes. These criteria are then reflected in the model of accountability reporting proposed at the end of the chapter.

### Completeness

Taking as given that none of the attributes of effectiveness is redundant, the first question of any set that purports to be comprehensive is whether it is complete. Does anything have to be added? Any proposals for extension have to be balanced against the need to keep the set manageable, but there are several possible areas for development. Five illustrations are offered. The most obvious is the omission of the compliance component of accountability. Accountability for compliance with authorities of various kinds is one of the three components included in the scope of comprehensive auditing, and a representation on compliance should be added to the list of attributes. Second, while questions of values and ethics may be considered to be implicit in the Management Direction attribute, it is arguable that the issue is sufficiently important to warrant a separate representation. Third, although the question of service quality may be implicit in attributes such as Management Direction, Achievement of Intended Results, and Acceptance, there is both sufficient public interest and sufficient illustrative representation of quality in the literature to justify its explicit inclusion as an additional representation. Fourth, the important insight into internal systems provided by the Working Environment attribute might usefully be extended generally or specifically to include a broader set of 'overhead support systems'. For instance, a representation on the nature and scope of general administrative support would address an area that is not only of central interest to, but is usually misunderstood by, constituencies such as boards and funders. Fifth, the credibility of representations as a diagnostic tool for managers – quite apart from the assurance provided by external audit – would be enhanced by a representation on management systems for internal audit and evaluation. This could be part of the Monitoring and Reporting attribute, but is arguably too important to be left in an implicit category.

*Criterion a:*
*The scope of the set of attributes should be extended as necessary to reflect the nature of the programme and the information requirements of programme constituencies.*

## Clarification

Practise with the attributes suggests some ambiguity and possible misunderstanding of intended focus. Three relatively common such areas may suffice to illustrate the point. First, the major contribution of the attributes in extending the concept of effectiveness from its original specific focus on the achievement of objectives has tended to leave the Achievement of Intended Results attribute in something of a residual category, used to indicate achievements in areas that are not treated in other attributes. For instance, intended results related to service quality and customer satisfaction could be dealt with under Acceptance, those in a complementary programme under Secondary Impacts, and those related to, say, hiring and training, could fit nicely under Working Environment. Without some guidance on distinctions here, variations in usage could diminish the consistency and comparability of reports, and, perhaps worse, obscure what we argue later should be the central focus on the Achievement of Intended Results attribute. Second, while the Costs and Productivity attribute is interpreted generally as the traditional efficiency component of the old value-for-money question, ambiguity and some redundancy are common in establishing the distinction between this attribute and *Appropriateness*, interpreted as a 'best methods', 'how things are done' attribute. One solution here would be to see Appropriateness as part of a strategic perspective in which best methods are determined, and then to use Costs and Productivity to show how these methods are implemented; but what is important is clarification of intended meaning and therefore consistency in interpretation. Third, the contribution of the attributes approach in pointing to the distinction between operating results (internal and external) and management systems and practices is frequently diminished by lack of both explicitness and clarity on where to draw the line. Flexibility is obviously desirable, but again consistency and comparability may require some guidance on necessary basic structure. While some attributes such as Monitoring and Reporting and possibly Protection of Assets refer essentially to management systems, most can imply both systems and operating results. For instance, Acceptance would be dealt with most thoroughly by describing both the management systems in place to determine customer satisfaction, service quality, etc., and the actual operating results obtained by using these systems. Similarly, Management Direction requires information on the management systems used to determine, say, strategic direction and build budgets, and also the actual operating statements of objectives, budget targets, etc.; and a similar argument obtains for attributes such as Working Environment. What would seem most useful would be guidance that made this distinction clear and required both sorts of evidence; some suggestions for, at least, explicitness in this distinction were offered in the set of general standards proposed in Chapter 5.

> *Criterion b:*
> *The attributes should be clearly and specifically defined and distinguished before their use in a programme report, and any areas of possible ambiguity resolved; resolving ambiguity includes making a clear distinction between management systems and operating results.*

## The nature and perspective of the information presented: from description to a theoretical model; from a checklist to prioritization and key success factors; and from a static cross-section to a dynamic moving picture of organizational performance

These are big issues, and they all have their roots in the nature and purpose of the message a set of management representations using the attributes is intended to convey. The questions are interdependent, indeed cumulative, and, in an attempt at clarity of argument, will be treated in order.

*Description or theoretical model?*

The composite picture offered by the 12 perspectives on effectiveness may be seen as more than the sum of its parts, even in a simple listing. But is this potential synergy simply an inference to be drawn subjectively by each beholder, or is there a logic to the list that can be articulated as a broad theoretical model of programme performance, where the attributes constitute the set of model variables? In short, is there some logic and order to the shopping list that goes beyond description to convey systemically a sense of how programmes work? Even in list form, it is clear that the attributes will not generally be independent. For instance, outstanding performance in programme unit costs (under Costs and Productivity) might be achieved at the expense of customers (Acceptance) and staff (Working Environment). A full set of representations by management should therefore include reference to the relationships among attributes and the relative weights assigned to each. This is obviously true where attributes are in conflict; but it is also true where they are complementary or relatively independent – since scarce resources have to be allocated among various management systems, and managers cannot optimize 12 attributes simultaneously. So a start could be made to moving from description to a model of programme performance by identifying and revealing, first, management's perception of the relationship among attributes, and, second, and in the light of these perceptions, management's assigned priorities among the attributes. Making explicit management's perceptions and priorities is important, since these perceptions and priorities may not be shared by other programme constituencies, such as clients and funders.

> *Criterion c*
> *Reports using the attributes should make explicit management's perceptions of the relationship among the attributes, and, in the light of these perceptions, management's assigned priorities.*

*From a checklist to prioritization and key success factors*

The logical next question is whether prioritization can be postulated in a more generalizable sense. In short, can the set of attributes be prioritized generally in terms of *intrinsic* significance for programme performance? Any such prioritization which is generalizable to the point of being generally accepted, would be reflected in the promulgation of the attributes as a set of standards for reporting performance information, and would not preclude approaches to programme-specific and time-specific prioritization.

One approach to such general prioritization is summarized in Figure 10.1; the classification draws on a set of interviews with public sector programme managers and central agency staff on the use of the attributes in reporting performance. The attributes were initially classified into those that are primarily of an instrumental nature, relating to management systems, and those that are primarily of a consequential nature, relating to operating results. The attributes were then prioritized into two categories, described as 'core' and 'supplementary'. Two attributes are defined as both instrumental and core in nature: Management direction, which provides for prioritized programme objectives (programmatic direction) and the translation of these objectives into budgets (financial direction); and Monitoring and Reporting, which provides information on the extent to which intended programmatic and financial direction has been achieved. Three attributes are defined that are both core in nature, and relate to actual operating results: Achievement of Intended Results; Costs and Productivity; and Financial Results. The core framework thus includes management systems that provide programmatic and financial direction and the monitoring and reporting of the extent to which that direction has been achieved, and results measures that include both accountability for value for money – defined broadly as cost-effectiveness, and including both traditional effectiveness and efficiency – and financial accountability. This core information could stand alone as a set of performance accountability representations. The remaining seven attributes are classified as supplementary, as providing useful additional information which, however, cannot stand alone but require the context of the core set. Relevance, Appropriateness, Responsiveness, Working Environment, and Protection of Assets are all classified as supplementary management systems, and Acceptance and Secondary Impacts, as supplementary operational results. Although there was no disagreement among managers and board members interviewed that there should be a core set of attributes, and indeed that the five identified attributes should all be part of that core, a few managers expressed some concern with our relegation of Acceptance to the supplementary category. The position we defended was that success under the Achievement of Intended Results would be partially a function of success under Acceptance, whereas the converse would not necessarily hold. But this discussion begins to foreshadow the subsequent discussion on focus and logic models of programmes.

The point we seek to make here is that the classification of a sub-group of the attributes as generally more important amounts to postulating a set of *general key success factors* in organizational performance. Any such ranking should therefore be carefully debated, and should not preclude programme-specific and/or time-specific ranking by managers. Further, any approach to prioritization should not be at the expense of the comprehensive, eclectic scope of the 12 attributes. That scope reflects the interests of the various constituencies of non-profit sector programmes, and what is seen generally

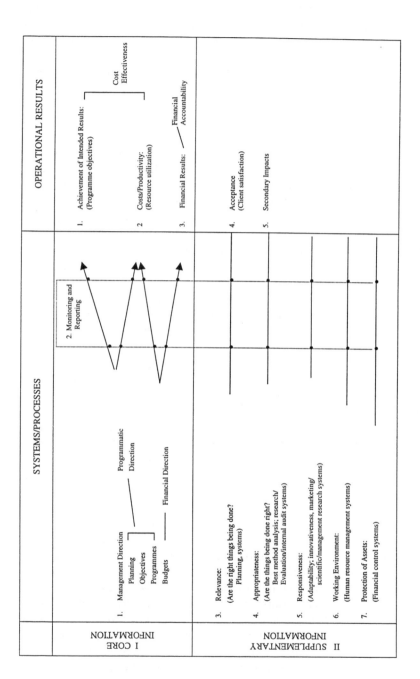

*Figure 10.1* An approach to prioritization of the CCAF/FCVI framework.

as a key success factor, or is seen particularly by a manager at a point in time as a key success factor, may not be persuasive to members of other constituencies, such as clients or funders or even programme staff, who may have a highly focused, perhaps one-dimensional, view of what constitutes success.

*Criterion d:*
*For like programmes, consideration should be given to determining general priorities or key success factors among the attributes, and any such priorities should be clearly communicated to programme managers and users of reports.*

*From a static cross-section to a dynamic moving picture of programme performance:*

Prioritization offers one perspective on viewing the set of attributes systemically. Quite consistent with prioritization, another perspective which could contribute to a more systemic view would be to argue that the attributes potentially offer much more than a static perspective, a mere cross-section at a point in time, as it were, of organizational performance.

The very arrangement of the attributes in Figure 10.1 postulates implicitly a relationship between the attributes – the variables in a model of organizational performance – over time. Management is seen as establishing purpose and direction, and as putting in place management systems to pursue that purpose and direction. The implementation of purpose and direction through these systems results over time in consequences – in operating results of various kinds. In short, the picture implicitly is a moving one, of a cycle of management activities that result in consequences. The core attributes are arranged in such a picture as an accountability framework over the management cycle, or as the basic infrastructure of such a framework.

The attributes would, of course, be brought together in an end-of-year report by management, and to that extent they still represent a longitudinal cross-section at a point in time; but they would be presented in that report in such a way that the picture reflects explicitly the management cycle of activities: What did management set out to do? How did management keep an eye on progress? And how did things turn out over the year as a whole relative to intentions? By contrast, the dynamic of the management cycle is implicit in a simple list of the attributes in the conventional manner. In short, by presenting the attributes explicitly in the dynamic context of the management cycle, managers can bring the picture to life by offering to users of the representations what can be viewed as a 'movie' of the past year rather than a snapshot of the year-end.

The presentation of the attributes as a dynamic accountability framework also suggests their use for accountability purposes in the parts of the management cycle prior to the end-of-year report. The relevant attributes could indeed be used as a way of representing accountability information in a consistent way at various stages of the cycle, as a way, in effect, of representing accountability terms of reference at the beginning of the cycle, and how these terms of reference were pursued across the cycle, culminating in the comprehensive end-of-year report.

One approach to such a general framework was proposed in Chapter 4 and developed in Chapter 5. Reflecting continuing discussions with managers and board members in the agencies, and testing of the proposal, a development of the framework that is designed specifically to be used as an end-of-year programme annual report is offered as the final section of this chapter after a brief discussion, relevant to the proposed annual report, of the nature of evidence used in reporting the various attributes. At this stage, it is worth capturing in a formal criterion the argument made in Chapters 4 and 5 and here that there is merit to arranging the attributes, for whatever purpose, in a way that reflects the management cycle.

> *Criterion e:*
> *To serve a variety of purposes across the management cycle, from planning to external reporting at the end of the year, the attributes should be arranged to reflect that cycle of intentions, activities and achievements, and thus to 'tell the story' or present a moving picture of the programme.*

## The nature of the evidence presented under each attribute

Given the scope of an accountability report based on the 12 attributes, and the arrangement of the information to permit both prioritization of various kinds and a dynamic perspective on management activities, it remains to consider briefly some characteristics of the evidence adduced under each attribute, which would provide for validity and reliability, and usefulness to senior management.

## Measurability

In principle, valid and reliable evidence should be measurable. But the concept of measurement is an elusive one, ranging along a spectrum from firm and easily measured quantitative evidence such as the number of clients served, through less firm and less easily measured information such as client satisfaction along measurement scales of various kinds, to essentially non-quantitative information such as clients' comments and associated anecdotal evidence. Technically, even this last category can be 'measured' or at least systematically represented through content analysis or other methods, but the value of such evidence to users lies much more in the additional perspective it offers than in any precision in measurement. The moral of the story, in designing an accountability framework, is that it is better to be approximately right than precisely wrong, and that a comprehensive perspective is a more important consideration than one based on that which can be easily measured. The temptation is always to stick to what can be measured easily; the dangers are that what can be measured easily may be a poor surrogate for, or worse, actually perverse in relation to, the desired output or outcome; that managers then manage to and report on what they can measure easily; that senior managers get an incomplete and possibly misleading perspective on accountability; and that managers, in turn, are given incentives that reward ease of measurement rather than successful performance. Validity and reliability should thus be seen in very practical terms that require the avoidance of the trap of relatively easy measurement, and the presentation of all the information on each attribute that senior management needs in order to understand programme performance.

*Criterion f:*
*Validity and reliability should be seen in very practical terms that require the presentation of all the relevant information on each attribute that those using the information need to understand programme performance.*

## Succinctness

Although senior managers need all the information under each attribute that is necessary to understand programme performance, they do not need and should not get more than is necessary. Validity and reliability thus require that completeness of perspective be balanced against succinctness, and the associated structural characteristics of understandability and accessibility. A major flaw in the performance indicators industry, particularly with respect to indicators relating to such attributes as Cost and Productivity, is the presentation of large numbers of indicators which swamp decision-makers and defeat the purpose of accountability reporting. So senior management should get all the information it needs, but only what it needs, and it should get it in understandable and accessible form.

*Criterion g:*
*Senior management should get all the information it needs, but only what it needs, and should get it in an understandable and accessible form.*

## Causality

Management representations constitute an accountability statement by programme managers. The question that follows is whether they should therefore be confined to performance over which managers have control – that they 'cause' – and for which they can therefore legitimately be held accountable. The most obvious example would be that managers can be held accountable for direct and controllable programme costs, but cannot legitimately be held accountable for the allocation of, say, organizational overhead costs which are part of total programme costs. Now total programme costs are obviously of interest to senior management and a complete representation within the Costs and Productivity attribute should contain such information. But the limits of programme management's control and therefore accountability should be clearly identified. On the other side of the value-for-money equation, a similar argument applies to the matter of outputs and outcomes. Managers in, say, a training programme, can control, or at least significantly influence, and can there-fore be held accountable for, outputs such as curriculum content, the number of candidates, and even the quality of candidate performance. But managers have much less influence on subsequent consequences such as the number of job offers or the first salary offers obtained by successful graduates, and virtually no influence on ultimate consequences such as the differential income and productivity of graduates or their career path. Consequences therefore lie along a spectrum from those that occur up to the point of programme completion – usually referred to as outputs – to those that occur at various stages after completion – usually referred to as outcomes. Completeness in reporting to senior management requires that as much information as possible, including outcomes, be reported – indeed the key attribute of Relevance may require the identification of outcomes – but fairness in the assignment of accountability also requires that management's accountability be confined to outputs, that is, to those consequences that they can control or influence significantly.

*Criterion h:*
*Fairness in the assignment of accountability requires that management's account-ability be confined to consequences that management can control or influence significantly, such as direct costs and outputs.*

*Operationality*

The 12 attributes, arranged in the original way, or prioritized and rearranged in some of the ways discussed above, are standards for what performance information should be collected and monitored across the management cycle and brought together in a comprehensive end-of-year report. They are not standards of performance. Operational usefulness to senior management requires for any programme that the attributes be operationalized through criteria or benchmarks of success for each kind of performance information. There are no 'generally accepted criteria of performance' for non-profit programmes, but progress could be made towards developing, essentially negotiating, illustrative performance criteria for like programmes of comparable size, say, cost and productivity criteria for training programmes in comparable organizations. In the absence of external benchmarks, criteria are still necessary for operational usefulness to senior management. Such criteria must be acceptable to senior manage-ment (the users of the information) and to programme management (the producers of the information) and therefore need to be negotiated. Since the end-of-year report deals with performance in relation to declared inten-tions, the time for the negotiation of acceptable criteria is when budgetary targets in relation to each of the attributes are determined; such targets may obviously be adjusted, again by negotiation, in the light of changing circumstances over the year. Targets can relate to the design and working of management systems as well as operating performance, and are programme-specific rather than general in nature. So the prescribed infor-mation components of the end-of-year report are operationalized by the use of general performance criteria where such criteria are available, and, in the absence of general criteria, by programme-specific criteria which reflect directly the declared and negotiated intentions of programme management at the beginning of the annual management cycle, and changing circumstances over the cycle.

*Criterion i:*
*The prescribed information components in the end-of-year report should be opera-tionalized by the use of general performance criteria where such criteria are available, and otherwise by programme-specific negotiated criteria.*

## Objectivity and verifiability

An essential contribution of the CCAF/FCVI approach to reporting is its recognition of the appropriate area of expertise of both programme managers and auditors. Programme managers are best equipped to make representations about programme performance, and, subject to general guidance on the 12 categories of information, they are appropriately cast in that role. Management representations constitute, however, an accountability statement, essentially self-disclosure, and the question arises whether managers can be expected to treat the opportunity in confessional mode and provide complete and accurate information even where they are concerned that such information might redound to their disadvan-tage. The evidence presented is bound, at least in significant part, to be subjective in nature, and managers can reasonably be expected to put the best possible construction on events. At worst, management diagnostics might translate into the creation of a smokescreen that would vitiate the accountability objective. This potential compromise of the validity and reliability of evidence presented in the CCAF/FCVI framework can be addressed by the additional, interdependent criteria of objectivity and verifiability.

Objectivity requires that evidence provided in a set of management representations be supplemented to the greatest extent possible by evidence provided by third parties. The objectivity of the set of evidence as a whole would be improved by the use under, for instance, the Acceptance and Working Environment attributes, of evidence provided by clients and staff, respectively. Objectivity would also be improved by clear identification of relevant management systems and operational results in relation to specified criteria, and by clear substantiation, albeit in summary form, of the sources and methods of analysis by which evidence is derived. In short, the evidence should also be verifiable.

A first level of actual verification could involve the provision to senior management of an internal audit opinion on the completeness and accuracy of the set of representations. Reinforcement of the accountability loop to senior management, and completion of that loop beyond senior management and boards to external users of information such as funders, requires the assurance provided by an external attest audit in which the audit report is in the public domain. External auditors could, of course, rely as appropriate on any internal audit work that had been done. Both internal and external auditors would thus play the role most appropriate to their expertise – the verification of the completeness and accuracy of management representations.

*Criterion j:*
*The information presented in management representations should be, to the extent possible, objective and verifiable, and, again to the extent possible, should include audit assurance, both internal and external.*

## A proposed format for end-of-year reports based on the 12 attributes

A format for end-of-year reports based on the 12 attributes is proposed in the Appendix to this chapter. The proposal reflects the preceding discussion, and the set of criteria for the assessment of reports.

The proposal has several features. First, it includes all 12 attributes but adds a few additional attributes in the interests of comprehensive accountability reporting. Second, an explicit distinction is drawn between management systems and operating information. Third, the three levels of accountability – financial accountability, accountability for compliance with authorities, and accountability for value for money – are explicitly distinguished. Fourth, the attributes are presented in a dynamic framework that reflects the management cycle of activities over the year. Fifth, the limits of management accountability for value for money – outputs as distinct from outcomes and direct controllable costs as distinct from full costs – are identified. Sixth, the format incorporates criteria – or benchmarks of success – in the form of targets established at the planning and budgeting stage of the cycle, and such general or 'industry-wide' criteria as are available. Seventh, the format requires that subjective evidence presented by management be supplemented to the extent feasible by external, third-party evidence.

Eighth, self-evaluation by management is incorporated in the form of a situation analysis summary of strengths and challenges, and used as the basis of a statement by management of proposed actions, and of a set of recommendations for decisions by senior management. Ninth, an internal audit opinion is incorporated to provide assurance to senior management, and an external audit opinion incorporated to provide assurance to the board of the organization and the general public. Finally, a subset of attributes is suggested as the core logic – key success factors – of the approach; the other attributes by implication may be seen as supplementary.

Consistent with previous chapters, the focus here is on a major function, defined as a client service programme, within a non-profit agency. We learned quickly in our discussions with the agencies that the programme level was the most practical and helpful focus and that performance in the agency as a whole could best be approached through aggregation from the programme level. A client service programme is defined, following the discussion on costing in Chapter 7, to include direct client service activities – defined in Chapter 7 for purposes of cost calculation as mission centres – and those support or overhead activities that serve and are necessary for the delivery of direct client services, and thus service clients indirectly.

In essence, the proposed format is intended to come alive as a moving picture, to tell the story of what happened over the year in the programme in a way that captures both the temporal and conceptual relationship among the set of attributes. The attributes, with some supplementation, are thus seen as the variables in a model of programme operations. The model explicitly links reporting back to those parts of the agency's strategic and business plans relevant to the programme, and, after a self-evaluation situation analysis of strengths and weaknesses, forward to a proposed set of actions by management and recommendations for action to senior management.

Following a brief, descriptive introductory section, the proposed format deals with the strategic perspective of the programme at the end of the year, in the light of changing circumstances over the year, and how that perspective relates to the strategic plan of the agency. Entitled 'Where We Fit: Our role in the Agency and the Community', the section includes two attributes. First, the Relevance attribute describes and assesses the role of the programme with respect to the problems for which it was designed. Second, the Responsiveness attribute describes and assesses how the programme has adapted to changes in external circumstances over the year. For both attributes, the description and assessment would include reference to the relationship of the strategic perspective of the programme to that of the agency. The information provided also distinguishes between the nature and functioning of the management systems set up to determine the strategic perspective, and the actual operating information produced by these systems: an end-of-year statement on Relevance which would include reference to outcomes or consequences in the community as a result of programme activities; and an end-of-year statement on Responsiveness which would describe the extent of adaptation to changing circumstances over the year.

The rationale for the continued existence of the programme leads directly to the next section: What We Set Out to Achieve and How We Did It: Ends and Means in Our Service Programme. The section includes two attributes: Management Direction, dealing with ends, and Appropriateness, dealing with means, and should reflect directly the business plan of the programme within the agency business plan. For both attributes the information provided distinguishes between the management systems set up to determine ends and means (planning, budgeting and quality assurance systems for Management Direction, and programming and methodology analysis and selection systems for Appropriateness) and the actual operating information for the programme produced jointly by these systems: values; mission; the set of prioritized objectives and corresponding programme design (and, if necessary, sub-programmes or activities); the financial plan which shows revenue and expenditure targets for the year (setting the stage for financial accountability); and a programme plan which shows cost and productivity targets for the year (setting the stage for accountability for the traditional efficiency component of value for money) and a variety of output targets for the service programme, including at the general level output targets for all service programme objectives, and, more specifically, targets for client acceptance of service outputs, targets for output quality, and targets for intended secondary impacts. The general service outputs foreshadow accountability for Achievement of Intended Results, and the other output targets foreshadow accountability for Acceptance, Quality (which has been added to the CCAF/FCVI list), and Secondary Impacts. The set of output targets set the stage for accountability for the traditional effectiveness component of value of money. As a set of accountability terms of reference, targets are confined to outputs over which programme management can exercise control. It would be desirable in this section to elaborate on the intended outcomes foreshadowed under Relevance, but to distinguish such outcomes clearly from outputs and to confine the accountability of programme management to the latter. The targets provided in this section become the primary criteria for assessing the achievements of the programme later in the set of representations.

Before turning to achievements, however, it is necessary to include accountability terms of reference for support activities in the programme. This section is titled: How We Managed Our Affairs: Ends and Means in Our Support Activities. Three of the CCAF/FCVI attributes (Working Environment, Protection of Assets, and Monitoring and Reporting) are included in this section, and two additional attributes (Management Overhead and Evaluation and Audit) proposed for inclusion. Compliance is an essential part of any accountability framework, and the section includes a description of the nature and functioning of the management system(s) set up to ensure compliance with authorities and the actual compliance targets (degree of compliance and the associated cost of compliance activities) for the year. The Working Environment attribute is included in this section, but is given the rather broader title of People Management. Like the treatment of compliance, the approach here requires a description of the nature and functioning of the management systems set up for people management, and the actual operating targets (output targets for matters such as hiring and training, and the associated cost of people management activities) for the year. The Protection of Assets attribute is included here as a support activity related to financial, material and human assets; the approach includes a description of the nature and functioning of these management systems and the actual operating targets for the protection of assets, and corresponding costs. On the grounds that People Management provides too narrow a perspective on support systems, a Management Overhead attribute is proposed to cover the general administrative support area which is so frequently misunderstood and therefore unfairly criticized and inadequately funded. The approach includes a description of the management systems set up to provide general administrative support, and associated output targets and costs. Monitoring and Reporting is included in this section as a support activity, and the approach includes a description of the management systems set up for monitoring and reporting accountability information – for both service programmes and support programmes – and a description, and possibly illustration, of the periodic reports provided internally to programme management and those provided to senior management, and a statement linking such periodic reporting to the primary output of the systems: the end-of year report which forms the next section of the representations. Operating information on this attribute also includes the target cost of operating monitoring and reporting systems. The final component of this section deals explicitly with Evaluation and Audit. What is proposed here is a description of management systems set up to deal with evaluation within the programme, systems to coordinate with the internal audit group within the agency or perhaps federated funding agency, and systems to coordinate with the external auditor of the programme. For all three interrelated systems, this section also requires a description of the targeted operating information to be produced by each system. This includes the following: regular evaluation reports from internal evaluation systems; regular internal audit reports from the internal audit group, culminating in an internal audit opinion on the end-of-year accountability report; and the opinion provided by the external auditor on the comprehensive (financial, compliance, value for money) accountability report produced by programme management at the end of the year.

Having set the strategic and operating stage, the next section of the end-of-year report describes and assesses what actually happened over the year: What We Achieved: Our Accountability Record. This section distinguishes explicitly among statements on the three levels of account-ability (financial, compliance, and value for money), which in combination form the comprehensive accountability statement. For each category of accountability information, the management systems which produce the required information have already been described, and the information is therefore limited to operating results.

Under financial accountability, the Financial Results attribute provides the traditional set of financial statements including explanatory notes on variance from budgeted financial targets for revenues and expenditures, including a self-evaluation by programme management on financial control over the year.

The Compliance attribute provides a statement on and assessment of the extent of compliance with authorities and the cost of compliance, in both cases relative to targets. Although targets are the primary criteria used in the self-evaluation by programme management, the compliance area might provide some external benchmarks from, say, similar organi-zations, on the extent and cost of compliance, which, if available, should also be used in the self-evaluation.

The largest part of the accountability report is the report on account-ability for value for money. In the proposed approach, this part in divided into two sub-parts, the first dealing with the service programmes as a whole, the second with that component of the service programme that relates to support activities. The former subsumes the latter, by definition, but is included to provide a more complete statement on how the programme has functioned, and also indeed to draw attention to the frequently neglected, and underfunded, support activities.

For the service programme as a whole, the approach includes repre-sentations by programme management on four CCAF/FCVI attributes – Achievement of Intended Results, Acceptance, Secondary Impacts, and Costs and Productivity – and one additional attribute: Quality. The Costs and Productivity attribute provides an accountability statement covering the traditional efficiency component of value for money, and the other four attributes, including Quality, provide an accountability statement covering the traditional effectiveness component of value for money in general terms, and some specific aspects of effectiveness. Under the four attributes related to traditional effectiveness, the approach includes a state-ment of actual outputs achieved compared to targets, and, wherever possible, to externally derived criteria such as industry standards. The approach also requires that to the extent possible, evidence provided by management be supplemented by third-party external evidence, that evidence and analytical trails be clear and auditable – essentially, that management's representations be clearly substantiated, not merely asserted – and that outputs, for which programme management is directly account-able, be distinguished from outcomes, which programme management does not control directly and for which it cannot therefore be held directly accountable. Correspondingly, under Costs and Productivity, the approach includes actual costs and productivity measures compared to targets and, wherever possible, to externally determined criteria. The approach also requires, as for outputs, that evidence and analytical trails be clear and auditable, and that direct controllable costs, for which management is directly accountable, be distinguished from full programme costs, which programme management does not control and for which it cannot therefore be held directly accountable.

Under support activities, the approach includes three CCAF/FCVI attributes: Working Environment (re-named People Management), Protection of Assets, and Monitoring and Reporting; and two additional attributes: Management Overhead and Evaluation and Audit. As for the service programme as a whole, the approach includes a statement of actual support programme outputs and associated costs compared to the targets and any external criteria, and a summary self-evaluation by programme management, and requires that evidence and analytical trails be clear and auditable.

The penultimate section of the report by programme management takes the form of a Situation Analysis – a summary of the strengths and challenges identified under each attribute, and actions proposed by programme management to maintain areas of strength and meet challenges. The summary of strengths and weaknesses would bring together management's self-evaluations in the record of achievements in both service and support programmes, and management's evaluation of strengths and weaknesses under the various 'stage-setting' attributes – the strategic perspective under the Relevance and Responsiveness attributes, direction and methodology under the Management Direction and Appropriateness attributes, and internal management under the Compliance, People Management, Protection of Assets, Management Overhead, Monitoring and Reporting, and Evaluation and Audit attributes. The proposed actions by management would be within management's authority and budget limits for the past year; essentially, management would say in this section what it would do differently next year if given the same budget again.

The final section of the representations by programme management includes recommendations for action to senior management. These could deal with such matters as clarification of direction or approval of new methodology, and could foreshadow later budget and/or personnel requests to address particular weaknesses.

The final two sections comprise the two audit opinions. In the first, the internal audit opinion on the completeness and accuracy of the representations is provided by the funding agency internal audit branch or evaluation group within the organization and is intended to provide assurance to senior management. The second opinion on the completeness and accuracy of representations is provided by the external auditor, relying as appropriate on internal audit work done, and is intended to provide assurance to all internal and external stakeholders, including funders, clients, staff, volunteers and the general public.

Reflecting the discussion of prioritization, the final page of the proposed reporting format suggests a core logic – the 'key success factors' – for both programme management and senior management. The core set includes seven attributes, three of a 'stage-setting' nature, and four dealing with results achieved. The argument is that a programme exists in a vacuum unless its Relevance is identified; that this relevance must be translated into action under Management Direction; that progress in intended direction must be monitored and reported (Monitoring and Reporting); and that core results refer to the traditional three areas of accountability: Financial Results (financial accountability); Compliance (accountability for compliance with authorities); and Achievement of Intended Results and Costs and Productivity ( the core elements of traditional effectiveness and efficiency). Without treatment of *at least* these attributes, senior management lacks the information to judge the reason for and the success of a programme. The other attributes are not classified as unimportant, but as supplementary to the core logic of the basic set. This prioritization is, of course, of a general nature. Particular users of accountability information might choose a different core logic, or might be interested in only one attribute as a key success factor. Programme staff, for instance, might focus on People Management, and clients on Acceptance.

## III Conclusion

The response of management and boards in the agencies to the proposed end-of-year reporting structure was broadly favourable. All parties agreed that a reporting framework that described performance in relation to explicit intentions at the planning and budgeting stage of the cycle was a more complete and fairer approach to accountability. The common currencies and associated criteria were established at the beginning and were observed through the reporting and evaluation stages. There was also broad endorsement of the explicit identification of the role of support activities which otherwise tended to receive little credit and to be regarded as expendable. Concerns about the complexity of the approach were alleviated by our identification of the core elements – key success factors – in the framework, and by our insistence that extension of the framework should reflect agreement by the board, senior management, and programme management, that the benefits of the extension exceeded its inevitable additional costs. One nagging question remained. The very comprehensiveness of the approach required a rather lengthy answer to any request for a summary statement on programme success. Further, it also became clear that comprehensiveness at the reporting stage presented a rather diffuse target at the planning and budgeting stage. Programme managers obviously seek to do as well as possible for given resources, but managers pointed out that they could only optimize one thing at a time, and that it would be useful to explore further how, consistent with the inevitable multiple objectives and varying interests of different constituencies, some planning focus could be introduced. So to this task we turned our attention, recognizing that any progress in providing focus at the prospective part of the cycle would have to be reflected through the cycle and in the accountability reports and evaluations done at the end.

## Note

1   CCAF/FCVI, *Effectiveness Reporting and Auditing in the Public Sector* (Ottawa, CCAF/FCVI, 1987).

## APPENDIX: NON-PROFIT ORGANIZATIONS
## END OF YEAR (EOY) REPORT FOR A CLIENT
## SERVICE PROGRAMME

### TABLE OF CONTENTS

(a)   Introduction: brief description of the programme; budget; staff and other resources

(b)   Where we fit: our role in the agency and the community

| Attribute | Information | |
|---|---|---|
| | **Management Systems** | **Operating Information** |
| (i)   Relevance | Nature and functioning of management system. ⟶ | EOY assessment of relevance, (including reference to outcomes.) |
| (ii)   Responsiveness | Nature and functioning of management system. ⟶ | EOY statement of adaptation over the year to changing circumstances. |

Note: This section deals with the strategic perspective of the programme as part of an agency at the end of the year, in the light of changing circumstances over the year.

(c)    What we set out to achieve and how we did it: ends and means in
our service programme

| Attribute | | Information | |
|---|---|---|---|
| | | **Management Systems** | **Operating Information** |
| (i) | Management Direction: | Nature and functioning of planning, budgeting, and quality assurance systems. | a.  Values |
| | | | b.  Mission |
| | | | c.  Set of Prioritized service objectives and corresponding programmes. |
| (ii) | Appropriateness: | Nature and functioning of systems for programming and choice of programme methods. | d.  Financial plan: <br> – revenue targets: <br> – expenditure targets. |
| | | | e.  Programme plan: <br> – cost and productivity targets; <br> – output targets for service objectives; <br> – client acceptance targets; <br> – secondary impact targets. |

Note: This section sets out the accountability terms of reference ('marching orders')
for the service programme of the agency, and reflects directly the agency's business
plan. The targets provided in this section become the primary criteria for assessing
the achievements of the programme.

(d) How we managed our affairs: ends and means in our support
    activities

| Attribute | Information | |
|---|---|---|
| | **Management Systems** | **Operating Information** |
| (i) Compliance: | Nature and functioning of systems to ensure compliance with authorities. | Compliance targets (outputs, $) |
| (ii) People Management (working environment): | Nature and functioning of people management systems. | People management targets (outputs, $) |
| (iii) Protection of Assets: | Nature and functioning of systems for protecting assets. | Financial, material and human assets protection targets (outputs, $) |
| (iv) Management Overhead* | Nature and functioning of systems for general administrative support | Administrative support targets (outputs, $) |
| (v) Monitoring and Reporting: | Nature and functioning of systems for monitoring and reporting accountability information. | Monthly reports on service and support programme targets, culminating in full EOY report. |
| (vi) Evaluating and Audit* | Nature and functioning of three inter-related systems: | |
| | (a) evaluation within the agency | (a) regular evaluation reports; |
| | (b) co-ordination with funding agency internal audit branch; | (b) regular internal audit reports, culminating with EOY internal audit opinion; |
| | (e) co-ordination with external auditor. | (c) EOY external audit opinion. |

* Added to CCAF/FCVI list

Note: This section deals with the accountability terms of reference for the support
or overhead activities of the programme.

(e)  What we achieved: our accountability record

| Accountability Category | Attribute | Information (all Operating Results) |
|---|---|---|
| 1. Financial Accountability. | Financial results | Financial statements |
| 2. Accountability for compliance with Authorities. | Compliance* | Statement of extent of compliance with authorities |
| 3. Accountability for Value for Money:<br><br>(i)  Service Programme<br><br>–aspects of traditional effectiveness | (a) Achievement of intended results.<br><br>(b) Acceptance.<br><br>(c) Secondary impacts.<br><br>(d) Quality.* | –Actual outputs achieved compared to targets, and, wherever possible, to external criteria (e.g. industry standards):<br>–External third-party evidence wherever possible;<br>–Evidence trails auditable;<br>–Output distinguished from outcomes (accountability limited to outputs). |
| –traditional efficiency | (e) Costs and productivity. | –Actuals compared to targets, and, wherever possible, to external criteria;<br>–Evidence trails auditable;<br>–Direct controllable costs distinguished from full costs (accountability limited to direct controllable costs). |
| (ii) Support Activities | (a) People management (working environment).<br><br>(b) Protection of assets.<br><br>(c) Management overhead.*<br><br>(d) Monitoring and reporting.<br><br>(e) Evaluation and audit.* | –actual outputs compared to targets, and, wherever possible, to external criteria;<br><br>–evidence trails auditable. |

* Added to CCAF/FCVI list

(f)   Situation analysis: a summary of strengths and challenges identified for the set of attributes, and program management's proposed action with respect to those strengths and challenges

| Attribute | Strengths | Challenges | Proposed Action |
|---|---|---|---|
| 1.  Relevance<br><br>2.  Appropriateness<br><br>3.  Etc. ... | | | |

(g)   Recommendations to senior management

(h)   Internal audit opinion:

- Provided by the funding agency internal audit branch (or by the internal audit or evaluation group within the organization.)

- This opinion is intended to provide assurance to senior management and the board

(i)   External audit opinion:

- Provided by an external auditor

- This opinion is intended to provide assurance to all internal and external stakeholders, including funders, clients, staff, volunteers and the general public.

(j)   Core logic of report

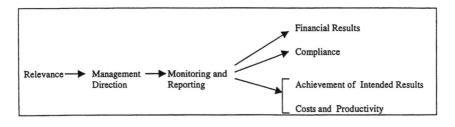

# 11 Performance measurement in non-profit organizations

## A note on integration and focus within comprehensiveness

## I Introduction

Performance in commercial organizations is generally defined from the perspective of shareholders around the central focus of profitability and corresponding return on shareholders' equity. It is clear what kinds of information are relevant, and, through generally accepted accounting principles, how success is measured in terms of that information. There is, however, no such obvious unifying focus in public and private non-profit organizations which do not sell their products or services.

Some interesting attempts at systematizing the kinds of information to be included in a definition of performance in non-profit organizations appear in the evolving Canadian literature on accountability, and have been discussed in previous chapters. There is broad agreement that the set of information presented about organizational performance should include both procedural and consequential components. The procedural components include financial information on the extent of compliance with authorities of various kinds. The consequential components include various attempts to develop a surrogate for profit in the form of evidence on 'value for money', usually defined to include the use of resources (efficiency) and the achievement of organizational purposes (effectiveness). In its work on comprehensive auditing, the CCAF/FCVI defined the scope of organizational performance which should be addressed in a comprehensive or broad-scope performance audit to include the three components just described,[1] and the Canadian Institute of Chartered Accountants (CICA) elaborated formally on the definition of value for money and how its attainment should be assessed.[2] The CCAF/FCVI pursued the matter under the generic head of 'effectiveness', and proposed that this be defined comprehensively using the twelve attributes explored in the preceding chapter.[3] Most recently, a committee representing senior public servants and the Office of the Auditor General in British Columbia proposed an eclectic approach couched broadly in the traditional framework (financial results, compliance, and value for money, the last described as 'operational results') but drawing heavily on the CCAF/FCVI set of attributes in its interpretation and elaboration.[4]

The considerable achievement of these various approaches to defining performance in non-profit organizations – particularly the CCAF/FCVI set of attributes – is to draw attention to the comprehensiveness necessary to reflect the interests of various constituencies. They have addressed primarily the external reporting part of accountability, and, with some creativity in rearrangement and perhaps prioritization, they can serve to 'tell the organizational story' much more thoroughly than earlier approaches that simply offered financial statements (which, by definition in non-profit organizations which do not sell their outputs, say nothing about value for money) and some sort of description of activities and perhaps clients. However, even the developed and reorganized version of the CCAF/FCVI attributes that demonstrates the chronological cycle of governance (strategic) and subsequent management activities remains essentially a cross-sectional slice of performance along the cycle. It does take the important step of defining the attributes in a chronologically dynamic sense, but it does not provide a causally integrated dynamic model of programme performance that could serve conceptually and operationally as the basis of governance and management control. Such an integrated model would have to address the matter of focus. Multiple attributes of performance cannot be simultaneously optimized, and an operationally helpful model of programme performance in non-profit organizations would include the articulation of unifying or fundamental purpose, how the various components of the model contribute to that purpose, and how the achievement of that purpose is to be measured.

If multi-attribute approaches to defining performance in non-profit organizations are to serve as a basis for governance and management control, what is required is focus and integration within comprehensiveness. One approach to multi-attribute performance measurement designed for the private commercial sector – the Balanced Scorecard[5] – offers explicit focus and integration and is indeed designed to serve as a way of translating organizational strategy into action. The balance of this chapter summarizes the Balanced Scorecard approach; explores the applicability of such an approach to public sector commercial organizations and then to public and private non-profit organizations; and ends by proposing that the CCAF/FCVI 12-attribute system be developed as an alternative balanced scorecard, as an approach to a comprehensive but also focused and integrated model of performance in non-profit organizations which would continue to serve the purpose of external reporting to a variety of constituencies, but would also set the stage for more meaningful reporting by serving as the basis of governance and management control across the cycle of organizational activities.

## II The Balanced Scorecard

The Balanced Scorecard approach to conceptualizing and measuring performance in private commercial organizations defines the maximization of long-term profit (long-term revenue minus long-term expenses) as the long-term or strategic operating objective of private commercial organizations. This focus is defined from the perspective of the shareholders whose owners' equity (net wealth) in the organization is maximized through the operating objective of long-term profit maximization. Achieving this long-term objective requires, however, that those who govern and manage the organization have information at any point in time on a cross-section of information – a Balanced Scorecard of performance attributes – including financial results, which indicate short-term or intermediate-term progress towards the long-term goal of profit maximization, and information on three other categories of information all of which are not ends in themselves but rather are instrumental in serving the single, focused long-term objective. The Balanced Scorecard thus complements short-term financial measures of past performance with measures of the drivers of future performance. Given one, unifying strategic focus, of which short-term financial results provide simply the most recent historical evidence, all other components of the Scorecard are defined as instrumental in the achievement of the long-term objective.

The other perspectives in the multi-attribute set of information which constitutes the Balanced Scorecard include the following: the customer perspective, measured by such indicators as customer satisfaction and retention, and market share; the internal business processes perspective, measured by such indicators as operating cost, product quality, and product innovation; and the learning and growth perspective, measured by such indicators as employee satisfaction, training and productivity, and information system availability. The set of measures in the Balanced Scorecard is, however, much more than a static cross-section of various bits of performance information. Rather it is a logic model, a dynamic, chronologically and causally integrated, model of organizational performance, which can therefore serve as basis of strategic management – of governance and management control focused on the attainment of the long-term objective. In the simplest representation, outcomes in the area of learning and growth are causally and chronologically linked to outcomes in the area of internal business processes, which in turn are linked directly to long-term expenses and indirectly, through the area of customer satisfaction and growth, to long-term revenues. Strategy is the translation through budgeting and resource allocation of a set of hypotheses about cause and effect into objectives and outcomes in a set of integrated variables (the components of the Scorecard) all of which are focused on a single long-term objective. Figure 11.1 illustrates the Balanced Scorecard model in its simplest form; Kaplan and Norton, who developed it, provide a range of more detailed practical illustrations.[6] The strategic objective of long-term profit maximization is translated into a set of objectives, strategies, and associated outcomes in the four components of the Balanced Scorecard. The chronological and causal integration of these objectives,

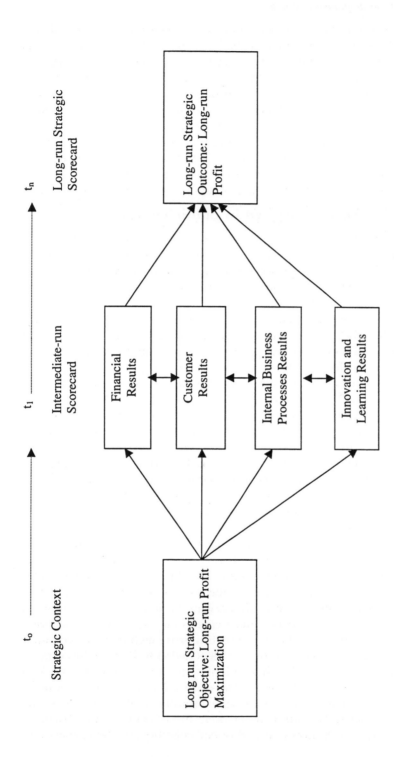

*Figure 11.1* The Balanced Scorecard (private commercial organizations).

strategies and 'intermediate' performance outcomes serves the unifying strategic outcome of long-term profit. In Figure 11.1, the formal logic model, or implied causal sequence, is implicit. The performance measurement framework, either as a prospective means of determining what to do, or as a retrospective means of determining realized success, is explicit.

The question to which the balance of this paper is addressed is whether the Balanced Scorecard approach can be used in other than private commercial organizations. The discussion begins by considering public commercial organizations, and then turns to various categories of non-profit organizations.

## III The Balanced Scorecard in public commercial organizations

Publicly owned commercial organizations which are self-financing through the sale of services – such services as transportation and power – may be seen as directly analogous to private commercial organizations. The shareholders in this case are ultimately the general public and in practice their representatives in elected governments. On behalf of these shareholders, self-financing public commercial organizations pursue the primary operating objective of long-term profit maximization in order to maximize the owners' equity of their public shareholders.

In principle, publicly owned commercial organizations are different from private commercial organizations only with respect to the broader shareholder base. In practice, governments acting on behalf of these shareholders may place qualifications on the pursuit of long-term profitability in public commercial organizations. Such qualifications may take the form of a requirement to provide all services to certain categories of users – say, the elderly – at preferred prices, or to provide specific unprofitable services – say, transportation routes to remote areas. The long-term profit objective is thus constrained by these requirements, which may be seen as additional objectives whose achievement is at the expense of – that is, has to be traded off against – the primary objective of profit maximization. If the additional qualifications were complementary rather than in conflict with the primary objective, they would be defined as instrumental in the attainment of that primary objective and would form part of the causal logic model culminating in that attainment. In simple terms, long-term profit is lower because of these qualifications or constraints. The profit foregone as a result of these constraints can generally be fairly accurately calculated, and thus can be specifically identified either as a reduced profit and thus a subsidy from the corporation to the public or as the basis of a subsidy from government to meet the constraints. The long-term profit maximization objective then has to be reformulated either as the pursuit of constrained profit maximization – where the long-term profit foregone as a result of the constraints imposed is explicitly identified in dollar terms as a subsidy from the corporation to the public – or as unconstrained long-term profit maximization defined to include the specifically calculated public subsidy (either on the cost or revenue side, or both) required to pay for the pursuit of the additional objectives. It should be added that if the decision criterion for determining a course of action at the prospective stage of the cycle, or indeed for determining success at the ongoing or retrospective stages, is one of satisficing rather than optimizing,[7] the distinction between objectives and constraints essentially disappears, and the prospective or retrospective decision criterion may be expressed in terms of satisfactory performance in any or all of the set of performance measures. This alternative currency of success could form the basis of an accountability framework, but is inferior in terms of incentives and potential performance to the alternative of constrained optimization.

As for private commercial organizations, other objectives, strategies and performance outcomes from the customer, internal business processes, and learning and growth perspectives are instrumental, through a dynamic, integrated causal model, in the pursuit of the single over-arching organizational strategic objective of long-term profit maximization.

Figure 11.2 illustrates this approach in its simplest form, and includes three types of variables (for which objectives and strategies – ends and means – and associated outcomes must be specified): the long-term unifying variable of profit maximization; the set of intermediate variables which are instrumental in the pursuit of long-term profit, and intermediate measures of that intended long-term outcome; and, for publicly-owned commercial organizations – or, for that matter, privately-owned but publicly regulated organizations – explicitly specified constraints or limitations on the pursuit of long-term profit maximization. Whereas the set of instrumental variables complement, indeed are preconditions of, the pursuit of long-term profit, constraints are by definition in conflict with, and limitations on, long-term profit. Clarity in defining organizational objectives and performance requires that the nature and effects of these constraints, and their role in the logic model of organizational performance, be explicitly specified.

## IV The Balanced Scorecard in private membership non-profit organizations

Private membership organizations such as clubs, professional organizations, and cultural organizations, are established for the exclusive or at least primary benefit of members, corresponding to shareholders in commercial organizations – the members (customers) are also the funders. The primary operating objective of such organizations may therefore be considered to be the maximization of long-term net benefit (the value of long-term gross benefits minus long-term expenses). The expenses side of the equation can obviously be measured in dollars, and the benefit side can also

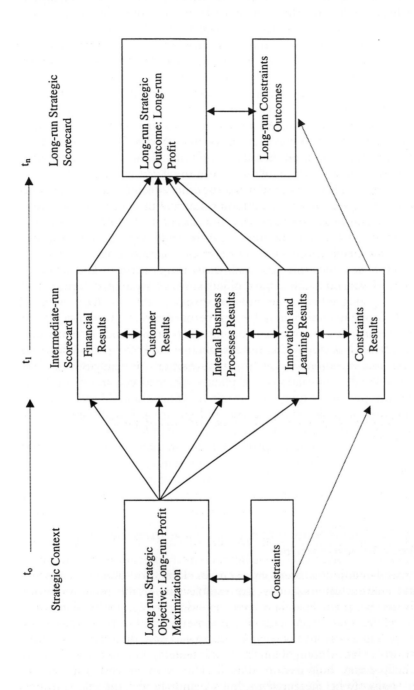

$t_0$        $t_1$        $t_n$

Strategic Context     Intermediate-run Scorecard     Long-run Strategic Scorecard

Long run Strategic Objective: Long-run Profit Maximization

Constraints

Financial Results

Customer Results

Internal Business Processes Results

Innovation and Learning Results

Constraints Results

Long-run Strategic Outcome: Long-run Profit

Long-run Constraints Outcomes

*Figure 11.2* The Balanced Scorecard (public commercial organizations).

probably reasonably be imputed or inferred in dollar terms using such reference points as membership fees and waiting lists for membership. If memberships can be sold, the analogy with owners' equity in the commercial sector can be directly drawn. Members thus seek to maximize the value of their membership in dollar terms in the long-term. It is clear that members are very interested in other benefits such as privacy, the quality of the playing surface, and exclusive dining facilities, which are distinct from economic net benefit. Does this mean, however, that the primary net economic benefit objective must be supplemented by other non-monetary performance measures? The Balanced Scorecard approach would include such broader evidence as essential but intermediate to the pursuit of the maximization of net economic benefit. The additional components of performance noted above could all be subsumed under the customer perspective of the Balanced Scorecard, and, in chronological and causal integration with performance in internal business processes (such as cost of operations) and innovation and learning (such as staff training and satisfaction) defined as components of a model of organizational performance focused on the maximization of long-term net economic benefit. Even a seeming constraint such as preferred prices for youth members may be interpreted as instrumental in promoting long-term membership growth and therefore long-term profit and ownership equity. So the Balanced Scorecard illustrated in Figure 11.1, or perhaps the modified version in Figure 11.2 which includes constraints, can serve as an approach to strategic management and performance measurement in membership non-profit organizations; net economic benefit is equivalent or directly analogous to profit.

## V The Balanced Scorecard in other non-profit organizations

### Introduction

The situation becomes more complex where customers and funders are separated. This is true of tax-funded services provided by public departments and institutions and services provided by charitable private non-profit organizations which are funded exclusively by donations, exclusively by public subvention (from general tax revenue), or, most commonly, by some combination of these two sources. Public or private non-profit services funded exclusively from general tax revenue can be broadly divided into two groups: first, those in which the primary objective is the provision of a defined quantity and quality of a non-profit service of some kind, in areas such as transportation and education, but which may also have some redistributive effects (intended or unintended); and, second, those in which the primary objective is redistributive, such as cash transfers to defined groups of eligible recipients, but which may also have some effects (intended or unintended) on private economic behaviour and other non-profit services. These are treated in turn – the former in more detail reflecting the wide variety of publicly financed non-profit services – and are followed by a discussion of services provided by private, donation-funded, charitable non-profit organizations.

### Non-redistributive services

For all non-redistributive services funded from general public tax revenue and provided without charge or at a nominal charge it can still be argued that their implicit primary objective is the maximization of long-term net benefit (the 'value' of long-term gross benefits minus the value of long-term costs) from the perspective of the public at large – who are the 'shareholders' of public organizations. The cost side can certainly be calculated in terms of dollars; the public shareholders are also taxpayers and have an obvious interest in the resources used to provide public services. But what about the benefit side? In principle, the public as voters (and taxpayers) who vote (in the majority) to initiate or continue a public service can be seen as expressing implicitly through the political process the view that the imputed or inferred dollar value of the service exceeds its costs, and can also reasonably be assumed to favour the maximization of that difference over time. But the political process provides at best a general implicit message on willingness to pay, or, more strictly, willingness to be coerced by taxation. From the point of view of the public policy analyst charged with providing administrative information for accountability purposes on the benefits side of the equation for a specific programme, the appropriate conceptualization and definition of primary focus or long-term objective depends on the type of public organization and service. Non-redistributive services can be classified along a continuum from those in which benefits are clearly separable and external effects trivial, to classic public goods in which benefits are not separable and all benefits are, in effect, external. The spectrum of cases is dealt with below.

#### Services with clearly separable benefits

Consider first those services provided more or less exclusively by public non-profit organizations – in such areas as health, education, transportation, social services, recreation, housing, cultural services, and administrative services – where, for at least the major part, the benefits derived from the service are separable (i.e. where beneficiaries can be identified and excluded), where external effects are trivial, and where, as a consequence, it would be possible to obtain a measure of willingness to pay through user pricing. Even if user pricing is not to be used in financing such services, it would be possible experimentally to determine willingness to pay for various levels of service and thus to estimate directly their dollar value. In this case, the appropriate primary long-term objective is the maximization of net social benefit, where both costs and benefits are defined in dollar terms, the latter determined (and monitored) experimentally where the service is funded entirely or primarily from general tax revenue. As for public commercial organizations, other objectives which are complementary to the primary objective serve to support that primary focus, and other objectives which are specified as constraints on net benefit maximization should be explicitly costed and incorporated in the primary objective as a formal limitation or identified as an explicit subsidy within the primary objective. An obvious example of a constraint would be a geographic redistributive constraint that obliged those who provide the service to provide the service in remote areas. On the public balance sheet, the long-term objective of social benefit maximization serves to maximize social or public equity, or net wealth, in the service; the analogy with private wealth is direct, although current public sector accounting practices would have to be revised to incorporate the 'flow' effects on revenue and expense statements (ironically, current practice acknowledges only the expense side!) and the 'stock' effects on statements of financial condition. Given necessary adjustments to accounting practice, the Balanced Scorecard approach shown in Figure 11.2 would serve as an appropriate model of planning and reporting in services with clearly separable benefits.

## Merit goods

Moving along the continuum, consider the case of so-called 'merit goods' – where benefits are separable and beneficiaries are excludable, but where external benefits, which cannot be determined directly, in practice, or experimentally, by revealed consumer demand, are considered significant. For such services, as a whole or with respect only to the valuation of external effects – which exercise would, in effect, serve to increase (or decrease) revealed demand – willingness to pay could be determined not directly but by imputation through cost-benefit analysis. In such cases, appropriate adjustments could be made to market-revealed prices relevant to the analysis, and external effects (benefits as well as costs) which are not revealed in market transactions included. As for services with separable benefits and trivial external effects, the primary objective could still, in principle, remain the maximization of long-term social benefit (and therefore shareholder equity in the service), where both costs and benefits are defined in dollar terms, including information obtained practically or experimentally on direct consumer valuation, and information on external benefits and costs obtained indirectly through cost-benefit analysis. All other complementary objectives would support, that is, be instrumental in the attainment of, this long-term objective, and any constraints would be valued in dollar terms and incorporated in or associated with the long-term objective as a specific limitation or as an explicit subsidy. On the balance sheet, the maximization of net social benefit serves to maximize social equity in the service; of course, the revision to public sector accounting practices for both flows and stocks would have to be even more heroic than in the previous case. Given such adjustments, the Balanced Scorecard could again serve as the appropriate model for planning and reporting. It is, however, clear that by this point on the spectrum the analogy with profit – and therefore the applicability of the original Balanced Scorecard – is becoming somewhat contrived, certainly in practice if not in theory. An alternative approach will be discussed in the context of the pure public goods case at the end of the spectrum.

## Classic public goods

The classic public goods case poses much greater difficulties with respect to demand revelation and therefore output valuation – it is always possible to tell in dollar terms what services cost! Services of this kind include defence, public health, external relations, and justice. Their nature is that benefits cannot be separated and beneficiaries cannot be excluded. There is therefore no incentive to reveal demand – indeed there is an incentive to conceal demand where any such revelation would be construed as measuring willingness to pay. All benefits are external, and are enjoyed uniformly by each individual. The general argument holds that, implicitly, the political decision to supply the service implies a decision that the 'value' of the service exceeds its cost, but this is not very helpful to the analyst charged with the development of accountability information, either prospectively or retrospectively. Although theoretical approaches have been suggested for determining demand for public goods,[8] a more practical approach to defining a primary objective in such cases would probably be to argue that the benefit side now needs to be operationally defined in non-dollar terms such as programme quality, and that the primary objective then be the maximization of long-term service effectiveness for a given budget (or cost) constraint, or the converse: the minimization of costs for the attainment of a specified minimum effectiveness level. The former is the more likely configuration, and the one that will be pursued in this argument. It is important to emphasize that optimization using cost-effectiveness as distinct from cost-benefit implies the use of two incommensurable variables (one in dollars, the other in some measure of service effectiveness), and therefore the optimization of *one* of the two variables for a specified level of the other. In specifying the objective in this way, the analyst still serves the public as shareholder by attending to tax costs. Arguably the analyst also serves the public generally by attending to the effectiveness of the publicly financed programme. Other complementary objectives are secondary to and instrumental in the attainment of the primary focus on long-term effectiveness for a given budget. Any constraints on the attainment of the service objective – as distinct from the budget constraint – must be explicitly specified and their effects on the primary objective – increased cost and/or reduced effectiveness – explicitly incorporated in the statement of the primary objective which is the basis for accountability measurement and reporting.

Although conceptually it is possible to argue that the maximization of long-term effectiveness for a given budget serves to maximize social equity in the service, in practice the analyst may have practical difficulty in accumulating 'bits' of effectiveness; the extent of the change in the (measurable) long-term strategic objective over the life of the programme could, defensibly, be taken to represent the accumulated 'effectiveness equity' in the programme. At the very least, the analyst can demonstrate the long-term budget costs (constraints) of the programme and the associated long-term evidence on effectiveness. The link of cost-effectiveness to the traditional balance sheet defined in dollar terms is obviously tenuous; perhaps there is room for some creativity in designing the equivalent of a balance sheet for accumulated cost-effectiveness information – but the current state-of-the-art makes this of theoretical rather than immediate practical interest. Two other qualifications to the cost-effectiveness argument may be useful.

First, the analyst must remember that those who fund such services are different from those who consume them – this is the primary distinction between public departments and institutions and charitable non-profit organizations, on the one hand, and commercial organizations and membership non-profit organizations, on the other. Further, it has been argued that for services at the public goods end of the continuum, there are no practical ways – direct or indirect – of determining willingness to pay and therefore valuing services in dollar terms. How then can the interests of the specific client group for the service, say, the frail elderly or children with reading deficiencies, be considered in determining the appropriateness of the effectiveness level (*not* the appropriateness of cost since these clients do not pay)? At the very least, it seems reasonable to postulate that the interests of specific non-paying clients are part of the equation, and that in the definition of the primary effectiveness objective, the appropriate level of effectiveness reflect an explicitly or implicitly negotiated compromise between what the taxpaying public wants (or is willing to pay for) and what specific clients want. By analogy with the Balanced Scorecard, other performance information is necessary but only in so far as it serves the long-term primary objective of service cost-effectiveness.

Second, the 'neatness' of this proposed cost-effectiveness analogy to cost-benefit and commercial profit is challenged, of course, by the difficulty of defining one over-arching measure of effectiveness that would be served and supported by other objectives. The simpler solution would, of course, be to settle for a satisficing rather than an optimizing decision criterion (prospective or retrospective) but it is worth pursuing the more rigorous concept of optimization. The concept of optimization does require a single focus – only one thing can be maximized – but it can also be argued that this particular thing may have to be a carefully defined composite of several aspects of effectiveness. For instance, quality of care could be defined as a single measure, but a single (more complex) measure derived from a composite (using the same scale of measurement) of measures of, say, attainment of the direct medical objective, recurrence rate, and complication rate. This approach is widely used in the health field where the composite measure is defined as 'utility' rather than effectiveness, and the analytical perspective correspondingly defined as cost-utility rather than cost-effectiveness.[9] Where constraints are specified which are in conflict with effectiveness (or utility), the approach suggested above for public commercial organizations could be used. Effectiveness (or utility) which is to be maximized for a given budget would then be defined as a single primary performance indicator subject to a set of constraints or limitations, reflecting target levels (floors) in an associated set of objectives which are defined as constraints on the attainment of the primary objective; it is worth repeating that if these additional considerations were complementary to rather than in conflict with the attainment of the primary objective, they would be defined (and measured and reported) in the causal logic model as instrumental in the pursuit of the primary objective. This all makes life more complicated, of course, but the central argument still holds that a focused, and therefore operationally helpful, approach must be taken to the 'value' side of value for money, if the analyst is to get beyond simply expressing descriptively a set of indicators (corresponding to a set of objectives).

The Balanced Scorecard illustrated in Figure 11.1, or in modified form in Figure 11.2, is not practically useful for goods and services that lie towards the pure public goods end of the spectrum (including all public goods and services where external effects can be shown to be significant) since its unifying long-term objective is profit or its equivalent. But the obvious question is whether the Balanced Scorecard concept can be adapted to such goods and services. Kaplan and Norton do treat non-profit organizations briefly,[10] but do not work through the formal adaptation of their model. An adaptation is suggested in Figure 11.3 following brief discussion of two other categories of non-profit services which require similar adaptation: public redistributive services; and services provided by private charitable non-profit organizations.

## Public redistributive services

The argument for services that fall into the public goods end of the continuum applies directly to purely redistributive services, such as cash transfers. The primary objective in such cases could be determined as the maximization of long-term effectiveness where effectiveness is defined in relation to the specifically defined redistributive target – say, bringing a target population up to a defined absolute income level – and cost is, as always, defined in terms of the budget constraint – the dollars *available* to achieve this target. Note that 'available' does not equal 'necessary'; the cost-effectiveness criterion here could be stated in terms of minimizing the budget *necessary* to achieve the prescribed effectiveness target. Minimizing cost is a non-trivial matter: many redistributive programmes are administratively costly and/or are poorly targeted and therefore wasteful. Returning to the standard formulation of cost-effectiveness or cost-utility (maximize effectiveness or utility for a given budget), other complementary objectives – say, relating to family stability – and constraints – say, excluding certain age categories of beneficiary – could be treated as suggested above, retaining the focused clarity of one over-arching primary objective.

### Charitable non-profit services

Services provided by charitable non-profit organizations fall in between those provided by membership non-profit organizations and those provided by government departments at the public goods/redistributive services end of the continuum. They are set up privately in order not to serve members but to serve a defined client group, say, persons suffering from multiple sclerosis. The members will help to fund the organization by membership fees and donations, but this funding will be supplemented by a variety of other private and government sources. Direct benefits will be enjoyed by defined clients – who do not pay or do not pay enough to cover costs – and indirect benefits by members who resemble supportive taxpayers in the case of public services. While in formal conceptual terms the primary or over-arching objective could be stated in traditional Balanced Scorecard terms as the maximization of long-term net benefits (the imputed dollar value of services minus long-term expenses), in operational terms the over-arching objective would be to maximize long-term service effectiveness for a given budget constraint, where members and funders are served by attention to the cost side, and the appropriate level of effectiveness reflects an explicitly or implicitly negotiated compromise between the interests of clients served directly by the programme and the various groups of funders, including members. As in the other categories, additional bits of performance information are needed, but only in so far as they sustain the primary objective. As for public services at the cost-effectiveness end of the spectrum, the concept of owners' equity can be considered in conceptual terms, but is difficult to define operationally other than in terms of accumulated improvement over time in the designated measure of effectiveness. The difficulty of defining effectiveness in a single measure also obtains here, but probably less severely than for public non-profit programmes; charitable non-profit organizations are often quite focused around a central long-term objective. In any event, the problem could be addressed as in public non-profit programmes by defining utility as a composite measure of effectiveness.

### An adapted Balanced Scorecard

It has been argued that for certain categories of non-profit organization – specifically, those providing public services in which external effects are significant, public redistributive services, and private charitable services – the traditional Balanced Scorecard must be adapted to the reality of cost-effectiveness rather than profit or its equivalent. Figure 11.3 suggests an approach to such adaptation.

The Strategic Context generates as a function of governance the mission of the organization and from that mission a single, focused long-term strategic objective, defined in terms of long-term service effectiveness or utility, which is to be maximized for a given set of budget constraints over time. Obviously, the governance exercise here also includes the determination of feasible revenue constraints over time, and probably also – although the matter is not formally incorporated into Figure 11.3 – the determination of strategy and the allocation of budget to the matter of fund-raising (revenue maximization over time). The articulation of an operational long-term strategic objective, that is, one for which valid and reliable performance evidence can be gathered and analysed, is challenging – Hodgkinson notes that 'true purpose is rarely enunciated . . . [and that for an easier life!] the administrator colludes in this'[11] – but is a necessary condition for the transformation of a smorgasbord of performance information into a focused, chronologically and causally linked, model of organizational performance and a basis for serving accountability across the governance and management cycle – from strategic planning through budgeting and monitoring to reporting and evaluation. In Figure 11.3, the long-term objective of profit maximization is replaced by long-term service effectiveness or utility maximization for a specified revenue target or constraint. The broken-line box within the strategic context incorporates the possibility of the specification, as part of the accountability terms of reference, of target performance levels in other objectives which are constraints on the pursuit of the primary objective.

Governance control sets the context for management control. Intermediate evidence on service effectiveness performance (as distinct from short-run profit) is provided as part of the set of information – the Balanced Scorecard – needed for decision-making by both managers and board members – the former for day-to-day management control, the latter for control of progress toward the polestar of the long-term strategic objective. The other components of that Scorecard include information from the other three perspectives in the Balanced Scorecard – customer, internal business processes, and innovation and learning – and two further dimensions. The first, Financial Results, is defined separately from the second (Revenue Constraint Results, defined below as a constraint) to include revenue results drawn from that second component but also evidence on financial expenditure which will serve, together with revenue information,

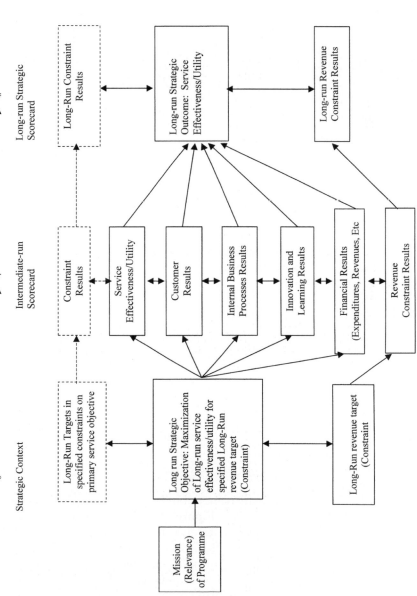

*Figure 11.3*
The Balanced Scorecard (public and private non-profit organizations).

as a means of providing procedural accountability information in the form of financial statements, and independently as a means of generating programme cost information. Careful attention to resource utilization is clearly relevant to service effectiveness maximization – getting as much as possible from a limited budget. These various components are then integrated chronologically and causally in a logic model which is implied, but not specified in Figure 11.3, geared to the achievement of the long-term service effectiveness objective. The intermediate results on service effectiveness are intermediate evidence on the desired long-term strategic outcome; the other components are all instrumental, in a defined model, in the pursuit of that outcome. The broken-line box shows intermediate results in the other, non-revenue, constraints.

The Revenue Constraint Results are, of course, an integral part of ongoing (intermediate and long-term) evidence, but evidence of a constraint or limitation on performance rather than performance itself (abstracting from fund-raising performance). The long-term 'bottom-line' equivalent to long-term profit is long-term service effectiveness or utility for a given long-term budget constraint. This optimization criterion for the determination of strategy or the assessment of results becomes a constrained optimization criterion where constraints on the pursuit of the primary objective, other than the fundamental revenue constraint, are specified.

## VI An alternative Balanced Scorecard using the CCAF/FCVI attributes

The CCAF/FCVI set of attributes represents a uniquely Canadian approach to multiple-component performance reporting, and this final section of the chapter considers briefly whether that framework could be used as an alternative Balanced Scorecard for non-profit organizations in which the long-term objective cannot be operationally defined in terms of profit or its equivalent.

The CCAF/FCVI framework includes the 12 attributes of effectiveness defined and discussed in some detail in the previous chapter. Figure 11.4 suggests one approach to incorporating the CCAF/FCVI attributes in a Balanced Scorecard framework which would serve not only as a basis for reporting but also as basis for planning and budgeting, in short, as a basis of both governance and management control across the cycle of organizational activities.

Three of the 12 attributes (which are in bold face) are incorporated in what is defined as the Strategic Context in Figure 11.4: Relevance is defined as the basis of the organizational mission statement, and Management Direction defined to require the translation of the mission into a single strategic service effectiveness objective which is to be maximized subject to the long-term revenue constraint. The possibility of constraints other than the fundamental revenue constraint is shown in the broken-line box. Appropriateness is also

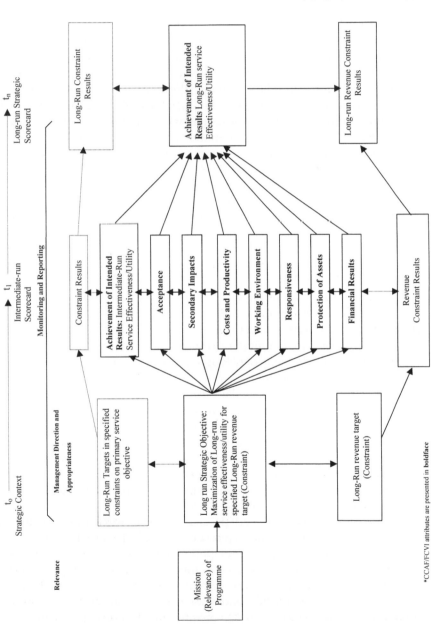

*Figure 11.4* The CCAF/FCVI * framework: a Balanced Scorecard for non-profit organizations (public and private non-profit organizations).

The following text appears within the figure:

Relevance

Strategic Context

t_o ———— t_l ———— t_n

Management Direction and Appropriateness

Monitoring and Reporting

Intermediate-run Scorecard    Long-run Strategic Scorecard

Long-Run Constraint Results

Achievement of Intended Results Long-Run service Effectiveness/Utility

Long-run Revenue Constraint Results

Constraint Results

Achievement of Intended Results: Intermediate-Run Service Effectiveness/Utility

Acceptance

Secondary Impacts

Costs and Productivity

Working Environment

Responsiveness

Protection of Assets

Financial Results

Revenue Constraint Results

Long-Run Targets in specified constraints on primary service objective

Long run Strategic Objective: Maximization of Long-run service effectiveness/utility for specified Long-Run revenue target (Constraint)

Long-Run revenue target (Constraint)

Mission (Relevance) of Programme

*CCAF/FCVI attributes are presented in **boldface**

included under Management Direction, and requires the strategic specification of programme designs – the means to pursue the strategic end defined
in the long-term service effectiveness objective.

The Monitoring and Reporting attribute is defined in an over-arching
way in Figure 11.4 as the management system through which intermediate and long-term performance is monitored and reported.

The intermediate-run Scorecard in Figure 11.4 incorporates the remaining eight CCAF/FCVI attributes in a variation of the traditional Balanced
Scorecard. First, intermediate-run evidence on the Achievement of Intended Results is defined to give evidence of intermediate-run achievement of
service effectiveness or utility. The other components, Acceptance, Secondary Impacts, Costs and Productivity, Working Environment, Responsiveness, Protection of Assets, and Financial Results, are all defined as
instrumental components of performance, which, in an integrated, chronologically and causally linked logic model of organizational performance,
serve the achievement of the long-term service effectiveness for the given
budget constraint. There would be objectives and strategies for each of these
components, but their outcomes would not be ends in themselves, but
means to the single long-term strategic end.

There are obvious parallels with the traditional Balanced Scorecard.
Acceptance parallels the customer perspective; Costs and Productivity
parallels the internal business processes perspective; and Working
Environment and Responsiveness parallel the innovation and learning
perspective. What is interesting is the Balanced Scorecard perspective
through which these various pieces of intermediate-run evidence on performance – with the exception of the intermediate-run evidence on the
achievement of the service effectiveness objective – are not ends in themselves but parts of a logic model of organizational performance designed
to maximize the single focus of a long-term service effectiveness objective
for a given budget constraint.

As in Figure 11.3, the intermediate-run Scorecard includes evidence on
progress in meeting the long-term revenue objective which serves as a
constraint on the pursuit of the long-term service objective. Intermediate
performance in the non-revenue constraints is shown in the broken-line box.

The final component of the model in Figure 11.4 shows information on
long-term strategic performance – Achievement of Intended Results in the
long-term showing long-term service effectiveness or utility, achieved for
the long-term revenue constraint result.

Although chronology is specified, the causal logic model is implicit in Figure
11.4. Figure 11.5 illustrates one step towards a formal causal logic model by
incorporating some of the ideas developed about the CCAF/FCVI attributes
in Chapter 10. A distinction is drawn in Figure 11.5 between support activities and operating results, and the extended set of attributes developed in
the previous chapter illustrated under each head. The set of four support
activities shown in Figure 11.5 (Monitoring and Reporting remains as an

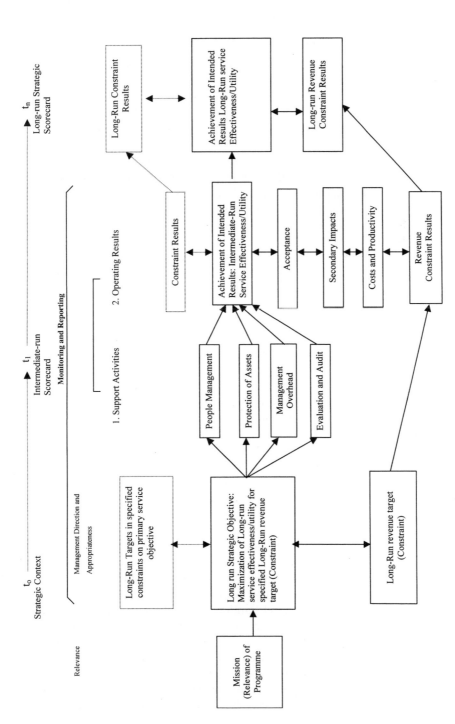

*Figure 11.5* The CCAF/FCVI framework: a Balanced Scorecard for non-profit organizations: development towards a formal causal logic model.

over-arching management system relevant to the whole management cycle) include People Management, Protection of Assets, Management Overhead, and Evaluation and Audit. These activities are seen, quite literally, as supporting or making possible the actual results achieved. Under operating results, the causal model by which the Acceptance, Secondary Impacts, Quality, and Costs and Productivity attributes support or make possible the maximization of long-term service effectiveness or utility, remains implicit.

## VII  Conclusion

It is generally accepted that a sufficient and appropriate definition of performance in non-profit organizations requires multiple components. The argument of this chapter is that such a multiple-component definition of performance is much more useful if it can serve not only as a basis of performance reporting but also as a basis of governance and management control over the cycle of organizational activities. The Balanced Scorecard developed for commercial organizations offered one useful way of transforming a performance reporting framework into a strategic management framework, and can be adapted directly for use in public sector commercial organizations and private non-profit memberships organizations, and, with more creativity, for public and private non-profit organizations. This same Balanced Scorecard approach can be used to broaden the applicability of the CCAF/FCVI set of effectiveness attributes from a method of reporting to a framework for strategic management. The argument has been developed at the major function or programme level; the next stage would be aggregation to the organizational level.

The articulation of an operational long-term strategic objective is easier said than done. But what does seem clear is that a long list of objectives and performance indicators only becomes operationally useful as a tool of strategic management if a clear focus is defined, and a logic model of performance constructed to achieve that focus. It is also interesting to note the crucial role of governance control as a context for the more conventional management control, and to reflect on the incentive provided by the proposed approach to pursue integration and complementarity, rather than conflict, among objectives and outcomes. It is intuitively obvious that satisfied clients are an essential building block in long-term service effectiveness; this approach forces the articulation of such links.

Management and board members in the agencies in the research project in Toronto and Victoria reacted cautiously but favourably to the argument of this chapter. There was, of course, considerable unease about the generation of an over-arching strategic objective, but at the same time an intuitive grasp that focus was necessary if clear 'marching orders', that is, clear understanding about common currency and criteria, were to be given, and, further, that such a focus could greatly strengthen performance reporting and success in competitive fund-raising.

The work also generated an interesting debate about the difference between the optimizing and satisficing decision criteria. When we were able to move the debate from mathematics to common sense or practicality, there was broad agreement that optimization, even in its constrained variant, presented a clearer basis for prospective decisions on whether to proceed with a programme and retrospective decisions on the success of a programme. In short, the optimization of cost-effectiveness or cost-utility was considered a more tractable surrogate for profit, a better basis for performance accountability, than the more loosely defined satisficing alternative.

The matter of focus also helped to bring some resolution to the discussion in the agencies about generating evidence on outcomes. Agency management, in particular, had expressed reservations about conceptualizing and measuring evidence on outcomes for a broad range of performance measures; their argument was that the costs of this exercise might simply exceed the benefits. Our argument was that work on outcomes should be done only to the point where benefits exceeded costs, and that the best way to ensure this would be to concentrate on conceptualizing and measuring outcome evidence – which, by definition, is intermediate- and long-term evidence – relevant to the components of the optimization or constrained optimization strategic decision criterion; in short, to concentrate on what is most important.

So we reached the point at this stage in the project where we had illustrated to the agencies the feasibility and usefulness of generating accountability information which would make possible direct comparison of programmes with commensurable cost-effectiveness or cost-utility decision criteria. For instance, two competitive programmes both geared to optimizing cost-utility, where utility was defined, say, as a composite indicator dealing with youth education and job training, could be directly compared using commensurable technical evidence at the prospective and retrospective stages of the cycle. But the agencies were quick, and right, to point out to us that we had not taken them to the next stage. What did we have to say about comparing programmes with incommensurable performance measures, where the effectiveness or utility measure of programme 1 was different from, and incommensurable with, that of programme 2? Was this the point at which administrative rationality using technical evidence had to be abandoned, presumably leaving the field to political rationality? Or could we offer any suggestions about this next, and inevitable, stage? To this matter we turned out attention in the final stage of the project.

## Notes

1 CCAF/FCVI, *Comprehensive Auditing: An Introduction* (Ottawa, CCAF/FCVI, 1994).

2 Canadian Institute of Chartered Accountants, Public Sector Accounting and Auditing Committee, *Value-for-Money Auditing Standards* (Toronto, CICA, 1988).

3 8. G. LeClerc, et al, *Accountability, Performance Reporting, and Comprehensive Audit: An Integrated Perspective* (Ottawa, CCAF/FCVI, 1996).

4 Auditor General of British Columbia and Deputy Ministers' Committee, *Enhancing Accountability for Performance: A Framework and an Implementation Plan* (Victoria, BC, Office of the Auditor General, April 1996).

5 R.S. Kaplan and D.P. Norton, *The Balanced Scorecard* (Cambridge, Mass., Harvard Business School Press, 1996).

6 Kaplan and Norton, *Balanced Scorecard*, 160, 240–1.

7 H.A. Simon, *Administrative Behaviour*, 3rd edn (New York, Macmillan, 1976), 38–41.

8 E.H. Clarke, 'Multipart pricing of public goods: an example', in S. Mushkin (ed.) *Public Prices for Public Products* (Washington, The Urban Institute, 1972), 125–30.
  T.N. Tideman, ed., Special Supplement to *Public Choice*, 29: 2, Spring 1977.

9 Ministry of Health, Government of British Columbia, *Health Services Outcome Reporting* (Victoria, BC, Ministry of Health, 1996).

10 Kaplan and Norton, *Balanced Scorecard*, 179–88.

11 C. Hodgkinson, *Administrative Philosophy* (New York, Elsevier Science Inc., 1996), 182.

# 12 The Value Sieve

## Accountable choices among incommensurable programmes

*Christopher Corbett*

## I Introduction

The development and utilization of commensurable measurement scales is driven by the desire of decision-makers to compare apples with apples. Comparable measures serve the need to understand the resources required to achieve an output or an outcome and hence value for money. Commensurability rests at the heart of efficiency and effectiveness measures and ensures that discussion regarding different approaches to achieve the same outcome can be accomplished in a technical and unemotional assessment which utilizes the full benefit of a rational, objective approach. When such a scale is available an accountable decision-maker (agent) may use the scale to select from among the available alternatives and to defend their choice to their supervisor(s) (principal).

However, in practice decision-makers are often faced with incommensurable measures and are still required to make choices to optimize the expected utility created by their allocation of scarce resources. The Value Sieve,[1] is a resource allocation methodology developed to assist managers and administrators of organizations who must make choices using incommensurable, apples vs. oranges, measures. Further the Value Sieve creates both procedural and consequential accountabilities to better manage the problems which are associated with decision-making under conditions of complexity, risk, ambiguity and ignorance.[2]

## II The problems of non-commensurability

At its core, commensurability encompasses traditional measurement validity and reliability concerns. Validity issues ask if the variable measured is indeed a reasonable representation of the dimension of interest within the applied setting. Reliability asks if the measure of a variable can be taken consistently. While validity and reliability are most commonly associated with experimental procedures they must also be considered within the context of quasi-experimental procedures and programme evaluation.[3]

The rigour of experimental process is often unobtainable within an applied setting. This fact will surely frustrate those individuals who wish

to ensure their programmes are fully supported by experimentally validated outcome measures. However, this difficulty should not be used to
support the argument that measurement is too difficult to use in organizations. Given the organization has a purpose, there must be an information
system which provides the essential feedback to the decision-makers and
indicates the organization is (or is not) moving in the prescribed direction.
Without such an information system there can be no meaningful,
purposeful action. While an information (feedback) system is a requirement for the goal-directed action of an organization, highly detailed
measurement systems may not be.

For example: Organization A teaches children to swim and measures
their swimming proficiency with a general test. The test indicates success
or failure on a number of variables and results in an overall pass or fail
for each swimmer. While more detailed and stringent tests and testing
conditions are possible, the general test meets the Organization A admin-
istrative/management requirements. Organization B also teaches children
to swim and tests the children's ability to meet specified competencies in
a similar but not identical method to Organization A. Both Organization
A and Organization B publish a list of children they have taught to swim.
Questions raised by the example include the following.

- Given differences in measurement between Organization A and
  Organization B, is the measurement 'children taught to swim' commensurable?
- To what extent should the organizations invest scarce resources to
  ensure that their measures of swimming competencies are commensurable?
- Under what circumstance can we envision the organizations individually or collectively investing in measurement improvements?
- What prevents any measurement system of 'children taught to swim'
  developed today from being refined to a more descriptive and specific
  representation in the future?
- How should accountability be allocated in relation to choice of
  measurement?

The purpose of the example is to suggest that while the desire to develop
perfection[4] in measurement is laudable, the conditions necessary for measurement perfection are not necessarily cost-effective or certain to improve
decision-making. Further, the notion of commensurability is in many cases
an arbitrary agreement about the level of detail/differentiation required by
the decision-maker. The compass of the information can only be determined when the purpose(s) of the decision-maker(s) is/are made clear.
Therefore in the applied settings of organizations, our challenge is to
develop decision systems which: utilize the information available; simplify
arguments where appropriate; avoid measurement dysfunction; point to

practical improvements in the activities of the organization (this can include measurement improvements); identify those activities which together maximize the outcomes of the organization given the resources available to the organization are limited; and ensure that those accountable for various aspects of performance understand and accept their accountability.

## Multiple measures and non-commensurability

For most decision-makers the desire to create a single commensurable measure with which to compare possible actions/programmes is very great. The benefit of a valid and reliable measure is that the measurements themselves, when reported on the scale, provide the decision-maker with a defensible, de facto course of action. Under this condition the accountable decision-maker is protected from error by the measurement system.

In most cases applied programme measurement will include more than one variable of interest and as a consequence multivariate techniques will be required to develop an equation which predicts a single commensurate dependent variable. Without the proper use of multivariate techniques great caution is required when decision-makers decide to 'prescribe a procedure' to aggregate the measures of individual variables. In all cases it is impossible to know whether the combinatorial of the model created provides anything more than a veil of rigour. It is better to provide the quantitative and qualitative information to the decision-makers without the addition of questionable combinatorial metrics. In previous chapters it has been argued that clarity in accountability relationships requires that multiple performance measures be focused through programme logic modules on one strategic outcome measure to be optimized for a given budget. It is also noted, however, that decision-makers are still faced with choices using incommensurable strategic outcomes, e.g. juvenile crime rates and quality of care for the elderly.

The consequence of this is that the decision-making process must facilitate decision-making using current incommensurable information and must accept that the objective function will be measured subjectively in terms of expected utility for the resources available. In other words, expected utility will be based upon the values/assessment of the decision-maker(s).

## Decision-making vs. problem solving

It should be recognized that when confronted with a choice, many individual decision-makers begin to direct their attention to solving the problem that is the subject of the choice instead of making a decision. Whatever the reason for this, it is important to realize that decision-makers confronted with difficult choices will tend to procrastinate and seek measurement tools which will assist them in deciding what to do. This is a problem if the decision-making process is time sensitive and/or the problem is too complex to resolve.

### Hierarchy, specialization, supervision and measurement dysfunction

Organizations develop hierarchies to better manage the variety of specialized activities which take place within and between themselves and organizations beyond their boundaries. The result of specialization is differentiation of the processes within the organization and consequently the utilization and development of specialized knowledge. A consequence of this specialization is that a principal does not necessarily understand the measures or the justifications used by an agent. In these circumstances the desire to aggregate information to develop a commensurable measure which can be used by the principal, e.g. an external funder, for decision-making may lose essential information needed for decision-making by the agent.

The goal of commensurability is to ease the difficulty of decision-making by establishing appropriate metrics. However, if the goal of commensurability is poorly managed it can result in principals reducing the significance of all of the information required by the agent alone to only the information required by the principal. The disparity of information between the principal and the agent is the central theme of measurement dysfunction. This is an important issue in relation to accountability because it suggests that a failure to understand the information relationship between principal and agent and their respective decision-making responsibilities can result in perverse/unintended organization outcomes. An accountable decision-maker must accept the distinction between control based upon the power of their office, and control based upon the power of information or knowledge.

### Politics, facts and judgement

When selecting a course of action decision-makers should be capable of substantiating their choices in such a way as to make distinctions between decisions based upon information (measures ) and decisions made based upon power of position (judgement). In practice we know that decisions based upon multiple measures will likely require the use of judgement by the decision-maker and hence it will be value-based. In other words the information provided is interpreted by the decision-maker(s) and they use their personal understanding of the circumstances and their best judgement to determine a best course of action. The use of personal insight and judgement is necessary in multiple variable and incommensurable decision-making and this fact places a special burden for accountability upon the decision-maker.

The special burden requires the justification of one choice versus another without the benefit of a clear measure which represents 'better' from all possible perspectives. In this regard there is very little difference between technical judgement[5] and personal politics. Both require the decision-maker to use a personal heuristic or value-based reckoning to result in a choice. The values of others may be quite different from the values of the accountable decision-maker(s) and as a consequence it is probable that debate about the elements of the heuristic will result in delaying problem-solving behaviour instead of decision-making.

However, the notion of judgement and related individual differences in technical judgement is taken to the extreme within the notion of pure politics. Pure politics can be argued as the use of position and power to make choices which prioritize personal ambition and directly or indirectly provide benefit. This frustrates the stated goal of using the available resources to maximize expected utility for the specified objective function. The negative use of pure politics is using the power of position to spend the expected utility intended for the stated objective function on an alternative, undisclosed objective function. For example, a decision-maker chooses an option preferred by an important board member or senior manager (even though the decision-maker knows the choice will have negative consequences for the enterprise) in order to curry favour.

Figure 12.1 shows technical certainty on the $y$ axis and judgement required on the $x$ axis. Technical certainty is highest when there is a single objective measure of outcome which is accepted by all participants. As more measures are used the problem becomes less technically certain as the relationship between the measures and the outcomes becomes more complex. Judgement required is highest when personal values and heuristics must be used to make decisions and lowest when empirically based decision-making is possible. The dotted line on the graph shows the concept of commensurability. Commensurability is highest when there is an agreed single measure with technical certainty which supports an empirically based judgement for decision-making. At the other end of commensurability is the point where many measures of quantitative and qualitative information require the decision-maker to use personal heuristics and values to determine the preferred choice. This is because even though some of the measures used to compare one programme with another may be the same (commensurable) the full description of the outputs and outcomes generated by the programme are not. Therefore, even though the independent variables used to describe the resources required to produce the output and outcomes may be the same (commensurable) it is unlikely that they will be identical quantities (commensurate).

Figure 12.1 shows an X on the graph of commensurability because in applied settings most choices are based upon the evaluation of multiple quantitative and qualitative measures for which there is no technically certain method of choosing and so requires the decision-maker to use

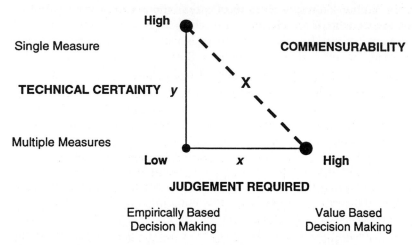

*Figure 12.1* Commensurability – the relationship between technical certainty and judgement required.

personal values in arriving at a conclusion. When technical certainty is high the decision-maker will rely more upon empirically based judgement than personal values. However, it must be acknowledged that the decisions which require no personal values or heuristics from the decision-maker occur at only a single point on the graph. These decisions are so clearly supported by technical information it is unlikely that the decision-maker would realize that they had made a decision at all. This being the case, the accountable decision-maker in an applied setting will most frequently expend their energies in comparing and then choosing among alternatives which require the use of personal values to balance incommensurable measures of alternative actions.

Individual differences are likely, given the required use of individual heuristics. The outcome of this will be that multiple decision-makers should be expected to have their interpretations vary around a mean. This does not suggest the difference will be insignificant among a small group of decision-makers who may represent broad differences of opinion and personal heuristics. Therefore it should be expected that disagreements will most frequently take place when technical information is low and judgement is high; when there is discrepancy in the knowledge required to utilize the information available; and when pure politics and power are used to direct resources to create personal benefit in the face of better options.

# III The Value Sieve – decision-making among incommensurable actions

## *Overview*

The Value Sieve is a 'choice'[6] prioritization process which results in a decision-maker choosing among alternative programmes in order to maximize an objective function for which they are accountable. Optimization is based upon the decision-maker's estimate of the expected utility of each programme's contribution towards the objective function, in relation to resources required. Expected utility is a composite measure of the expected outputs and outcomes of the component parts of the objective function. This ratio of expected utility to resources required is defined as *Value for Money* (VfM) (see Figure 12.2). Given the measures for each programme are not commensurable the expected utility of one programme vs. another is determined through direct comparison of the available choices by the decision-maker. The result is an ordinal scaling based upon the VfM of each of the choices available to the decision-maker. The ordinal scaling of the VfM of the choices provides the highest expected utility for a given total resource budget. From a resource allocation perspective this allows an opportunity for an existing budget to be optimized based upon VfM or a new budget to be estimated based upon what the decision-makers believe must be accomplished.

The heart of the Value Sieve methodology is the systematic use of information within a consistent accountability structure. This is essential for the coordination of information feedback so that the programmes of the organization can be adjusted to better meet their individual and collective organizational goals and objectives. The Value Sieve maintains the following fundamentals regarding the accountability of a decision-maker. A decision-maker:

- identifies the goals and objectives they are accountable for and how those goals and objectives are nested within the overall goals and objectives of the organization;
- is responsible for ensuring that in selecting their actions intended to reach their goals and objectives , as many choices are available/ considered as possible;
- is responsible for making choices among the available alternatives;
- is responsible for using the best information available;
- is responsible for understanding the impact of their choices which constrain the ability of other decision-makers; and
- is required to convey as much information about their choices as possible.

Therefore the value sieve starts with the notion that decision-makers must be able to list or inventory their options available. This is most

$$\text{Value For Money (VfM)} = \frac{\text{Expected Utility}}{\text{Resources Required}} = \frac{\text{Anticipated Outputs \& Outcomes}}{\text{Resources Required}}$$

In the literature, Value for Money is variously defined using different measures of value from productivity to outcomes. In this chapter we will use the above definition of Value for Money and abbreviate it as VFM.

*Figure 12.2* Value for Money (VfM).

realistically done by specifying actions that can be taken or programmes that can be implemented.

### The purpose of information

The purpose of information is to reduce uncertainty. Thus information can be interpreted as reducing the number of choices available which could be the correct answer to a question. One way of measuring information is to consider the change in the number of choices available (see Figure 12.3).

In this regard there are three things that are desired from any measurement strategy: Can the information eliminate my uncertainty about the choices available? Can the information reduce my uncertainty about the choices available? Can the information help someone else reduce their uncertainty about their choices available?

Therefore, data and measures collected which do not reduce a decision-maker's uncertainty among their choices, are not information. Similarly, if the decision-maker is constrained to a set of choices and does not have the power to recruit new choices, then data and measures which do not relate to the available choices are not information to that decision-maker.

### An inventory of choices

Information is used to reduce uncertainty about choices. Consequently, the Value Sieve requires that decision-makers identify their choices before they begin to determine their best course of action. This inventory of possibilities allows the decision-maker and their personnel (or other interested parties) to identify possible actions and the resources required to carry out the actions. Further, each action plan will include the specification of appropriate information which can demonstrate outputs and outcomes. Options may or may not rely upon relationships with other programmes or organizations, and some choices which are technically possible will not be eliminated from possible action because they do not conform to fixed organizational constraints.

### *The importance of a priori programme statements*

Cognitive psychology and experimental economics have been very useful in the demonstration of the impact of human bias in the forecasting, interpretation and explanation of data. The results suggest that creating a programme and explaining what will occur should be managed very much like the experimental process of describing an experimental model and then testing it. Accordingly a demonstration of understanding the dynamics of a programme must be based upon the ability to predict correctly the resource requirements, the outputs and outcomes before they come to pass. This is particularly important since the Value Sieve uses both resources required, and outputs and outcomes, in the decision-maker's determination of any programmes VfM.

It follows that measurement systems are not objectives in themselves but are means by which decision-makers receive feedback which can be used to better direct their efforts and resources they control. The central significance within experimental procedure is not the fact that there is measurement but the fact that the decision-maker/researcher must state, a priori, the question and how the question will be answered using some kind of repeatable observation and measurement system.

The a priori statement for a programme must provide the means by which an individual can demonstrate, test and improve a programme. Further, through the open provision of the a priori programme statement, including resources required, objectives, testing plan, data measures and decision process, others may participate in the improvement of the programme or the rejection of the programme in favour of another. An improvement to the programme may include showing that the programme does not explain all the facts in an appropriate way or that there are unforeseen consequences which occur but have not been taken into consideration by the decision-maker.

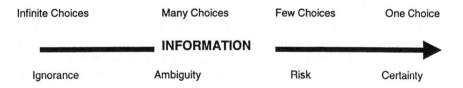

*Figure 12.3* Information, judgement and uncertainty.

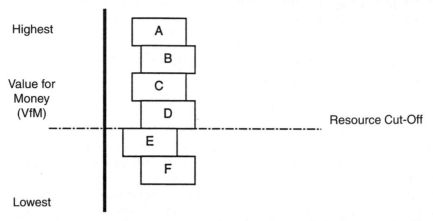

*Figure 12.4* Value for money ranking demonstrating optimized expected utility of a basket of programmes within the context of a specific objective function and resources available.

## Utility and objective functions

It is expected that incommensurable measures will be interpreted by a decision-maker within the context of an objective function. In social services an example of an objective function could be 'a set of objectives designed to reduce juvenile violence'. Thus each available alternative programme addressing juvenile violence could be considered within the context of its ability to, in new or complementary ways, contribute to the reduction in juvenile violence. The integrated measure (in the mind of the decision-maker) is the VfM of an alternative in addressing the objective function.

If only a single programme alternative was available then it would, by virtue of it being the only choice, be the best choice available and would thus have the highest VfM measure of the objective function. If two programme alternatives were available and the organization could afford only one, then the programme which offered the highest VfM for the objective function, from the perspective of the decision-maker, would be the programme selected. The pattern should be clear that through the use of comparison of one programme's VfM for the objective function with another a series of programmes could be compared which would demonstrate an ordinal measurement system of the VfM of the available choices for the objective function of interest. Such a system is shown in Figure 12.4.

A cheese sandwich with a given resource cost given to a young person would rank higher in expected utility for the objective function of youth hunger than would a cheese sandwich given to a senior citizen. The expected utility of the same item can be different when considering it in relation to the objective function of interest.

Thus a programme's expected utility for an objective function can only be determined when it is placed within the context of the available alternative programmes and the total resources available which can be applied to the objective function by the decision-maker. When an organization has the resources to fund one or more programmes towards the goal of an objective function, the collection of programmes which maximize the VfM for the objective function will be chosen.

An organization can be imagined as a hierarchy of objective functions, lower level objective functions being 'nested' within higher level objective functions. More senior decision-makers are accountable for the specification and coordination of junior decision-makers' objective functions. The Value Sieve ensures that each 'nested' objective function is optimized by the accountable decision-maker. Decisions which adjust the maximization of VfM of a single nested objective function in relation to a superincumbent objective function are made through the choices of a superior decision-maker who is responsible for maximizing VfM by balancing a collection of nested objective functions within their superincumbent objective function; i.e. when junior managers report to a senior manager, the senior manager is responsible for balancing and coordinating the actions/choices of the junior managers such that the VfM produced by their combined efforts is maximized for the senior manager's objective function. The obligation of junior managers is to make choices which maximize the VfM of their own objective function. The obligation of the senior decision-maker is to ensure that combined VfM is maximized and the expected utility producing efforts of the junior managers are coordinated. In this way programmes and their specific objective functions can be combined/'rolled up'[7] to create well-organized aggregates which correspond to the programmes and objective functions of decision-makers who are senior in the hierarchy of the organization. Rolling up the set of individual paired choice comparisons among programmes into an aggregate provides optimization at the aggregate or organizational level. The series of paired comparison choices involves the decision-maker's judgement about ranked contribution to VfM, where the concept of VfM involves assigning a common currency to both incommensurable outcomes and commensurable but incommensurate resources. In aggregate this provides for the maximization of expected utility for a total given budget.

VfM can be maximized by each decision-maker for their objective function. From the equation in Figure 12.2 it can be seen that VfM can be increased in one of two ways. The first is by holding the outputs and outcomes and therefore expected utility constant and trying to reduce the resources required to achieve those outputs and outcomes. The second is by holding the resources constant and then raising the outcomes and outputs. Conversely, a loss of VfM should result when the delivered outputs and outcomes are lower than originally estimated or the resources required are higher than the original estimates. It follows that a decision-maker cannot compare programmes and maximize VfM for an objective function until the 'best available'[8] information is provided for each of the choices that will be included in the decision-making process.

The ability to determine the VfM of an object or of a programme in relation to an objective function is inherent in all people. However, the estimate of VfM is not necessarily the same among all people and should therefore be expected to reflect individual differences.

Moving resources from one activity to another results in an improvement in VfM when there is a net increase in expected utility produced by the redirection of resources. VfM is determined through the medium of a specified programme's relationship with alternative programmes and an objective function. Value is a relative term which means the choice with the most VfM. An objective function in and of itself does not have expected utility. Consequently, investing resources to determine the optimal objective functions is only useful when there are sufficient degrees of freedom to redirect resources to programmes which can produce VfM for the new objective function(s). Further, the redirection is only appropriate if the new expected utility being created is greater than the expected utility being lost.

VfM is estimated by the a priori provision of information. VfM is determined by what was delivered. Accountability requires decision-makers to explain the difference between what was estimated and what was delivered and to adjust their future decision-making accordingly.

### Focusing on actions and not theory

While the Value Sieve can be applied to any sort of decision process, its great strength is in application environments. It has been specifically designed and tested in applied settings where choices must be made using the available incomplete information within short periods of time. These conditions are not conducive to extended philosophical discourse. Consequently the process focuses attention on actions that can be accomplished that have an impact upon the objective function. This approach accepts that a number of decision-makers may agree to a course of action as being the best available even though they are each agreeing for different reasons. In other words individuals participating in the decision-making process may assign a choice a high level of VfM for very different reasons.

For example – a city plot is declared by the city council as green space. Council members may feel this is the correct thing to do for a variety of reasons. Some members might value green space for environmental reasons while other may value green space because it increases property values in the adjoining area.

The central notion is that when individual differences of VfM do not affect the overall choice to proceed, it is immaterial that all participants agree with the choice for the identical reasons. Where differences of opinion become important are when the VfM estimates made by different members of a decision-making body disagree about whether the action should be taken or not, i.e. one group see the action as having high VfM and so wish to fund the programme while another group see the action as having low VfM and do not wish to fund the programme.

In practice the prioritization based upon the perceived VfM tends to show that in general there is much agreement among participants about programmes and that disagreement tends to take place at the margins where the differences in VfM are low; because these programmes are competing for resources around the cut-off they can stimulate important discussion.

### Combining individual differences

Individual differences assume that more than a single individual has a formal voice in the decision-making process. A benevolent dictator, no matter how carefully he or she listens, still makes the final decision. In this case and in many administrative positions, administrators and managers have no requirement to take into consideration differences of opinion. They have been designated as accountable and as a consequence the organization has trust in their decision.

In situations where groups of individuals are involved in developing a decision, the Value Sieve uses a preferential voting mechanism to combine perspectives on decision-making panels. There are different kinds of voting procedures that can be used, but these technical arguments are best left to more detailed explanation of the voting and the Value Sieve.

### Coordinating within and between boundaries in complex systems

The ordinal scale of programme VfM is an extremely informative record of the thinking of the decision-maker. The comparisons allow others to understand the priorities of the decision-maker in a much more comprehensive way than simply knowing the objective function. In looking at the relative utilities the ordinal measure can provide evidence of weighting of preferences within a budget envelope. Further, it lets other specialized areas understand the impact of changes in perceived VfM within a specialized group.

In the case of non-profit organizations the revealed prioritization of actions may be extremely important to ensure that continued collaborative action is possible.

For example, an outreach programme for youth is going to cut back on its swimming recreation time for street juveniles. This will impact the health of street youth because the swim programme has been used as a method of ensuring the youth take a shower before they enter the pool, and has been an opportunity for providing unobtrusive counselling for health and safety concerns as well as for keeping a reasonable estimate of numbers of street youth. The result will be an increase in demand for services at a local drop-in center.

A programme which was the last funded within an organization's budget knows that it is most likely to be eliminated if it cannot improve its performance. A programme which was the first not funded programme knows that in the next funding cycle it needs to demonstrate greater VfM than the last programme funded.

## IV Hypothetical application of the Value Sieve process

### *Value Sieve summary*

The Value Sieve is a decision process which maximizes the expected utility which can be produced by an organization for a specified collection of resources. The process requires decision-makers to specify their objective function(s) and within the context of that objective function compare the available programme alternatives. The VfM of each possible alternative programme is assessed using a paired comparison approach which ultimately creates a priority list of the alternative programmes. The prioritized list shows the maximum contribution towards the objective function which can be achieved given different levels of resource, i.e. the least VfM is provided by the last programme funded within the specified objective function.

Organizations with multiple objective functions can optimize the overall expected utility by moving resources from one prioritized list of programmes within one objective function to another prioritized list of programmes for an alternative objective function. In so doing, decision-makers are using the Kaldor[9] criterion to shift resources from one objective function to a different one. By extension this suggests that there may be a prioritization of objective functions for the overall organization.

The Value Sieve requires the following steps:

- the identification of the decision-maker(s);
- the identification of the objective function;
- the identification of the general level of resources that will be available;
- an inventory[10] of programmes/activities which may be used to address the objective function, (this process can be as open or closed as required);
- invitation to provide addition information regarding any programme within the inventory (this process can be as open or closed as required);
- prioritization of the programmes comparing the VfM of one programme vs. the VfM of another programme in relation to the objective function;
- a voting procedure if there is more than a single accountable decision-maker; and

- 'publication' of the prioritization of the programmes in the inventory (distribution can be as open or closed as required).

The Value Sieve is designed to be customized to meet the needs of the specific organization. In preparing the following example some assumptions and simplifications have been made to focus attention on the overall form and function of the methodology.

### Community Aid Society (CAS) – a Value Sieve hypothetical application

The Community Aid Society (CAS)[11] is a regional, charitable organization which promotes and collects charitable donations from the citizens of a geographic region and then directs them back into the communities of the region. The donations are provided to various CAS member organizations which provide charitable services to the people of the region. CAS conforms to the model of a federated funding organization (FFO).

On an annual[12] basis the member organizations provide their requests for funding to CAS and in turn CAS determines which service programmes it should fund. For the purposes of this hypothetical case I will assume that there are 60 funding requests, within 3 categories of programme: Youth Services, Seniors Services, and Family Services. Further I will assume that these programmes request approximately $3 million per year, which is based upon the average of the charitable donations which are raised each year. Each year there is no guarantee that $3 million will be raised and consequently some care must be taken to manage the expectations of the charitable agencies regarding continuity of funding, i.e. organizations which receive support from CAS have no guarantee of programme funding continuity.

The mission of CAS is to improve the well-being of the community through the provision of services to at-risk elements of the population. The general at-risk elements of the population have been identified by CAS as Youth, Seniors, and Families. The divisional structure of the Society reflects these focuses and consequently the objective of each of the divisions is to direct the resources each division receives to maximize the well-being of their target population within the community. Each service programme funded by a CAS division is regarded as providing the best value for money from among the service choices available.

The selection of the specific primary objective function is reviewed at the beginning of every third resource allocation cycle. The three-year review of primary objective functions was chosen over a one-year review process, to manage the expenditures of time and effort associated with a proper review. It was also determined that the three-year period provides stability for both CAS and the service provision organizations. The selection of the specific primary objective functions is usually done by board members and the senior staff through a combination of public discourse and needs survey. A significant benefit of this process is that it encourages CAS to communicate with the service providers, key organizations and members of the community.

The result of the process is an objective function: a prioritized (not weighted) list of primary objectives which are intended to guide the VfM estimates of the various programmes by the accountable decision-makers. The CAS generated the following objective function:

- Priority One: to reduce the number of families living below the designated poverty line;
- Priority Two: to improve the health and independence of emancipated youth who live in poverty;
- Priority Three: to enable programmes which aid youth in becoming economically self sufficient;
- Priority Four: to improve the independence of the elderly within the community;
- Priority Five: to increase volunteerism in the community;
- Priority Six: to restore and fortify families in distress.

This ranking of the component objectives in the objective function which articulates the over-arching mission 'community aid' is an important communication tool to the community, the decision-makers and the service providers. It represents a predisposition for actions which are consistent with the CAS priorities.

The Value Sieve process is used by CAS as both an optimization and as an accountability device. Optimization occurs through the selection of the highest VfM programmes which address the objective function. Accountability occurs by ensuring that the process is open, and participants document their deliberations/decisions .

In consideration of its accountabilities CAS must ensure that:

- the donors feel that CAS is the most appropriate mechanism to provide the maximum benefit to the target populations within the community, i.e. that CAS spends the funds wisely;
- the individuals within the target population who are receiving services get the quantity and quality of services which have been paid for by CAS;
- the available resources address the most important needs of the target populations;
- the service providers believe that the allocation process is fair and works to ensure that the most useful services are provided to the target populations;
- a reasonable strategy is employed to determine the needs of the specific target populations within the community;

- the resources provided to service organizations to acquire services are based upon fair pricing policies;
- there is consequence for service providers failing to provide the quantity and quality of services contracted and the outcomes predicted;
- the community believes the allocation process is responsive to the needs of the community, the target populations, and the organizations which provide the services; and
- the process is stable and establishes a base of trust in the process by service providing organizations.

*Resources available*

In this hypothetical case it will be assumed that there are 60 proposals for services requesting funds totaling $3,153,000. However, fund-raising this year has not been as successful as expected and there are only $2,800,000 available. Therefore there is a funding shortfall of $353,000. A shortfall can be managed in a number of ways but in this case the CAS board has determined that each division must demonstrate the impact of a reduction of the full $353,000. While it is unlikely that the board would manage the shortfall by reducing a single division it is not unreasonable to believe that such an open approach would demonstrate that the board is willing to review hard choices in order to ensure the health of the remaining service programmes.

The details of 60 different service requests are not necessary for the example; however it is useful to provide some sense of the services under consideration and the ability of the Sieve process to assist in making choices. Please note these service descriptions are hypothetical examples and are not intended to provide service-related insights.

*Sample services*

The hypothetical Youth Services projects are (see Table 12.1):

- YS3 ($14,000): Criminal Records checks for youth service workers.
- YS9 ($140,000): Swimming Safety Service, which maintains a community pool and provides opportunity for swimming instruction. Services are directed to young people aged 3 to 15. The programme trains 1,100 children to swim each year.
- YS14 ($201,000): Youth Accommodation Building allows homeless youth up to 90 days' accommodation while they find alternative safe housing. Expenses include cleaning, plumbing, maintenance, yard work, room set-ups and capital improvements.
- YS20 ($98,000): Street Outreach Service provides a social worker and vehicle to drive to various youth collecting locations in the city to ensure the young people are aware of community health and social

*Table 12.1* Value Sieve – proposals organized by division and unique identifier

| Youth project proposals | | Seniors project proposals | | Family project proposals | |
|---|---|---|---|---|---|
| *ID* | *Cost ($)* | *ID* | *Cost ($)* | *ID* | *Cost ($)* |
| YS1 | 113,000 | SS1 | 240,000 | FS1 | 4,000 |
| YS2 | 44,000 | SS2 | 65,000 | FS2 | 18,000 |
| YS3 | 14,000 | SS3 | 17,000 | FS3 | 28,000 |
| YS4 | 18,000 | SS4 | 96,000 | FS4 | 8,000 |
| YS5 | 175,000 | SS5 | 31,000 | FS5 | 36,000 |
| YS6 | 75,000 | SS6 | 38,000 | FS6 | 80,000 |
| YS7 | 25,000 | SS7 | 51,000 | FS7 | 10,000 |
| YS8 | 6,000 | SS8 | 12,000 | FS8 | 6,000 |
| YS9 | 140,000 | SS9 | 8,000 | FS9 | 160,000 |
| YS10 | 33,000 | SS10 | 39,000 | FS10 | 2,000 |
| YS11 | 58,000 | SS11 | 24,000 | Sub- | |
| YS12 | 64,000 | SS12 | 56,000 | total | 352,000 |
| YS13 | 35,000 | SS13 | 33,000 | | |
| YS14 | 201,000 | SS14 | 68,000 | | |
| YS15 | 12,000 | SS15 | 79,000 | | |
| YS16 | 28,000 | SS16 | 15,000 | | |
| YS17 | 60,000 | SS17 | 28,000 | | |
| YS18 | 19,000 | SS18 | 90,000 | | |
| YS19 | 22,000 | SS19 | 32,000 | | |
| YS20 | 98,000 | SS20 | 5,000 | | |
| YS21 | 105,000 | SS21 | 181,000 | | |
| YS22 | 37,000 | SS22 | 28,000 | | |
| YS23 | 20,000 | Sub | | | |
| YS24 | 10,000 | total | 1,236,000 | | |
| YS25 | 4,000 | | | | |
| YS26 | 110,000 | | | | |
| YS27 | 29,000 | | | | |
| YS28 | 10,000 | | | | |
| Sub- | | | | | |
| total | 1,565,000 | | | | |

safety net programmes. The social worker provides food and basic medical and hygiene supplies.
- YS25 ($4,000): Financial Hardship Offset provides required fees for children of low income families to participate in school events and enrichment activities.

Hypothetical Seniors Services Projects are:

- SS4 ($96,000): Seniors Yoga for Cardiac Patients provides an opportunity for seniors with cardiac health issues to congregate at a local recreation center and participate in a safe exercise regimen.
- SS6 ($38,000): Meals Delivery works with another project to provide hot meals to senior citizens in their homes. This programme covers the

cost of gas and automobile depreciation for volunteer drivers. These volunteers deliver approximately 200 meals each night of the year.

* SS12 ($56,000): Outreach for elders in abusive relationships. The counselling service provides education, counselling, and referrals.
* SS16 ($15,000): Membership Fees provides fees to low income seniors so that they may participate in enrichment and community activities.
* SS21 ($181,000): Seniors Group Counselling programme for management of depression. The service provides multiple workshops, and group and individual counselling opportunity for seniors who are experiencing depression.

Hypothetical Family Services projects are:

* FS3 ($28,000): Pre-school programme for young single parents and their children. The programme provides well-structured social and educational opportunities for the children and an opportunity for young single parents to establish healthy relationships with their children and promote social networks for themselves.
* FS6 ($80,000): Alcohol and Drug Counselling provides individual and group counselling to individuals and families of individuals with drug and/or alcohol dependency issues.
* FS9 ($160,000): Supported Independent Living. The goal is to provide skills to young parents (aged 17 to 24) who are living on income assistance. The goal is to aid in finding safe, affordable housing and provide skills and supports to find training and employment.

*The organization of decision-making*

The organization of the resource allocation process requires that CAS establish several mechanisms which will direct the resource allocation process. First CAS must have a clear mission statement for itself as an organization. This mission statement is a stable expression of the organization's vision. Second, the organization must create any specific goals and objectives for the business cycle it is in. As a community organization it may note that a specific issue is an increasing problem in the community and as a consequence it may direct the attention of service providers towards this issue by indicating that in this business cycle there is a desire to fund service programmes which direct attention/energy to that issue. Illustrative issues could include: literacy, inter-generation harmony, hunger, or violence.

The determination of the focus for the business cycle could be considered the objective function of the organization for the business cycle. Within that organizational objective function each funded programme will be prioritized. In the case of CAS, the divisional structure encourages the development of a secondary objective function which directs the attention of resource allocators to their specific target population (for example youth) within the context of the overall objective function (for example literacy).

Each of the divisions of CAS (youth, seniors and families) has a coordinator that receives requests for funding and confirms that they are complete. Service proposals must specify which division they are requesting to compete within. There are no limits to the number of proposals that can be submitted by a service provider and their is no constraint on a service provider who wishes to propose services to different divisions. Service providers which address more than one target population must demonstrate the costs associated with each target population/division.

There are a variety of different approaches which can be used in determining the specific decision-making process. This includes several strategies for proposal verification that may be carried out in the decision-making process. This example is based upon an organization making choices which are intended to benefit target members of the community who frequently, for a variety of reasons, have no voice of their own. This first requires that service providers requesting resources completely document their proposal and are satisfied that it fully and accurately represents the proposed programme. This includes costs, deliverables and the mechanism(s) (empirical and/or theoretical) through which the deliverables are produced.

For example: YS20 ($98,000), Street Outreach Service, the service that provides a social worker and vehicle to drive to various youth collecting locations in the city with food, basic medical, and hygiene supplies.

The project expects to provide services for 30 to 50 youth per evening of operation; the programme is expected to operate 6 p.m. to 2 a.m. Wednesday to Sunday, 48 weeks per year. We expect to provide services 9,600 times during the year (40 youth average per night, 5 nights per week, 48 weeks per year results in 9,600 contacts). This amounts to $10.20 per contact.

These are new programmes and there is little empirical evidence of the extent of the impact upon street youth and the community. However, it is our expectation that there are multiple positive circumstances which will occur as a result of this programme. These include:

- a reduction in youth related street crime in the downtown core areas where street youth congregate;
- a reduction in street youth numbers because those who can be assisted will be referred to existing support agencies;
- a reduction in young deaths due to exposure or extreme poverty;
- an increase in the ability to manage and monitor the street youth population for individual health concerns;
- an increase in the ability to manage and monitor the street youth population for public health concerns;
- an opportunity to establish and maintain a dialogue with street youth so that issues and/or alternative approaches can be identified which will improve the quality of life for all within the community.

There are concerns that such projects may encourage youth who live at home to move onto the street and/or youth from other regions and communities to move here to live on the street. We do not expect this to be the case and have found no evidence in the limited literature of such occurrences. It is, however, a consistent concern raised in newspapers by critics in areas where such projects have been undertaken.

Initially we intend to collect the number of contacts made, and the type of services received during each contact. In addition discussions are taking place with other service providers and municipal officials to determine our ability to develop new or use existing indicators which would test our above mentioned project expectations. The project will work to identify these additional and appropriate measures within 90 days of being funded.

*Resource allocation process – CAS*

LEVEL ONE – MEMBERSHIP

A first step in the resource allocation process is when individual organizations self-select to apply and successfully become a member of CAS. The membership in CAS specifically defines the requirement for cooperative action with CAS. Further, membership provides competitive, collaborative, and cooperative opportunities between member organizations.

LEVEL TWO – DIVISION APPLICATION

As a member, an organization can apply to as many of the divisions as they wish with as many different programmes as they wish. However, only completed proposals are accepted. As a part of its transparency philosophy, CAS has chosen to allow the requests for funding to be reviewed by any interested party. All parties may provide specific salient written feedback regarding any individual project proposal. A copy of the feedback is provided back to the originating organization. The originating organization may adjust, or clarify the proposal in response to the feedback at its own discretion. Feedback is retained by CAS and is provided to the proposal reviews along with the final project funding application.

Table 12.1 shows the project unique identification numbers, the requested funds for each project and the division within which it is competing for funding.

LEVEL THREE – DIVISIONAL APPLICATION REVIEW

The CAS believes that the expertise of the service provider members must be used to assist in the selection of projects to fund. Consequently, the representatives for each of the members of each division are used to create the division's resource allocation jury. This decision to use service providers

*Table 12.2* Value Sieve – youth proposals sorted by individual raters

| *Youth project proposal* | | | *Rater* | | | | | | | | *Sum* |
|---|---|---|---|---|---|---|---|---|---|---|---|
| *ID* | *Request ($)* | *Sort* | *A* | *B* | *C* | *D* | *E* | *F* | *G* | *H* | |
| YS3 | 14,000 | Low | 1 | 1 | 1 | 1 | 1 | 1 | 1 | 1 | 8 |
| YS9 | 140,000 | Low | 1 | 1 | 1 | 1 | 1 | 1 | 1 | 1 | 8 |
| YS14 | 201,000 | Low | 1 | 1 | 1 | 1 | 1 | 1 | 1 | 1 | 8 |
| YS20 | 98,000 | Low | 1 | 1 | 1 | 1 | 1 | 1 | 1 | 1 | 8 |
| YS25 | 4,000 | Low | 1 | 1 | 1 | 1 | 1 | 1 | 1 | 1 | 8 |
| YS18 | 19,000 | Med. | 1 | 1 | 1 | 1 | 1 | 1 | 2 | 1 | 9 |
| YS10 | 33,000 | Med. | 1 | 1 | 1 | 1 | 1 | 1 | 2 | 2 | 10 |
| YS12 | 64,000 | Med. | 1 | 2 | 1 | 1 | 2 | 1 | 1 | 1 | 10 |
| YS24 | 10,000 | Med. | 1 | 2 | 1 | 1 | 2 | 1 | 2 | 1 | 11 |
| YS15 | 12,000 | Med. | 2 | 2 | 2 | 2 | 2 | 2 | 1 | 2 | 15 |
| YS16 | 28,000 | Med. | 2 | 2 | 2 | 2 | 2 | 2 | 1 | 2 | 15 |
| YS19 | 22,000 | Med. | 2 | 2 | 2 | 2 | 1 | 2 | 2 | 2 | 15 |
| YS23 | 20,000 | Med. | 2 | 1 | 2 | 2 | 1 | 2 | 2 | 3 | 15 |
| YS2 | 44,000 | Med. | 2 | 2 | 2 | 2 | 2 | 2 | 2 | 2 | 16 |
| YS8 | 6,000 | Med. | 2 | 2 | 2 | 2 | 2 | 2 | 2 | 2 | 16 |
| YS27 | 29,000 | Med. | 2 | 2 | 2 | 2 | 2 | 2 | 2 | 2 | 16 |
| YS6 | 75,000 | Med. | 2 | 1 | 2 | 2 | 2 | 3 | 2 | 3 | 17 |
| YS11 | 58,000 | Med. | 3 | 2 | 3 | 3 | 3 | 2 | 1 | 1 | 18 |
| YS22 | 37,000 | Med. | 2 | 3 | 2 | 2 | 2 | 2 | 3 | 2 | 18 |
| YS1 | 113,000 | Med. | 2 | 2 | 3 | 2 | 2 | 2 | 2 | 3 | 18 |
| YS13 | 35,000 | Med. | 3 | 3 | 2 | 3 | 3 | 3 | 3 | 2 | 22 |
| YS7 | 25,000 | Med. | 3 | 3 | 3 | 3 | 3 | 3 | 3 | 2 | 23 |
| YS4 | 18,000 | High | 3 | 3 | 3 | 3 | 3 | 3 | 3 | 3 | 24 |
| YS5 | 175,000 | High | 3 | 3 | 3 | 3 | 3 | 3 | 3 | 3 | 24 |
| YS17 | 60,000 | High | 3 | 3 | 3 | 3 | 3 | 3 | 3 | 3 | 24 |
| YS21 | 105,000 | High | 3 | 3 | 3 | 3 | 3 | 3 | 3 | 3 | 24 |
| YS26 | 110,000 | High | 3 | 3 | 3 | 3 | 3 | 3 | 3 | 3 | 24 |
| YS28 | 10,000 | High | 3 | 3 | 3 | 3 | 3 | 3 | 3 | 3 | 24 |
| Sub-total | 1,565,000 | | | | | | | | | | |

in the review process is often challenged by observers; however, it forms an important element in the accountability system used by CAS. Instead of working to determine who else in the community has the expertise to know what can or can't be done and the appropriate cost and outcome relationships for non profit organizations, CAS requires its members to police themselves through a transparent review and prioritization of their own service proposals.

In the case of the youth project proposals there are 28 organizations proposing 28 projects. These members participate in the selection of 7 of their members to carry out the sort. The youth decision-making group is composed of 8 persons, 1 from each of the organizations and the division manager.

*Table 12.3* Value Sieve – prioritization results by division by proposal

| Youth project proposals | | | Seniors project proposals | | | Family project proposals | | |
|---|---|---|---|---|---|---|---|---|
| ID | Cost ($) | Sort | ID | Cost ($) | Sort | ID | Cost ($) | Sort |
| YS3 | 14,000 | Low | SS4 | 96,000 | Low | FS3 | 28,000 | Low |
| YS9 | 140,000 | Low | SS6 | 38,000 | Low | FS6 | 80,000 | Low |
| YS14 | 201,000 | Low | SS12 | 56,000 | Low | FS9 | 160,000 | Low |
| YS20 | 98,000 | Low | SS16 | 15,000 | Low | FS1 | 4,000 | Med. |
| YS25 | 4,000 | Low | SS21 | 181,000 | Low | FS4 | 8,000 | Med. |
| YS1 | 113,000 | Med. | SS3 | 17,000 | Med. | FS7 | 10,000 | Med. |
| YS2 | 44,000 | Med. | SS5 | 31,000 | Med. | FS8 | 6,000 | Med. |
| YS6 | 75,000 | Med. | SS7 | 51,000 | Med. | FS10 | 2,000 | Med. |
| YS7 | 25,000 | Med. | SS8 | 12,000 | Med. | FS2 | 18,000 | High |
| YS8 | 6,000 | Med. | SS9 | 8,000 | Med. | FS5 | 36,000 | High |
| YS10 | 33,000 | Med. | SS11 | 24,000 | Med. | Sub- | | |
| YS11 | 58,000 | Med. | SS13 | 33,000 | Med. | total | 352,000 | |
| YS12 | 64,000 | Med. | SS14 | 68,000 | Med. | | | |
| YS13 | 35,000 | Med. | SS15 | 79,000 | Med. | | | |
| YS15 | 12,000 | Med. | SS17 | 28,000 | Med. | | | |
| YS16 | 28,000 | Med. | SS19 | 32,000 | Med. | | | |
| YS18 | 19,000 | Med. | SS22 | 28,000 | Med. | | | |
| YS19 | 22,000 | Med. | SS1 | 240,000 | High | | | |
| YS22 | 37,000 | Med. | SS2 | 65,000 | High | | | |
| YS23 | 20,000 | Med. | SS10 | 39,000 | High | | | |
| YS24 | 10,000 | Med. | SS18 | 90,000 | High | | | |
| YS27 | 29,000 | Med. | SS20 | 5,000 | High | | | |
| YS4 | 18,000 | High | Sub- | | | | | |
| YS5 | 175,000 | High | total | 1,236,000 | | | | |
| YS17 | 60,000 | High | | | | | | |
| YS21 | 105,000 | High | | | | | | |
| YS26 | 110,000 | High | | | | | | |
| YS28 | 10,000 | High | | | | | | |
| Sub- | | | | | | | | |
| total | 1,565,000 | | | | | | | |

Each individual member carries out a paired comparison to generate a personal sort on the projects. The sort generates three groups of projects of the same size categorized as high priority, medium priority, and low priority. In the Youth division case there are 28 proposals and consequently each rater is requested to select 9 high (signified by the number 3), 9 low (signified by the number 1) and 10 medium proposals (signified by the number 2). The individual prioritizations are then collected from each member and then aggregated to show how each ranked the proposals. The example of the first prioritization is shown in Table 12.2. In this example it should be noted that the rankers uniformly agreed on 5 low ranked, 3 medium ranked and 6 high ranked proposals. Clearly the number of perfect agreements will vary, however experience

*Table 12.4* Value Sieve – youth division ranking

| Youth project proposals | | Rater | | | | | | | | Score | Rank |
|---|---|---|---|---|---|---|---|---|---|---|---|
| ID | Cost($) | A | B | C | D | E | F | G | H | | |
| YS3 | 14,000 | 1 | 1 | 1 | 1 | 2 | 1 | 1 | 1 | 9 | 1 |
| YS9 | 140,000 | 4 | 4 | 4 | 5 | 4 | 4 | 4 | 4 | 33 | 4 |
| YS14 | 201,000 | 2 | 2 | 5 | 2 | 1 | 2 | 2 | 2 | 18 | 2 |
| YS20 | 98,000 | 3 | 5 | 3 | 3 | 3 | 3 | 3 | 3 | 26 | 3 |
| YS25 | 4,000 | 5 | 3 | 2 | 4 | 5 | 5 | 5 | 5 | 34 | 5 |

*Table 12.5* Value Sieve – individual division lowest priority rankings

| Youth project proposals | | | Seniors project proposals | | | Family project proposals | | |
|---|---|---|---|---|---|---|---|---|
| ID | Cost (4) | Rank | ID | Cost | Rank | ID | Cost | Rank |
| YS3 | 14,000 | 1 | SS4 | 96,000 | 2 | FS3 | 28,000 | 10 |
| YS9 | 140,000 | 4 | SS6 | 38,000 | 5 | FS6 | 80,000 | 8 |
| YS14 | 201,000 | 2 | SS12 | 56,000 | 3 | FS9 | 160,000 | 9 |
| YS20 | 98,000 | 3 | SS16 | 15,000 | 4 | FS1 | 4,000 | 7 |
| YS25 | 4,000 | 5 | SS21 | 181,000 | 1 | FS4 | 8,000 | 6 |
| Subtotal | 457,000 | | Subtotal | 386,000 | | FS7 | 10,000 | 3 |
| | | | | | | FS8 | 6,000 | 4 |
| | | | | | | FS10 | 2,000 | 5 |
| | | | | | | FS2 | 18,000 | 2 |
| | | | | | | FS5 | 36,000 | 1 |
| | | | | | | Subtotal | 352,000 | |

to date would suggest that agreement occurs more frequently than was originally expected.

Looking at the medium ranked proposals, it should be noted that the various individuals did vary on these rankings and this is to be expected. By using the individual rankings a complete aggregated first prioritization will allow all raters to understand where the various proposals stand and this provides an opportunity for discussion on a proposal by proposal basis to listen to each member identify any unique elements they felt were important in their ranking or how others ranked a specific proposal.

In the example, Table 12.3 shows there was sufficient agreement within the Youth Division to unanimously identify 5 low proposals which in total requested $457,000. The Senior's Division also unanimously identified 5 low ranking proposals which totalled $386,000. The Family Division unanimously identified 3 low ranking proposals totaling $268,000. In order for the Family Division to meet the requirement of delivering the full shortfall, all of the service proposals within it will need to be ranked to total $352,000.

The next level of the Value Sieve requires the same divisional raters to prioritize the lowest ranking proposals in order to meet the targeted budget

*Table 12.6* Value Sieve – combined priority sort

| | Between division programmes and rankings | |
|---|---|---|
| ID | Cost ($) | Sort |
| YS20 | 98,000 | Low |
| YS25 | 4,000 | Low |
| FS3 | 28,000 | Low |
| FS6 | 80,000 | Low |
| FS9 | 160,000 | Low |
| FS1 | 4,000 | Med. |
| FS4 | 8,000 | Med. |
| FS7 | 10,000 | Med. |
| FS8 | 6,000 | Med. |
| FS10 | 2,000 | Med. |
| FS2 | 18,000 | Med. |
| FS5 | 36,000 | Med. |
| SS4 | 96,000 | Med. |
| SS6 | 38,000 | Med. |
| SS12 | 56,000 | Med. |
| SS16 | 15,000 | High |
| SS21 | 181,000 | High |
| YS3 | 14,000 | High |
| YS9 | 140,000 | High |
| YS14 | 201,000 | High |
| Subtotal | 1,195,000 | |

requirements. In the cases of the Youth and the Seniors proposals this meant prioritizing the proposals that had already been unanimously agreed as the lowest ranking. In the case of the Family Division this meant ranking the entire collection of Family proposals.

This ranking is done by starting with the low rated proposals only and individually ranking them using paired comparisons. At this level an additional prioritization or a preference voting method is used which results in an individual ranking of proposals 1 to $n$. In the example shown in Table 12.4, a simple ranking of 1 to 5 is demonstrated.

The combination of each rater's ordinal rank by programme yields a total score which translates into a proposal-specific ordinal level ranking by the division decision-makers. The combined results of such a process are shown in Table 12.5.

The divisions have now completed their responsibility by providing an ordinal level ranking of their divisional proposals. These divisional recommendations are provided to the board level decision-makers of CAS. The CAS executive decision-making group must now prioritize among the divisions' proposals in such a way that the budget constraints are met. It should be noted that the executive have access to the full proposals listed and the ranking results of each of the divisions. The executive have the power to ignore the recommendations of each of the divisions if they see fit. While it is anticipated that the executive decision committee will in most cases follow the recommendations of the divisions, the executive have the oversight responsibility to ensure that they are satisfied with the process and appropriateness of the divisional Value Sieve ranking.

The executive repeat the Value Sieve procedure that was used by the divisions. In this context the task may be seen as more challenging because the proposals that must be ranked are less likely to be comparable. Individual raters are requested to sort the 20 proposals towards an outcome of 7 low rank, 6 medium rank and 7 high rank.

In Table 12.6 the results of the individual low, medium, and high sort is shown. The raters unanimously agreed on 5 low and 5 high ranked proposals with 10 medium ranked proposals containing mixed results. The low sort proposals total $370,000. While it is possible to argue that the sorting process could end now, it is important to identify the specific ranking of these low rated proposals so that those operating within this domain understand the raters' perspectives of what is valued by CAS. Consequently the low and medium proposals will be ranked to provide an ordinal level ranking of each of these proposals. Implicit in this ranking is that if additional resources became available or if a further reduction of resources were to occur these lower ranking proposals would be the beneficiaries or the losers respectively.

In providing ordinal level ranking to the low and medium proposals the Community Aid Society is prioritizing the spending of $644,000. These dollars support the projects which provide services which are the least valuable of the services provided by funded proposals of the CAS. The notion of least valuable is clearly a relative term and is not intended to suggest that those proposals if funded would not accomplish worthy outcomes. What it does indicate is that the 'community VfM' of these services is ranked lower than that of other services.

The Value Sieve procedure has prioritized all proposals within each division and has prioritized the lowest ranked proposals across the Society. This results in a clear message from CAS to the community, the target population, and service providers *about* what the Society believes are programmes which provide, from the resources available, the most effective and efficient uses of the resources to better the target population. It focuses the arguments and discussion regarding service proposals on those proposals which are operating or will be operating at the margin.

A careful review of the ranking shown in Table 12.7 demonstrates that regardless of what is said by CAS decision-makers at the executive level, the Family proposals are not well ranked. With all 10 Family proposals operating in the bottom 12 of all 60 proposals reviewed it should be clear that the Family division service providers are either not performing well enough, or not proposing services which are seen to have relative value, or Family services are not a high priority for CAS when compared to their other service divisions.

Thus the value of the ranking is that it allows those organizations offering proposals which are operating on the margins to understand

*Table 12.7* Value Sieve – final ranking

| ID | Cost ($) | Rank | Cost |
|---|---|---|---|
| YS20 | 98,000 | 15 | 98,000 |
| FS3 | 28,000 | 14 | 28,000 |
| FS9 | 160,000 | 13 | 160,000 |
| FS6 | 80,000 | 12 | 80,000 |
| YS25 | 4,000 | 11 | |
| FS1 | 4,000 | 10 | |
| FS4 | 8,000 | 9 | |
| FS10 | 2,000 | 8 | |
| FS8 | 6,000 | 7 | |
| FS7 | 10,000 | 6 | |
| FS2 | 18,000 | 5 | |
| FS5 | 36,000 | 4 | |
| SS4 | 96,000 | 3 | |
| SS6 | 38,000 | 2 | |
| SS12 | 56,000 | 1 | |
| Subtotal | 644,000 | Subtotal | 366,000 |

this and determine if this information can be used in a constructive way. For example it may be the case that a proposing organization must find a method to reduce the costs associated with the outcomes/outputs in order to improve its ranking, i.e. its value for money. Or it may be the case that CAS no longer wishes to offer funding to proposals which offset the responsibility of existing government proposals, i.e. CAS does not want to become the financial support to programmes/projects which are the legal responsibility of the government. Or it may be that the proposal addresses a problem so vast that CAS does not feel it has the resources, or the proposal making agencies the knowledge or skills necessary, to address such problems.

Whatever the reason several extremely important elements are communicated as a result of the Value Sieve methodology.

The transparent sort, and subsequent ranking process, clearly demonstrates the ranking of proposals and shows which proposals were valued over others. An individual decision-maker is unable to indicate values of one kind and not support those values in their decision-making prioritizations. This is not to say that there will not be obfuscation at the margins with individuals potentially presenting the most politically acceptable explanations for their prioritizations.

## Technical summary

The Value Sieve establishes a stable and consistent model/methodology for decision-making within an organization. The model can be applied to any type of organization which wishes to ensure its decision-makers are accountable. The methodology does not constrain the application of judgement or personal insight to any decision but it does require that the decision-maker demonstrate the information used and solutions considered. It does this by requiring the decision-maker to identify the choices which were considered and to make evident the relative VfM of each for the objective function. This simple act establishes the bridge between technical and political accountability by making both the technical and judgement components of decision-making transparent. It accepts that both technical and political communities within an enterprise may have preferences which cause them to 'spend VfM' rightly meant for the specified objective function. Through the Value Sieve process it is possible to know if there was insufficient effort spent in developing alternatives, whether alternatives were based upon bad technical knowledge, or whether some other consideration must have been involved in the judgement associated with the prioritization of the available choices.

While the methodology cannot look into someone's mind and know the reason for their choices it is possible for a supervising individual or board or member of the public to note a disparity in the VfM judgement(s) of a decision-maker and take corrective actions. Consequently, accountability flows in the appropriate directions in order to minimize poor judgement of both technical and political natures. This feedback establishes a foundation for ongoing efforts to improve individual and overall expected utility produced by the organization within a specified level of resource. This is enhanced and coordinated through the 'roll up' which assists an organization in creating a stable model of decision-making which is designed to accept changes in technical knowledge and social preferences over time.

## Conclusion

The Value Sieve was developed to work in an environment which is almost entirely populated by well-meaning and industrious individuals working hard to do the right thing. It accepts that judgement and incommensurable measures will be present for the vast majority of decisions made, today and in the foreseeable future. It supports a decision-maker in using judgement to interpret the best available information and goes far in the way of ensuring procedural and consequential accountability. These accountabilities provide the opportunity for decision-makers, working in good faith, to adjust their actions to improve performance given new knowledge or a changing environment.

Further, the Value Sieve as a technique communicates the values of the decision-makers to the rest of their organization through the selection of actions, actions which provide insight into the underlying values of the decision-maker and their objective functions.

By specifying the methodology and techniques of an accountable decision-maker the Value Sieve creates a simple and unifying understanding of the purpose of management, and the foundation for an organization to maximize the expected utility it produces for a specified objective function for a given budget.

## Notes

1 J. Christopher Corbett 'A decision support system for the allocation of resources (DSSAR) by a regional health board', Masters Thesis, University of Victoria, Victoria, BC, 1994.
2 The Value Sieve continues to be a primary focus of my research efforts at the University of Victoria. My Interdisciplinary Ph.D. dissertation, which should be completed by the time this book is published, contains more extensive technical information regarding the Value Sieve methodology including conceptual underpinnings and implementation strategies.
3 While pure experimental approaches are not always possible, an organized approach to the evaluation of current practice and the acquisition of supporting knowledge is always appropriate.
4 Measurement perfection would be valid and reliable measurement commensurability which can remain valid and reliable within and between applied settings.
5 The distinction between technical judgement and personal politics is intended to point out that it is very difficult to determine the extent that a decision-maker has made a judgement based upon self interest at the cost of the best interest of the programme or organization. Indeed it is the impossibility of knowing the thoughts of an individual which makes the need for measurement of results imperative for the feedback of information and consequent control of a programme and an organization.
6 A choice may be a programme, an action, a project or any other identifiable alternative use of controlled resources. This paper will attempt to stay with the language of alternative programmes.
7 Rolled up is a common phrase used in management accounting which suggests that each layer in an organization's financial and business activities can be consolidated without distorting the underlying detail.
8 Best available is not intended to suggest that extraordinary efforts be employed to collect new or better information. As a start it simply requires the programme managers and staff provide the data they currently use for decision-making. This will include a clear statement of what they believe they accomplish with the resources they are provided.
9 Kaldor criterion – A change is an improvement if the people who gain from the change evaluate their gains at a higher dollar figure than the dollar figure the losers attach to their losses.
10 An inventory includes the available information about the programme. This would include resource costs, processes used, outputs and outcomes. In some cases it may also include supply availability and estimated demand for service.
11 Community Aid Society (CAS) is the name chosen for the hypothetical organization because to my knowledge there is no organization which represents itself with this name.
12 The sieve need not be used on an annual basis. One of the original design intentions of the fully documented process was to reduce the costs associated with resource allocation by increasing the time between allocations. In those cases the design recommends a contract provisions for 3 to 5 years.

# Summary and conclusions

1   A clearly defined accountability framework is the foundation of performance measurement, evaluation and reporting in non-profit organizations. The concept of accountability was defined to include both the hierarchical model of mandatory accountability (the requirement to render an account for a responsibility conferred) and the *voluntary* disclosure of relevant information to the various internal and external constituencies of a programme or organization. For both the narrow and extended models, we then argued that a meaningful framework of accountability must include: first, shared expectations about conduct and performance; second, a shared language or currency in which fulfilment of those expectations is described; third, shared criteria defined in that currency as to what constitutes fulfilment; and, finally, a means of communicating information about conduct and performance. The balance of Chapter 1 then explored the various dimensions of accountability, and foreshadowed the major arguments of the book by emphasizing the evolution of the categories of technical information used to fulfil accountability relationships – that is, the evolution of common currencies – and corresponding criteria of conduct and performance and ways of communicating that information.

2   In Chapter 2, the concept of evaluation that underlies any accountability information system was examined in detail. Evaluation can occur at differing levels (from individual to programme to organizational to system) and can be based on inputs, processes, outputs and outcomes. Methods of evaluation involve designing the process (which requires answering the questions: why is it being undertaken, what is to be evaluated, what type of evaluation is to be used, and who will do it); choosing the data-gathering modes (quantitative and/or qualitative) and deciding on the standards to be used in interpreting the data. A key concept in evaluation is that of the 'logic model'. Every evaluation contains one whether it is implicit or explicit. Assumptions are made about the nature of the links between inputs, processes and outcomes, and between the levels of performance they are examining.

Common fallacies in logic models were identified and the 'ideal' evaluation process for dealing with them was described. The problem

with the ideal process, however, is that it is rarely feasible to implement it when evaluations are carried out in the real world. This is due
to certain technical problems and pervasive psycho-social tendencies
among both evaluators and evaluatees. On the technical side, it is often
not feasible to gather all the information that is needed due to time, cost
and availability constraints and an inadequate understanding of the
causal connections between means and ends. On the psycho-social side,
there is a strong tendency for those being evaluated to want to 'look good
and avoid blame' vis-à-vis the evaluators. Secondly, when there is
ambiguity as to the meaning of the data produced in the evaluation
process (and there usually is), there is an almost inevitable tendency to
impose an interpretation consistent with pre-existing experiences and
beliefs.

3   Most of the points made in the general discussion of evaluation are
illustrated in Chapter 3 which presents the results of research carried out
by the authors which tracked in depth the actual evaluation process
followed by three funding agencies as they evaluated the performance of
two social agencies in a Canadian city. It was seen that the evaluators
each approached the process with somewhat differing concepts of who
they were evaluating (scope), what they were going to evaluate (focus), and
how they were going to evaluate (methods used). Since these differences
were never made explicit to the evaluatees they created problems. An
especially significant problem was the role of non-formal evaluation in the
process. An organization's unofficial reputation in the eyes of the larger
community of which the evaluators were a part unquestionably influenced
the conclusions of the evaluators. So, also, did the extent to which the
evaluatees conform to certain unspoken values held by the evaluators –
values never made explicit in the formal evaluation system.

4   In Chapter 4 we documented the challenges that arise when attempts
are made to improve the evaluation process. On the assumption that both
those who hold others accountable (evaluators) and those being held
accountable (evaluatees) would prefer to work with a process that is jointly
created, clear, and uniformly interpreted, we approached six of the organizations studied. The proposal was to reveal the problems and inadequacies
in their existing accountability information systems suggested by the data
gathered in phase 1 of the project. We would then work with all parties in
jointly developing 'new and improved' evaluation processes which they
would use on a pilot test basis for a year.
   The result of these efforts at 'action research' was that, broadly speaking,
they were politely refused. It appeared that both the evaluators and
evaluatees, for whatever reasons, believed that the benefits to be
derived from improving the process were not worth the costs incurred
in creating it.

5   In the absence of performance reporting standards, non-profit agencies face difficulties in accommodating the varied and changing information requirements of public and private funders, and other users of performance information such as clients, volunteers, management and staff. Faced with clear evidence of the lack of success which is likely to occur as a result of rushing to normative prescriptions without careful consultation, we proceeded to work more carefully with four of the agencies studied starting from their concerns and needs for information. We asked the range of internal and external constituencies what information they had, and what they would like to have, and used this as the basis for some more cautious normative suggestions. The proposed standards are standards for what categories of performance information should be reported across the management cycle, from planning and budgeting through to external reporting and auditing/evaluation. They are specifically not standards of performance. The development of such criteria or benchmarks of success for each category of performance information is a subsequent step. The sector is so diverse that it is unlikely to be fruitful to attempt the prescription of performance criteria applicable to all non-profit agencies. However, given the acceptance of an information framework of the sort proposed, primary users, including funders, could move to negotiate a set of general performance criteria – standards of performance – for each of the component parts of the information framework for non-profit agencies directed to similar objectives.

A gratifying consequence of the more cautious and consultative approach used in this part of the research project was that the staff and board members in the non-profit agencies involved in the project were generally persuaded that a general approach of the sort proposed would be useful both for internal governance and management control and for external accountability. We were therefore encouraged to take the next step of demonstrating the practical applicability of the accountability framework particularly with respect to the key components of performance such as service costing and service outputs and outcomes.

6   As a first step in dealing with practical applicability it was decided to step back and make a thorough examination of existing tools for evaluation that had been created by others for use in the non-profit sector. Chapter 6 reports the results of this survey. In brief, the conclusion was that there are, as yet, no perfect tools that will 'work' for all non-profit organizations. In fact, most existing tools are process, rather than outcome, based and are open to numerous problems with their logic models, methodologies and interpretation frameworks. The chapter concludes with the identification of those tools with the greatest potential for the future (which becomes the subjects of Chapters 11 and 12) and presents recommendations on how to introduce improvements to the accountability process. These recommendations were then applied in the remaining phase of the project.

7   Turning to specific components of accountability information, we looked next at the money side of value for money – the matter of programme and unit costs – in a case study of four human service non-profit agencies. We discovered that the concept of costs was not well understood, either by internal decision-makers or by external funders. Line-item financial information, either as budgets or financial statements, was frequently, and erroneously, taken to convey sufficient information on programme costs. In the case study we set out to demonstrate the importance of understanding and including in cost calculations the cost of the support or overhead activities that are necessary to sustain direct client service activities. The work attempted to demonstrate that information on the nature and role of overhead costs, and the derivative information on the full and unit costs of client service programmes, could be generated using a relatively simple model that invites managers to start with line-item information, and then to formalize the assumptions they are working with intuitively in the operation of programmes, and to explore the implications of these assumptions. The illustrative model was constructed for a hypothetical human service non-profit agency that combined the interesting features of the four client organizations. The first task was to determine which organizational activities could be classified as overhead, and calculate what proportion of total organizational costs could be attributed to them. The second task was to determine what drives the use of overhead activities by client service programmes and to use that cost driver information to load overhead costs down onto client service programmes. In this way the full cost – including an appropriate share of organizational overhead costs – of each client service programme could be determined. We also showed how this programme cost information could be combined with output information to determine unit cost – the average cost of a unit of service.

The argument was well received when presented to managers, staff and board members in the agencies studied. They seemed reassured about the practical feasibility of the approach, and recognized the various situations in which analytically justified information about total and unit costs would be useful for internal accountability and for reporting and contract negotiation externally.

8   In the first of two case studies on the value side of value for money – what is achieved by using resources? – we addressed the interest of the Capital Mental Health Association (CMHA) in meeting the requirements of its public and private funders for evidence of programme logic models, including outcome indicators, in both requests for funding and reports on performance. Compliance with the Executive Director's request that we deal with one strategic outcome for each programme was consistent with, indeed foreshadowed, our later research argument that the effective design of programme logic models requires a focus on one strategic, long-term

objective and associated outcome. The case study illustrates 5 of the 12 programmes examined in the complete study.

Two tables were produced for each programme. The first table shows the primary strategic programme objective, the assumptions underlying the programme, the stated target of the programme and its relevant indicators, and the appropriate programme evaluation method. In the second table, this information was recast in outcome terms and placed under the appropriate outcome category (initial, intermediate, and long-term) in a programme logic model. The programme logic model links the various stages implicit in a programme, from programme inputs and activities through to outputs and the various outcome categories. The causal relationships implicit in the logic model are simple, if heroic. If the specified outputs occur, there is a significant probability that the initial outcome will occur, and so on. So the causation that is assumed is probabilistic in nature, but is sustained by the expertise and experience of the professionals delivering the programme.

The proposed models were well received by the Executive Director, programme managers and board members at CMHA, and preliminary implementation of the approach for all 12 programmes began on 1 September 1997.

9    The second case study revisited the Art Gallery introduced in Chapter 4. It, too, focused on programmes rather than the whole organization; however, in this case, the programmes proved to be much more interdependent than in the case of the mental health organization. Nevertheless, the particular area of gallery operations that deals with special exhibits was selected to be reported on here. A logic model for this programme area was developed and applied. Existing sources of information were identified along with areas where new information could be gathered. Recommendations on how the Gallery could improve its accountability information system were developed and presented to the Gallery, this time with considerably more success.

10    Our next frontier was to respond to the concerns of all client agencies about how best to present their accountability information externally in the form of an annual report at the end of the funding year. Agencies wanted help with 'telling their story', and evinced particular interest in exploring the use of the 12-attribute approach proposed by the CAAF/FCVI. We began by emphasizing the three major, and interrelated, strengths of the 12-attribute approach. First, the attributes provide an eclectic, comprehensive definition of the concept of effectiveness, reflecting the perspectives of the varied constituencies of non-profit programmes. Second, managers rather than external evaluators are responsible for preparing performance 'representations' for the 12 attributes. And, third, the approach requires verification of the completeness and

accuracy of management representations by external auditors who thereby bring their skills to bear most appropriately in their traditional attest role. We then continued, however, with a discussion of some challenges presented by the approach, and developed some criteria for their use in annual reporting. On the basis of our critique, and using the proposed criteria, we then proposed a format for annual reports based on the attributes.

The proposal had the following features. First, it includes all 12 attributes but includes a few additional attributes in the interests of comprehensive accountability reporting. Second, an explicit distinction is drawn between management systems and operating information. Third, the three levels of accountability – financial accountability, accountability for compliance with authorities, and accountability for value for money – are explicitly distinguished. Fourth, the attributes are presented in a dynamic framework that reflects the governance/management cycle of activities over the year. Fifth, the limits of management accountability for value for money – outputs as distinct from outcomes, and direct controllable costs as distinct from full costs – are identified. Sixth, the format incorporates performance criteria, either in the form of targets established at the planning and budgeting stage or of 'industry-wide' general criteria. Seventh, the format requires that the subjective evidence presented by management be supplemented to the extent feasible by external, third-party evidence. Eighth, self-evaluation by management is incorporated in the form of a situation analysis summary of strengths and challenges, and used as the basis of a statement by management of proposed actions, and of a set of recommendations for decisions by senior management. Ninth, an internal audit opinion is incorporated to provide assurance to senior management and the board, and an external audit opinion incorporated to provide assurance to all other internal and external constituencies.

The response of management and boards in the agencies to the proposed reporting structure was broadly favourable. All parties agreed that a reporting framework that described performance in relation to explicit intentions at the planning and budgeting stage of the cycle was a more complete and fairer approach to accountability. The common currencies and associated criteria were established at the beginning and were observed through the reporting and evaluation stages.

11 Even the revised version of the CCAF attributes that demonstrates the chronological cycle of governance and management activities remains essentially a cross-sectional slice of performance along the cycle. While it does take the important step of defining the attributes in a chronologically dynamic sense, it does not provide a causally integrated dynamic model of programme performance that could serve conceptually and operationally as the basis of governance and management control. Such an integrated model would have to address the matter of focus. Multiple attributes of

performance cannot be simultaneously optimized. An operationally helpful model of programme performance in non-profit agencies would include the articulation of unifying or fundamental purpose, how the various components of the model contribute to that purpose, and how the achievement of that purpose is to be measured.

The Balanced Scorecard developed for commercial organizations can be used to transform a performance reporting framework into a strategic management framework, and, in the next stage of the research project, we developed the Scorecard directly for use in public sector commercial programmes and private non-profit membership programmes, and, with more creativity, for public and private charitable non-profit programmes. We also transformed the chronological version of the CCAF/FCVI reporting framework developed at the previous stage of the project into an alternative Balanced Scorecard.

12    The final chapter deals with the most difficult issue facing those using accountability information to make decisions: that of making choices between programmes with different administrative currencies. This we described as the problem of technical failure or incommensurability – comparing programmes where the central components of performance, the indicators that are to be optimized, are different. On the surface, this appears to be the point where administrative accountability bowed out, and political accountability took over. But we argued that while these two accountabilities were different, they need not remain as two solitudes. We attempted to build a bridge between these solitudes by demonstrating a decision process in which decision-makers are provided, first, with the best available technical information about alternative programmes with incommensurable outcome measures, and, second, with an ordinally weighted set of objectives to which all programmes under consideration are addressed. Decision-makers are then required to make paired choices that reveal explicitly the common currency they are using to make choices with respect to an implicit composite utility measure of achievement of the weighted set of objectives. Decision-makers are free, of course, to use a currency that is entirely defined in terms of sustaining their position of power – in short, maintaining political support – but the relationship of such choices to the administrative information available is made explicit; in such a case, otherwise concealed politics has become revealed politics. This approach seems to offer strong promise that the bridge can provide a mechanism for informed choice that both extends the scope of decisions based on administrative information and leaves explicit room for decisions based on political information.

# Bibliography

Adie, R.F., and Thomas, P.G., *Canadian Public Administration*, Toronto, Prentice Hall, 1987.

Alvesson, M. and Deetz, S., 'Critical theory and postmodernism: approaches to organizational studies', in S.R. Clegg, C. Hardy and W. Nord (eds) *The Handbook of Organization Studies*, Thousand Oaks, CA, Sage, 1996.

Anthony, R.N., Dearden, J., and Govindarajan, V., *Management Control Systems*, Homewood, Ill., Richard D. Irwin, 1992.

Anthony R.N., and Young D.W., *Management Control in Nonprofit Organizations*, 6th edn, Boston, Mass., Irwin/McGraw-Hill, 1999.

Ashforth, B.E. and Gibbs, B.W., 'The double-edge of organizational legitimization', *Organization Science*, 1: 1, 1990, 177–94.

Auditor General of British Columbia and Deputy Ministers' Committee, *Enhancing Accountability for Performance: A Framework and An Implementation Plan*, Victoria, BC, Office of the Auditor General, April 1966.

CCAF/FCVI, *Effectiveness Reporting and Auditing in the Public Sector*, Ottawa, CCAF, 1987.

CCAF/FCVI, *Comprehensive Auditing: An Introduction*, Ottawa, CCAF/FCVI, 1994.

Canadian Institute of Chartered Accountants, CICA Handbook Section 1000, Financial Statement Concepts (Toronto, Ontario, annually updated).

Cameron, K.S., 'The effectiveness of ineffectiveness', *Research in Organizational Behaviour*, 6, 1984, 235–85.

Canadian Institute of Chartered Accountants, Public Sector Accounting and Auditing Committee, *Value-for-Money Auditing Standards*, Toronto, CICA, 1988.

Canadian Institute of Chartered Accountants, Public Sector Accounting and Auditing Committee, *General Standards of Financial Statement Presentation*, Toronto, CICA, 1995.

Canadian Institute of Chartered Accountants, *Not-For-Profit Financial Reporting Guide*, Toronto, CICA, 1998.

Clarke, E.H., 'Multipart pricing of public goods: an example', in S. Mushkin (ed.) *Public Prices for Public Products*, Washington, The Urban Institute, 1972, 125–30.

Connors, Roger and Smith, Tom *Journey to the Emerald City: Achieve a Competitive Edge by Creating a Culture of Accountability*, Paramus, NJ, Prentice-Hall, 1999.

Corbett, J. Christopher, 'A decision support system for the allocation of resources (DSSAR) by a regional health board', Masters Thesis, University of Victoria, Victoria, BC, 1994.

Cutt, James et al., *From Financial Statements to Cost Information: Efficient Resource Utilization In Non-Profit Organizations*, Victoria, BC, Centre for Public Sector Studies, 1994.

Cutt, J., Bragg, D., Balfour, K., Murray, V. and Tassie, W., 'Nonprofits accommodate the information demands of public and private funders', *Nonprofit Management and Leadership*, 7: 1 (Fall 1996), 45–67.

Day P., and Klein, R., *Accountabilities: Five Public Services*, London, Tavistock Publications, 1987.

D'Aunno, T., Sutton, R.I. and Price, R.M., 'Isomorphism and external support in conflicting institutional environments: a study of drug abuse treatment units', *Academy of Management Journal*, 34: 3 (1991), 636–61.

DiMaggio, P. and Powell, W., 'The iron cage revisited: institutional isomorphism and collective rationality in organizational fields', *American Sociological Review*, 48 (1983), 147–60.

Dinsdale G., 'Enhancing performance at Capital Mental Health Association', MPA dissertation completed at the University of Victoria, reproduced in G. Dinsdale, J. Cutt and V. Murray, *Performance and Accountability in Non-Profit Organizations: Theory and Practice*, Victoria Papers in Public Policy, No.4, Victoria, BC, Centre for Public Sector Studies, 1998.

Elsbach, K.D. and Sutton, R.I., 'Acquiring organizational legitimacy through illegitimate actions: a marriage of institutional and impression management theories', *Academy of Management Journal*, 35: 4 (1992), 699–738.

Ernst and Young LLP, *Measures that Matter*, Boston, Mass., Ernst and Young Center for Business Innovation, 1998.

Financial Accounting Standards Board (US), Statement of Accounting Concepts, No.1, *Objectives of Financial Reporting by Business Enterprises*, Washington, FASB, 1978.

Goodman, P.S. and Pennings, J.M., 'Critical issues in assessing organizational effectiveness, in E.E. Lawler, D.A. Nadler and C. Camman (eds) *Organizational Assessment: Perspectives on the Measurement of Organizational Behaviour and the Quality of Work Life*, New York, John Wiley and Sons, 1980.

Glaser, B.C. and Strauss, A.L., *The Discovery of Grounded Theory: Strategies for Qualitative Research*, Chicago, Ill. Aldine Publishing, 1967.

Health, Ministry of, Government of British Columbia, *Health Services Outcome Reporting*, Victoria, BC, Ministry of Health, 1996).

Heffron, F., *Organizational Theory and Public Organizations*, Englewood Cliffs, NJ, Prentice-Hall, 1989.

Herman, R.D., 'Nonprofit organization effectiveness: at what, for whom, according to whom?', *Nonprofit and Voluntary Sector Quarterly*, 21: 4 (1992), 411–15.

Hodgkinson, C., *Administrative Philosophy*, New York, Elsevier Science Inc., 1996.

International Association of Psycho-social Rehabilitation Services, *Toolkit for Measuring Psycho-social Outcomes*, Columbia, International Association of Psycho-social Services, 1995.

Kaplan R., and Norton D., *The Balanced Scorecard*, Cambridge, Mass., Harvard Business School Press, 1996.

Kolter, P. and Adreason, A.R., *Strategic Marketing for Nonprofit Organizations*, 3rd edn, Englewood Cliffs, NJ, Prentice Hall, 1987.

LeClerc, G., et al., *Accountability, Performance Reporting, Comprehensive Audit: An Integrated Perspective*, Ottawa, CCAF/FCVI, 1996.

Lovelock, C.H., and Weinberg, C.B., *Public and Non-profit Marketing*, 2nd edn, Redwood City, CA, The Scientific Press, 1989.

Matek, S.J., *Accountability: Its Meaning and its Relevance to the Healthcare Field*, Hyattsville, Maryland, US Department of Health, Education and Welfare, 1977.

Mintzberg, H., *The Rise and Fall of Strategic Planning*, New York, Free Press and Prentice Hall International, 1994.

Morgan, G., *Imaginization*, Newberry Park, CA., Sage Publications, 1994.

Moynagh, W.D., *Reporting and Auditing Effectiveness: Putting Theory Into Practice*, Ottawa, Canadian Comprehensive Auditing Foundation, 1993.

Murray, V. and Tassie, W., 'Evaluating the effectiveness of nonprofit organizations', in R.D. Herman (ed.) *The Jossey-Bass Handbook of Nonprofit Management and Leadership*, San Francisco, CA, Jossey Bass, 1994.

Panel on Accountability and Governance in the Voluntary Sector, *Building on Strength: Improving Governance and Accountability in Canada's Voluntary Sector*, Ottawa, Panel on Accountability and Governance, 1999.

Quinn, R.E. and Rohrbaugh, J., 'A spatial model of effectiveness criteria: towards a competing values approach to organizational analysis', *Management Science*, 29: 3 (1983), 363–77.

Report of the Independent Review Committee on the Office of the Auditor General, Ottawa: Information Canada, 1975.

Scott, W.R., *Organizations: Rational, Natural and Open Systems*, Englewood Cliffs, NJ, Prentice-Hall, 1987.

Scott, W.R. and Meyer, J.W., 'The organization of societal sectors', in J.W. Meyer and W.R. Scott (eds) *Organizational Environments: Ritual and Rationality*, Newbury Park, CA, Sage, 1992.

Simon, H. A., *Administrative Behaviour*, New York, MacMillan, 1961.

Simon, J.G., 'Modern welfare state policy toward the non-profit sector: some efficiency–equity dilemmas', in H.K. Anheier and W. Seibel (eds) *The Third Sector: Comparative Studies of Non-Profit Organizations*, Walter de Cruyter, New York, 1990.

Tassie, A.W., Murray, V.V, Cutt, J. and Bragg, D., 'Rationality and politics: what really goes on when funders evaluate the performance of fundees?', *Nonprofit and Voluntary Sector Quarterly*, 7: 3 (September 1996), 347–65.

Taylor, M.E. and Sumariwalla, R.D., 'Evaluating nonprofit effectiveness: overcoming the barriers', in D.R. Young, R.M. Hollister, V.A. Hodgkinson and associates (eds) *Governing, Leading, and Managing Nonprofit Organizations*, San Francisco, CA, Jossey-Bass, 1993.

Thib M. L., 'Accountability information at The Art Gallery of Greater Victoria', MPA dissertation completed at the University of Victoria, BC, April 1999.

Tideman, T.N., ed., Special Supplement to *Public Choice*, 29: 2 (Spring 1977).

Waldo, 1983) Dwight Waldo, CEPAQ-ENAP, 'Debats sur L'Imputabilite', Actes du Colloque sur L'Imputabilite, Chateau Mont St. Anne, Quebec, 9 et 10 juin, 1983.

Williams, A.R. and Kindle, C., 'Effectiveness of non-governmental and non-profit organizations: some methodological caveats', *Nonprofit and Voluntary Sector Quarterly*, 21: 4 (1992), 381–90.

Young, D.W., *Financial Control In Health Care*, Homewood, Ill. Dow-Jones-Irwin, 1984.

Znaniecki, R., *Cultural Sciences: Their Origin and Development*, New Brunswick, NJ, Transaction Books, 1980.

# Index